Classroom-based Evaluation in
Second Language Education

CAMBRIDGE LANGUAGE EDUCATION
Series Editor: Jack C. Richards

This new series draws on the best available research, theory, and educational practice to help clarify issues and resolve problems in language teaching, language teacher education, and related areas. Books in the series focus on a wide range of issues and are written in a style that is accessible to classroom teachers, teachers-in-training, and teacher educators.

In this series:

Agendas for Second Language Literacy *by Sandra Lee McKay*

Reflective Teaching in Second Language Classrooms *by Jack C. Richards and Charles Lockhart*

Educating Second Language Children: The whole child, the whole curriculum, the whole community *edited by Fred Genesee*

Understanding Communication in Second Language Classrooms *by Karen E. Johnson*

The Self-directed Teacher: Managing the learning process *by David Nunan and Clarice Lamb*

Functional English Grammar: An introduction for second language teachers *by Graham Lock*

Teachers as Course Developers *edited by Kathleen Graves*

Classroom-based Evaluation in Second Language Education *by Fred Genesee and John A. Upshur*

From Reader to Reading Teacher: Issues and strategies for second language classrooms *by Jo Ann Aebersold and Mary Lee Field*

Classroom-based Evaluation in Second Language Education

Fred Genesee

McGill University

John A. Upshur

Concordia University

PUBLISHED BY THE PRESS SYNDICATE OF THE UNIVERSITY OF CAMBRIDGE
The Pitt Building, Trumpington Street, Cambridge, United Kingdom

CAMBRIDGE UNIVERSITY PRESS
The Edinburgh Building, Cambridge CB2 2RU, UK   http: //www.cup.cam.ac.uk
40 West 20th Street, New York, NY 10011-4211, USA   http: //www.cup.org
10 Stamford Road, Oakleigh, Melbourne 3166, Australia

First published 1996
Third printing 1998
Fourth printing 1999

Printed in the United States of America

Typeset in Sabon

Genesee, Fred
Classroom-based evaluation in second language education / Fred
Genesee, John A. Upshur
p. cm. – (Cambridge Language Education)
Includes bibliographical references.
1. Language and languages – Ability testing. 2. Language and
languages – Examinations. I. Upshur, John A. II. Title.
III. Series.
P53.4.G46 1996   96-3887
428'.0076–dc20   CIP

A catalogue record for this book is available from the British Library

ISBN 0 521 56209 0 hardback
ISBN 0 521 56681 9 paperback

Contents

98745

Illustrations

Chapter 8

Chapter 9

Chapter 11

Chapter 12

Chapter 13

Chapter 14

Tables

Chapter 11

Chapter 12

Chapter 13

Series editor's preface

A common view of the nature of language teaching and the work of second language teachers is that the primary concerns of language teachers lie with the process of instruction itself, that is, with helping learners acquire the language skills they need for a wide variety of purposes. Yet, for many teachers, decisions related to the assessment of student learning are an equally important part of their work. Such decisions relate to a wide spectrum of issues, including assigning grades to students, evaluating the suitability of textbooks, assigning students to an appropriate class in a language program, and deciding on the design and content of classroom tests. In order to carry out these tasks, teachers need more than access to different assessment techniques and instruments; they need an understanding of the nature and purposes of evaluation, procedures for collecting and interpreting different kinds of information about students and student learning, and the ability to make appropriate decisions about instruction and instructional plans that can have a significant impact on students. This book provides a comprehensive introduction to these issues and provides a framework for understanding both the nature and the processes of second language assessment and evaluation.

Drawing on a wide range of contexts, the authors present an accessible and practical guide to developing and conducting reliable and valid assessments in language teaching, discussing a wide range of both formal and informal evaluation techniques to improve second language teaching and enhance the success of second language learning. In addition to providing a thorough presentation of standard approaches to testing and formal assessment, the authors examine alternative approaches, such as classroom observation, portfolios, and student conferences. The book therefore provides a state-of-the-art introduction to current issues and approaches in second language assessment that will be invaluable to classroom teachers, teachers-in-training, and other language professionals. *Classroom-based Evaluation in Second Language Education* represents an important contribution to the field of second language education by drawing together current thinking and approaches in language assessment and by providing a conceptual framework that enables teachers to better understand the nature, purposes, strengths, and limitations of different approaches to second language evaluation.

Jack C. Richards

Authors' acknowledgments

We gratefully acknowledge the valuable collaboration of Carolyn Turner and Randall Halter. Their input and encouragement during the preparation of the book were much appreciated and have enhanced the final product immeasurably. We would also like to thank Janet Hanrahan-Brisse for assisting with the preparation of the preview and discussion questions and Neal Brengle, Else Hamayan, Naomi Holobow, Anne Katz, and Joy Kreeft Peyton for contributing valuable suggestions and sample materials.

1 Introduction to evaluation

- Introduction
- Coming to terms with evaluation
- Our approach
- The book

Preview questions

1. Why do you evaluate? When do you evaluate?
2. List all the methods of evaluation you use. Now list everything that you evaluate.
3. Who do you share the results of your evaluation with? Why?
4. What do you think are important characteristics of proper evaluation?
5. Are you required to assign students grades? How do you do this?
6. How would you evaluate the appropriateness of a textbook for your students?
7. How do you decide to go on to the next unit or chapter?
8. When students seem to be having difficulty grasping what you are teaching, how do you decide what changes need to be made to make the material more accessible to students?
9. What kinds of information or feedback do you use to indicate that your teaching is going well?
10. What kind of formal training in evaluation have you had? Was it useful? Why or why not? What do you wish you could do better? What do you hope to be able to do better after reading this book?

Introduction

We have selected the following scenarios to illustrate what we believe to be typical of second language evaluation from the perspective of teachers. When you read these scenarios, consider the questions these situations pose for teachers and how decisions in response to these questions can be made:

Elena Gonzalez, 7 years old, is a student at Highland Elementary School. For two hours each day, she is pulled out of her regular program for special classes in ESL. Her ESL teacher has recommended that Elena should no longer have to take ESL instruction. A committee of four people, the ESL teacher, Elena's regular teacher, Elena's mother, and the assistant principal of the school, will have to decide. They will review her performance in English, her work in the other school subjects, her adjustment to school, and the wishes of Elena and her family in order to reach a personally and academically sound decision.

John Sperling is an ESL teacher in a commercial language school in San Francisco. After the first week of classes, he notes that one of his students seems to be superior to all of her classmates. Should she remain in the class for seven more weeks until the end of the course? Should she be moved up to the next level? Should she perhaps be moved up two levels? John, together with the ESL coordinator and the teachers of other classes in which she might be placed, will have to make the decision. They will consider not only her performance in John's class, but also enrollments and the demands of the other classes.

Ellen Brady teaches first year English at Cornwallis High School. It is the 14th of November. She has prepared a lesson in which the students are to assume the roles of shoppers in a bakery. The class has hardly started when she gets a feeling that things are not going well. Should she continue with her lesson plan, or should she have her students spend the rest of the hour doing the next activity in their workbooks?

Bill Spears is head of the English Language Institute at Carleton University. He is responsible for the university's English courses for foreign students. The institute offers a variety of ESL courses. Bill wants to revise the institute's procedures for placing incoming students. In the past, they have given students a short interview and a quick written exam and used this information to place the students. But the instructors found that using this procedure resulted in misplacement of many students. Bill has to decide on a new procedure.

Ahmed Fawzi is a recent immigrant. He is taking basic English so that he can prepare himself to get a job as soon as possible. His course included a unit about job hunting and applications, but he wonders if his English is good enough for him to go for a job interview. There are several questions he will want to ask his teacher.

Sarah Weiss, a teacher at Cardinal LeBlanc High School, has just finished teaching the third unit in the new ESL program. She wants to decide, while the experience is still fresh in her mind, whether the unit should be revised in any major ways before using it again next term. Did the students accomplish what they should? Did they seem bored or interested? Was the unit too hard or too easy? There are many factors she must consider.

Vin Phong has been asked by the continuing education department of his local community college to teach ESL to a group of recently arrived Vietnamese immigrants. He has been told that he can do whatever he wants; the only restriction is that it will be an evening course that meets for three hours once a week for two months. He must decide what to do in the next month. This means preparing a course outline and lesson plans and selecting a textbook or other materials. In order to make these arrangements, he needs more information.

You can see from these brief scenarios that second language evaluation involves many different kinds of decisions: decisions about the placement of individual students in particular streams, levels, or courses of instruction; about ongoing instruction; about planning new units of instruction and revising units that have been used before; about textbooks or other materials; about student homework; about instructional objectives and plans; and about many other aspects of teaching and learning. There is more to evaluation than grading students and deciding whether they should pass or fail. In fact, decisions about students, although important, are few in number compared to the full range of decisions that are made daily in second language classrooms. In the vast majority of cases, second language evaluation is concerned with making decisions about instruction or plans for instruction. Even decisions about students usually affect instruction. For example, a new student placed in your class partway through the year will influence your teaching because you will have to accommodate this recent arrival.

More than anyone else, teachers are actively and continuously involved in second language evaluation – sometimes as the person making the actual decisions; sometimes in collecting relevant information for others who will make the decisions; or sometimes helping others make decisions by offering interpretations of students' performance. Even when teachers are not the actual decision makers, they are affected. For example, someone else may be responsible for the placement of students in second language classes, but teachers are responsible for teaching the students who are placed in their classes.

Parents, other teachers, noninstructional educational professionals (such as counsellors and remedial specialists), and students themselves are also important participants in evaluation. Teachers often consult or collaborate with other such people as part of the evaluation process: they consult with parents to decide whether more or different kinds of homework are called for to assist a student who is doing poorly; they consult with education specialists to decide whether second language learners should receive additional or special instruction; and they may consult with school principals or administrators responsible for placing students in different school programs. Teachers also plan activities that help students assess their own progress – for example, student conferences.

These opening scenarios also illustrate that second language evaluation relies on many different kinds of information. Although information about student achievement is certainly relevant, it is not the only, or necessarily the most important, information for making all decisions. Other factors can also be important – student behavior in class, their attitudes toward school or themselves, their goals and needs concerning the outcomes of second language learning, and their work habits, learning styles, and strategies.

Professional and physical resources in the school are also often considered in second language evaluation. Teachers' language proficiency, their professional qualifications, instructional preferences and attitudes, and availability can affect the appropriateness of particular instructional methods. Availability of class space, time, and instructional technology (overhead projectors, audio- and videocassette recorders or even paper, pencils, and textbooks) can determine the feasibility of particular second language objectives or methods.

Tests can be of great help in collecting information for second language evaluation. But tests are relatively limited because they can only tell us about certain aspects of student achievement; they cannot tell us much about the other factors that often figure in second language evaluation. Additional ways of collecting information are often called for in classroom-based second language evaluation. For example, information may be gathered through observation of student behavior during routine lessons, from comments by students during individual conferences, or from entries in students' journals. All of these can divulge important data about student learning and the effectiveness of instruction, as can information from school records, parents, and medical reports. These other sources are as critical as tests because of their broad scope. This may be surprising to those who think of evaluation only in terms of grades and decisions about passing and failing. As we pointed out earlier, however, there are many different kinds of decisions, besides passing or failing students, to be made in second language classrooms.

Coming to terms with evaluation

Second language evaluation is primarily about decision making. Indeed, the overall purpose of second language evaluation is to make sound choices that will improve second language teaching and enhance second language learning. Such decisions are based on informed judgment. They require the careful collection of relevant information and a thoughtful interpretation of that information. Three essential components of evaluation are information, interpretation, and decision making. It is important to distinguish among these three components because they are distinct. Information about teaching and learning is rarely meaningful by itself. It becomes meaningful when it is interpreted. Meaningful interpretations are needed in order to decide what actions to take or what changes to make to instruction.

Let us take the case of information resulting from class tests – that is, test scores – to illustrate these points. Imagine that Pedro scored 19 on a class test. By itself, Pedro's score is meaningless. We cannot tell from this score alone whether Pedro has done well. Moreover, if he has done poorly, we cannot discern the reason from his score alone. Therefore, we cannot decide whether to proceed with our teaching as planned or to take another course of action more appropriate for Pedro.

Pedro's test score would be more meaningful if we had additional information: the maximum possible score for the test; the test content and, in particular, the language objectives included in the test; how other students in the class did; how long Pedro has been in the class; whether he studied the night before the test; his health or well-being the day of the test (was he tired?); and so on. Once we have collected this information, we can make sense of Pedro's test score and decide what to do next.

First of all, we would want to know whether the test was a representative sample of what the students have been taught and were expected to learn. If so, then we are able to interpret Pedro's score in terms of how much of the instructional material he had learned. If we then speak to Pedro and find out that he was well rested on the day of the test and had studied hard the night before, and if we know that he has been in the class since the beginning of the year (like the other students, who all got higher scores), then we might interpret his test score to mean that he had not mastered the tested objectives. If this were the first time that Pedro had scored so poorly, we might interpret his performance to mean that he was simply having difficulty with this particular unit or these particular objectives. In this case, we might decide to give him additional individualized instruction and more homework to help him master the objectives in question.

Alternatively, if Pedro were an immigrant student attending an English-medium school for the first time and if he had consistently done poorly on previous assignments and tests (while all the other information remained the same), then we might interpret his test score in terms of difficulties he might be experiencing in adjusting to schooling in a new culture. In this case, we might decide to arrange a meeting with his parents to learn more from them about Pedro's home life and his parents' perceptions of his adjustment to school.

This simple example illustrates that sometimes intermediate decisions, such as to meet with parents or the learning specialist, are in order before making a final decision about appropriate action. You can also see that student performance can be interpreted in very different ways and, consequently, lead to very different decisions. Because second language evaluation is about making decisions, identifying the purpose or purposes for collecting evaluative information in the first place is essential. The nature of the purpose determines the type of information needed and the method of collecting that information.

In our example about Pedro, the purpose of evaluation was to plan

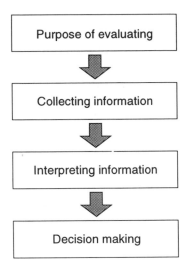

Figure 1   Aspects of classroom-based evaluation.

appropriate follow-up instruction for him given his current level of achieve-ment (in other words, to individualize instruction). This is undoubtedly a common and very important reason for classroom-based evaluation, but it is not the only one. One might undertake evaluation in order to make decisions about follow-up instruction for an entire class or to ascertain the effectiveness of particular instructional units with a view to improving them, if necessary, or to encourage student involvement in formulating personal learning objectives. Depending on the particular reasons for carry-ing out evaluation, different methods of assessment might be used; various kinds of information might be collected; and different kinds of interpreta-tions will be drawn.

For example, undertaking evaluation to ascertain the effectiveness of a particular instructional activity with a view to redesigning it or re-using it without modification might rely on observational information about how all or most students react to the activity; this could be done using a teacher checklist. In comparison, a teacher who wishes to encourage students' involvement in assessing and planning their own learning activities might decide to use conferences or dialogue journals in conjunction with students' own perceptions of their needs and personal goals with respect to alterna-tive instructional activities. The important point here is that there are differ-ent reasons for doing evaluation and these can influence the evaluation process. Thus, purpose is a critical aspect of classroom-based evaluation, along with information, interpretation, and decision making; see Figure 1.

Our approach

This book is concerned with second language learning that takes place as a result of instruction or other activities in classroom settings. It is intended to be useful and practical for teachers. It does not require specialized training in statistics, research methods, psychometrics (theory of testing), or any other technical domain.

Individual teachers face very specific challenges, and they must respond to these challenges in specific ways. Our audience is teachers with different kinds of learners, objectives, and means of attaining those objectives. Our approach is not based on a particular theory of language or language learning or on a particular instructional method or approach. It is intended to be adaptable to suit the specific characteristics and goals of a variety of classroom settings. In other words, we take into account the specific classroom contexts within which teaching and learning take place. Such an approach requires serious and careful consideration of the specific purposes, plans, and practices in each classroom. Teachers need to understand and be able to describe these aspects of their second language classrooms in order to plan appropriate and effective evaluation.

We include a strategy for conducting evaluation that should help teachers in four ways:

1. To determine what information would be useful for making particular kinds of decisions.
2. To devise ways of collecting relevant information.
3. To make sense of the evaluation information.
4. To make appropriate decisions.

Our strategy does not recommend or prescribe one particular way of doing evaluation. We do not believe that there is only one evaluation method that is applicable to all situations. It is the role and responsibility of individual teachers to choose a method that is responsive to their specific needs. We will suggest some possible ways of doing this. Individual teachers will need to choose from among these possibilities or devise alternatives better suited to their requirements.

We have adopted this approach to second language evaluation in order to better assist teachers:

- Plan relevant and effective evaluation
- Make sound and appropriate decisions, and
- Become effective agents of change within their classrooms or second language programs

To summarize, our approach is intended to be:

- Practical
- Classroom based and teacher driven
- Helpful in making instructional decisions
- Adaptable to different instructional styles and objectives
- Responsive to the needs of different audiences

Above all, our approach to evaluation is intended to help teachers enhance student learning.

The book

Our primary goal in this book is to develop teachers' evaluation skills so that they can improve second language teaching and learning in their classrooms. We use the term "second language" generically throughout the book to include foreign and second language teaching and learning. Our audience is primarily second language teachers or those working with second language teachers, (e.g., teacher educators, directors of second language departments or programs, those responsible for curriculum development, language and learning specialists, mainstream classroom teachers with second language learners), and anyone else who might be concerned with second language teaching and learning. We expect that most readers of this book will be teachers who are taking a course in evaluation or testing as part of a preservice education degree or in-service training. However, it could also be used by individual teachers who seek to improve their evaluation skills independent of formal instruction.

Although we use examples from English throughout the book, our approach to evaluation is applicable to the teaching and learning of any second or foreign language. We have taken examples from the English language because the book is written in English and, therefore, English examples will be understandable to most readers.

The book is divided into three parts. Part I describes the context of second language evaluation (Chapter 2), our framework or approach to second language evaluation (Chapter 3), and collecting information for evaluation (Chapter 4). Part II describes how to collect information using observation (Chapter 5), conferences and portfolios (Chapter 6), and dialogue journals, questionnaires, and interviews (Chapter 7). Part III is about tests, both objectives-referenced or classroom-based tests (Chapters 8–12) and standardized tests (Chapter 13). In the closing chapter (Chapter 14), we integrate and summarize briefly all of the preceding chapters.

More space is devoted to tests and testing than to alternative assessment methods, such as portfolios, conferencing, dialogue journals, and so on.

This difference does not reflect the importance we attach to these two general forms of assessment. Rather, it reflects the fact that the creation, scoring, and interpretation of tests are relatively technical, and considerable space is required for their discussion. Furthermore, tests and testing have been around for some time, and they have been discussed and examined extensively in scholarly and professional publications. In comparison, alternative assessment methods are relatively recent and have not been documented and discussed as thoroughly. Our coverage of these approaches reflects these differences.

We discuss conferences and portfolios together in Chapter 5 and dialogue journals, questionnaires, and interviews together in Chapter 7. This permits us to make certain comparisons that we think are useful. However, the reader should not interpret this arrangement as definitive. It is admittedly somewhat arbitrary, and, indeed, some readers would disagree with it. We encourage you to consider each method of assessment in its own right and to compare and contrast alternatives in a variety of ways.

A set of questions precedes and concludes each chapter. There are also questions and tasks within each chapter that are designed to facilitate your understanding and application of the ideas and suggestions presented in the chapter. Some of these require access to actual instructional materials, activities, or objectives. Readers who are currently teaching or have taught second language classes before can draw on their previous work. In the case of readers who are in preservice programs and have not yet taught, we suggest that you select a second or foreign language textbook that would be appropriate for the students you are likely to teach as the basis for working with these questions and tasks. Finally, at the end of each chapter is a list of suggested readings for those who would like more information on each topic.

In all chapters, we offer practical suggestions for doing evaluation in the second language classroom. Our approach is not prescriptive – we do not believe that there is a single right way to evaluate. The practical suggestions we offer are simply guidelines; practitioners will have to experiment with and adapt these procedures to best suit their specific needs.

Some key terms are used throughout the book. Sometimes we talk about evaluation within the context of a "course" of second language instruction. We use this term rather generally to refer to second language instruction that extends over a period of time, be it an intensive course of four to six weeks, the equivalent of a one-semester course of three to four months, or a year-long course of six to ten months. At other times, we refer to "units" and "lessons" as divisions of instruction within a course. Courses often consist of a sequence of units that, in turn, are made up of several lessons. Units extend over several sessions and are thematically integrated or united in some way. They are made up of lessons, which usually occur during one class session. Finally, lessons, in turn, consist of activities or tasks.

This terminology is not shared by all second language teachers. Elementary and secondary school second language teachers in many countries talk about teaching a subject rather than a course. Elementary school teachers often refer to units of instruction, but secondary school teachers and teachers in postsecondary or adult educational programs seldom do. For secondary school and college level instructors, a chapter within a textbook is often the equivalent of a unit of instruction, to use our terminology. "Lesson" is probably the most widely used and agreed-upon term used to refer to the instruction that takes place during a single class session.

You need not use the same terminology we do. However, it is necessary that you understand what our terms mean and what the corresponding unit of instruction is for you so that you can apply this material to your particular context. Most of all, it is important that you understand that the logic of our approach to evaluation applies to courses, units, lessons, and even activities in the same general way.

One final point – we have sought to avoid sexist language by using generic plural nouns and pronouns. However, where this strategy was unavoidable, we have used "he," "she," "him," "her," and so on, rather than the cumbersome "he/she," "him/her," "he or she" forms. We have used these singular forms randomly and more or less equally throughout the book.

Discussion questions

1. How do your views of classroom evaluation differ from those presented in this chapter?
2. Besides the kind of information you get from tests, what kinds of information do you consider in making decisions about your students and your teaching?
3. What do you do with the results of classroom tests? Would you use these results differently after reading this chapter?
4. Now that you have read this chapter, would you plan to do evaluation in your classroom differently? If so, explain how and why.
5. Are your students involved in evaluation in your classroom? If so, how? If not, why not? What do you see as advantages of student self-assessment? What are some disadvantages?
6. Does anyone else in your school or district make decisions that affect you? Who are they and how do their decisions affect you? Is there any way their decision making could be improved? If yes, explain.

7. What factors outside the classroom affect teaching and learning in your classroom? How do you find out about these sources of influence? And how do you use this information?
8. In your opinion, what are the advantages and disadvantages of tests?
9. What other methods of collecting information for evaluation do you use? What are the advantages and disadvantages of each?

Readings

Airasian, P. (1991). *Classroom assessment.* New York: McGraw-Hill.

Brindley, G. (1986). *The assessment of second language proficiency: Issues and approaches.* Adelaide, Australia: National Curriculum Resource Centre.

Cummins, J. (1984). *Bilingualism and special education: Issues in assessment and pedagogy.* San Diego: College Hill Press.

Finocchiaro, M., and S. Sako. (1983). *Foreign language testing: A practical approach.* New York: Regents.

Lazarus, M. (1988). *Evaluating educational programs.* Arlington, Va.: American Association of School Administrators.

Rea-Dickens, P., and K. Germane. (1993). *Evaluation.* Oxford: Oxford University Press.

PART I:
GETTING STARTED

2 *The context of second language evaluation*

- Introduction
- Instructional objectives
- Instructional plans
- Instructional practices
- Input factors
- Summary

Preview questions

1. Briefly describe your views of language and consider how they affect your teaching.
2. What kinds of language skills do you teach your students?
3. What are some theories of language you have studied? Have they had an effect on your teaching or your views of learning? Explain.
4. How do you know when your students have achieved your objectives?
5. Describe an authentic language activity you use. Is it successful in class? How do you know? If it is not successful, how could you make it more successful?
6. Do you make lesson plans? What do you include in them? How do you know if your plans are good? If you do not make lesson plans, how do you know what to teach and what to evaluate?
7. Describe how your instruction is organized over the course of the year or semester. Why is it organized this way? Is this useful or effective? If not, how would you reorganize it to be better?
8. What factors outside the classroom (in the school or outside the school) affect how you teach or the ability of your students to learn? If these factors have an adverse effect on teaching and learning in your classroom, what can you do about them?
9. What are some important characteristics of your students that affect your teaching? How do you know these things about your students?

Introduction

In Chapter 1, we pointed out that second language evaluation in the classroom is concerned primarily with improving instruction so that student

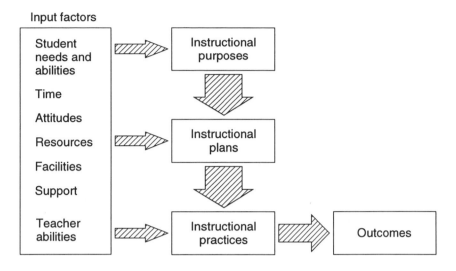

Figure 1   The context of classroom-based evaluation.

learning is enhanced. We also pointed out that classroom teachers, more than anyone else, are actively and continuously involved in evaluation. Students can also be active participants in assessing their own achievements and in planning how they will study and learn the language. In the next chapter, we describe a general strategy for making evaluation decisions. In order to talk about and carry out evaluation in the second language classroom, we need to define the important aspects of teaching and learning.

The discussion in this chapter is organized around the notions of instructional purposes, plans, and practices because instruction − whether we consider instruction of a course, a unit, or a lesson − consists of these three components. The purposes identify the objectives of instruction − the "why." The plans describe the means of attaining those objectives − the "how." And practices are what actually takes place in the classroom − the "what." We also discuss other factors that, strictly speaking, are not part of classroom instruction itself but that, nevertheless, can have a significant effect on second language teaching and learning. For example, community values and attitudes toward second language learning as well as incoming students' current levels of proficiency in the target language can determine the appropriateness of a particular second language course. Or current theories about teaching and learning may influence the effectiveness of the instructional approach of a second language course. We refer to these additional factors as "input factors." These four aspects of instruction (purposes, plans, practices, and input factors) are summarized in Figure 1.

The sources of influence listed in Figure 1 are not necessarily the only pertinent ones. You may want to modify or add to our list sources of influence that can be found in your classrooms and communities. Now let us look at some specific aspects of second language instruction and various ways in which they might figure in evaluation.

Instructional objectives

Types of instructional objectives

Instructional objectives describe the goals that you as a teacher aim for when teaching. On the one hand, they provide direction for planning appropriate instruction, and, on the other hand, they provide a basis for determining whether you have achieved what you set out to accomplish – they provide criteria for assessing the outcomes of your teaching. When identifying objectives to use in second language evaluation, it is important to use those objectives that best describe what you as an individual teacher want to accomplish. In some cases, your objectives may correspond closely to those included in curriculum guidelines, the text you are using, or other instructional documents. In other instances, your objectives might differ from the ones you are given. If you have not been provided with a clear statement of instructional objectives, it is essential that you articulate the objectives that you want to accomplish.

Different kinds of objectives guide classroom instruction: (1) language, (2) strategic, (3) socioaffective, (4) philosophical, and (5) methods or process. *Language objectives* refer to language skills that learners are expected to acquire in the classroom. We focus most of our attention in this book on language objectives because we believe that they are at the heart of second language teaching.

Increasingly, second language instruction also includes objectives that are concerned with strategies for communicating, learning, and critical thinking; collectively, we refer to these as *strategic objectives*. Learning strategies are "conscious processes and techniques that facilitate the comprehension, acquisition, and retention of new skills and concepts" (Chamot and O'Malley 1987, 239). According to Chamot and O'Malley, these may include metacognitive strategies (such as selective attention), cognitive strategies (such as summarizing and elaboration), or socioaffective strategies (such as questioning for clarification).

Socioaffective objectives refer to changes in learners' attitudes or social behaviors that result from classroom instruction; for example, changes in attitudes toward the target language, the target language group, or the learners' first language group. Here are some examples: "The learner will develop a greater appreciation and understanding of the target language culture" or "Students will engage in more extracurricular activities in the target language." Socioaffective objectives can be an important part of second language teaching. In most cases, however, they are secondary to language learning objectives. It is unlikely that socioaffective objectives will be specified without also specifying language objectives. Indeed, it is generally expected that changes in learners' attitudes will result from second language learning.

Philosophical objectives refer to changes in attitudes, values, or beliefs of a more general nature than those associated with socioaffective objectives. Moreover, the change often includes more than the participating students. It may be expected to occur in a community or a whole country. For example, "to strengthen democratic processes in the country" would be a philosophical objective if the effect is intended to spread beyond the students in the course. Philosophical objectives are also often associated with extensive second language learning and not merely a single course or year of instruction. The entire program of second language education in a country might have as an objective "to promote understanding among people of different cultures," but individual teachers are not likely to hold such an objective for single groups of students. These kinds of objectives are not considered in this book because they reach beyond individual classrooms.

Methods, or process objectives, refer to methods, processes, experiences, materials, activities, or other aspects of instruction. They may also refer to opportunities or experiences that learners are expected to have in the course of instruction; for example, "students will be given practice speaking conversational English"; or "students will be exposed to authentic English reading material." The objectives presented in second and foreign language textbooks are often stated in these terms. Because they provide criteria against which classroom practice can be compared, they are most useful for determining whether instruction is being implemented according to the stated aims of the textbook. Such objectives cannot be used to assess the outcomes of instruction because they do not identify changes in learners that result from instruction.

Not all of these objectives are equally useful for classroom evaluation. Philosophical objectives, for example, are minimally useful, and methods objectives are useful for evaluating only one component of instruction – the practices component. Strategic objectives help in understanding student performance in class and, thus, play an important role in instructional planning. They are, however, secondary to language acquisition; in other words, the effective deployment of certain strategies should lead to enhanced second language attainment and usage. Clearly, language objectives are fundamental to second language evaluation and are the focus of our attention. Teachers must be able to distinguish among these objectives

Table 1.   Types of instructional objectives

1. Language
2. Strategic
3. Socioaffective
4. Philosophical
5. Methods and process

so that they understand how each can or cannot be used in planning more effective classroom instruction (see Table 1).

Language objectives

Language objectives are often associated with an entire course of instruction as well as with individual units and lessons. We refer to the former as course objectives and the latter as unit and lesson objectives. The relationship between these is presented in schematic form in Figure 2. The difference between unit and lesson objectives, on the one hand, and course objectives, on the other hand, is a matter of specificity and scope. Unit and lesson objectives are much more specific and detailed than course objectives. They include the particular language skills and subskills to be taught, including exact words, grammatical rules, communicative functions, and so on. They are often identified in the teachers' manual or in the students' textbook. The content of a textbook is a good example of the specificity and scope associated with unit and lesson objectives.

Course objectives include and, at the same time, are more general than unit and lesson objectives. This is particularly true of courses that promote communicative competence or proficiency. In these cases, achievement of unit and lesson objectives may be necessary to achieve course objectives but, alone, they may not be sufficient. This situation can arise, in part at least, because some course objectives are very general and cannot be described completely or adequately in specific terms. Take, for example, an

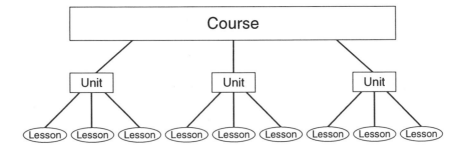

Figure 2   Organization of language objectives.

objective such as "The students will be able to communicate with native speakers of the target language of the same age in informal, everyday social situations." This objective is admittedly general (and subject to considerable difference in personal interpretation), but it is similar to objectives stated for many courses. In any case, it would be difficult to identify all of the specific language objectives that would be necessary and sufficient to achieve this broad goal. Overall achievement at the end of a course should be assessed with reference primarily to course objectives because they are the most inclusive statement of what students are expected to have learned.

Language objectives may have many different forms because there are numerous ways of looking at language. A great number of theories about language exist. They vary considerably. Some emphasize the structures and elements that make up language; some emphasize how language is learned; and yet others emphasize how language is used for social or communicative purposes. Some of these theories have had a significant impact on the second language teaching profession by influencing what and how we teach. For example, the audiolingual method emphasizes grammar, vocabulary, and the use of pattern practice exercises. This method is generally attributed to structuralist theories of language and behaviorist theories of language learning. More recently, pragmatic and sociolinguistic theories of language have emphasized the teaching of communicative notions and functions using a variety of interactive techniques, such as cooperative learning.

It is not our intention to review all of these theories or to describe their relationship to second language teaching. In fact, it is unlikely that this could be done since the relationship between various theories of language and second language teaching is too complex to make such an endeavor feasible. Moreover, such an attempt is not necessary since our approach is designed to be useful no matter what particular theory of language underlies your teaching. No single theory of language or language learning and, therefore, no specific category of second language objectives is considered more important than others in this book.

Moreover, individual teachers have their own notions of language and, although these may be informal and implicit, they influence what and perhaps even how they teach. Your particular notions about language will have a significant impact on what and how you assess and how you interpret the results of your assessment. Therefore, teachers need to make explicit the specific notions about language that underlie their objectives and teaching methods so that they can develop an appropriate plan for evaluation.

Our own notions about language are very simple. We believe that for purposes of second language evaluation in education, language is best viewed as a skill. It is possible to *know* a lot about a language without being able to *use* it. For example, many linguists are well acquainted with exotic languages – they know the grammar, the vocabulary, and the pronunciation rules of the language, but they cannot speak the language or use it in authentic ways. Although describing people's knowledge about language, independent of their ability to use that knowledge, is useful from a theoretical point of view, it is not helpful in teaching languages and evaluating second language learning. The focus in this book is on language as a skill.

Task 1

Use the questionnaire in Table 2 on page 21 to describe your theory of language.

Using language objectives in evaluation

The focus of this section is on course objectives. (We discuss unit and lesson objectives in more detail in the section on instructional plans.) One of the first and most important steps in evaluation is to assess the adequacy of course objectives relative to students' needs, background characteristics, and goals. A serious mismatch between student needs and course objectives would call for a revision in the objectives or, where possible, an alternative procedure for selecting students whose needs are more compatible with those objectives. By comparing course objectives with teachers' expertise and with the technical resources of the school, it is possible to determine the compatibility of the objectives with other input factors. Furthermore, by comparing course objectives with current theories of language learning, one can ascertain whether the objectives are compatible with current opinion.

A clear statement of course objectives is also relevant to the assessment of student achievement. Indeed, this is what most people think about when they think about second language evaluation. Student achievement is assessed in comparison with overall course objectives, which are also instrumental in assessing the adequacy of instructional plans and practices.

Explicit course objectives also help students understand how they will be able to use the language as a result of successful participation in a course. Thus, by comparing course objectives with their own language learning needs or expectations, they can decide whether a particular course will satisfy their needs. Similarly, by comparing objectives for different courses, students can judge how the language skills learned in one course will differ from those in other courses so that they can decide which particular course is likely to meet their needs, expectations, or desires best. A clear statement of course objectives can also serve as a criterion for students to assess their progress in language learning during a course of instruction.

Table 2.   Teachers' language theory questionnaire

Put a check mark in the appropriate column for each statement, depending on whether you agree or disagree.

Agree   Disagree

_____   _____   1. Language is a system of grammatical rules.

_____   _____   2. Vocabulary is the most important part of a language.

_____   _____   3. Language is basically a means of spoken communication.

_____   _____   4. Language is a means of establishing and maintaining social relationships.

_____   _____   5. Each language provides a unique way of organizing experience.

_____   _____   6. Learning grammatical rules is essential to learning a language.

_____   _____   7. Languages can only be learned by the conscious application of grammatical rules.

_____   _____   8. Language learning is best achieved by being exposed informally to authentic language in its native speech community.

_____   _____   9. Language learning is best when a teacher provides a carefully controlled exposure to the language.

_____   _____   10. Language learning is best promoted through using the language in authentic situations in the classroom.

_____   _____   11. Meaning is best conveyed through translation between the target language and the native language.

_____   _____   12. Language learning is best when the focus is on something other than the language itself.

_____   _____   13. There is no transfer from one skill to another when learning a language.

Source: R. V. White. (1988). *The ELT curriculum.* Oxford: Basil Blackwell, p. 159.

Course objectives should be described in such a way that anyone who reads them will gain a clear idea of how students will be able to use the second language if teaching and learning are successful. A clear statement of language objectives is important so that teachers can:

1. Plan appropriate instruction
2. Teach effectively
3. Evaluate the effectiveness of their instruction.

There is no simple or single way to prepare appropriate course objectives or to evaluate their appropriateness. A great deal of thoughtful judgment is called for. You may lack confidence in your judgment when first working with language objectives, but your confidence will grow with experience. Teachers should be prepared to assess and revise the objectives presented to them, regardless of whether they are contained in published second language materials or are found in local or district curriculum guidelines. Make sure that they are appropriate for your particular students and circumstances.

Although there are no definitive criteria for judging and preparing course objectives, some general guidelines can be of value. Well-stated and practical course objectives strive for the following five characteristics:

1. Course objectives should be general. A single course objective should cover a significant domain of second language performance. For example, "writing term papers," "conversing about common adolescent activities," and "comprehending the literal meaning of newspaper articles" are general and refer to significant domains of second language performance. In comparison, "will be able to use the correct forms of the present tense verbs" is too specific for a course objective.
2. Course objectives should refer to a single domain of language performance. A single course objective that refers to different domains of language should be rewritten and broken down into separate domains. For example, "Students will be able to read journal articles and write a summary of their reading" is better stated as two objectives: "will be able to read journal articles" and "will be able to write summaries of material they have read." Many of the specific things one might want to teach in order to develop reading ability might not be applicable to teaching writing. Moreover, a student might attain one objective but not the other – for example, to comprehend journal articles but not to write acceptable summaries; therefore, you could not assess attainment of this objective properly if both language domains were included.
3. Within a given language domain, course objectives should not overlap. That is to say, they should be as independent as possible. Separate but overlapping objectives should be combined into a single objective. For example, it would be better to combine these two overlapping objectives: "Students will be able to comprehend newspaper articles" and "Students will be able to comprehend classified ads in the newspaper." Often overlapping objectives can be restated in a hierarchical manner. For example, "Students will be able to comprehend newspapers: (a)

classified ads for literal meaning, and (b) news articles for literal and implied meanings."

4. Course objectives should refer to student performance, not to teacher performance. For example, to "teach" or "explain" or "illustrate" or "present" generally refer to teacher performance. Such statements as "students will be exposed to short radio excerpts" really refer to teacher activities. Such descriptions do not provide an adequate basis for evaluating student learning.

5. Preferably, course objectives refer to products of learning and to processes associated with language performance. For example, statements about students' ability to write a term paper or comprehend a weather forecast on the radio are about the products of learning. Similarly, statements about processes associated with certain kinds of language usage (such as preparing outlines of or revising written text) are useful forms of stating objectives for evaluation. It is best to avoid objectives that are stated in terms of processes related to learning itself; statements such as "students should practice," "improve," or "develop" are about the process of learning and are problematic because they are difficult to quantify. It is true that sometimes instruction aims to teach learning strategies, such as subvocal rehearsal of new material, watching TV in the second language, and so on. These are legitimate objectives for instruction, but they are not language objectives.

Instructional plans

Instructional plans specify what should be taught, and when and how it should be taught. They can be thought of as blueprints for achieving course objectives. Effective teaching requires detailed plans for an entire course, including plans for separate units and even individual lessons that comprise the course. Such plans are often referred to as the syllabus. A well-designed syllabus provides a great deal of specific information about all aspects of instruction, thus allowing teachers to implement the course appropriately and effectively and to assess it thoroughly. By comparing the instructional plans described in the syllabus with course objectives, teachers can assess whether the instructional plans prescribed in the syllabus are compatible with the course objectives. Syllabus plans that are not compatible with course objectives are not likely to be successful in achieving those objectives and, therefore, probably need to be changed. By comparing the syllabus with the needs and characteristics of a particular group of students and with the resources available at school, teachers can decide whether the syllabus is appropriate for their students and feasible given their particular professional resources. If the plans are judged to be inappropriate or not feasible, then changes in the plans are probably in order.

In the preceding examples, course objectives, professional resources, and student characteristics serve as a basis for assessing the syllabus. In other cases, the syllabus itself can serve as a basis for assessing other aspects of instruction. For example, if the syllabus appears appropriate and feasible relative to course objectives, student needs, and available resources, then following the syllabus faithfully becomes a necessary condition for achieving the course objectives. Not following the syllabus may result in failure to achieve the objectives. By comparing classroom practices with the syllabus, once instruction begins, teachers can monitor whether they are implementing the syllabus as prescribed. Knowing that the syllabus is not being implemented as prescribed might explain why instructional objectives are not being mastered by most of the students. Furthermore, it can indicate where classroom practices should be altered so that they align more closely with the syllabus and, thereby, improve your chances of achieving your instructional objectives.

Aspects of instructional plans

What facets of instructional plans are useful in second language evaluation? The following aspects of instructional plans can be considered:

1. Content (objectives)
2. Organization
3. Materials and equipment
4. Activities and roles

We describe each of these briefly now. You may want to modify the following descriptions of these items to be more suitable for your classroom.

CONTENT

At the very least, instructional plans can be described in terms of the specific language content, or objectives, to be taught and learned. The language objectives in unit or lesson plans identify interim learning outcomes and, therefore, provide criteria for assessing progress in learning during the course of instruction. If the interim objectives are not compatible with the course objectives, then changes to the syllabus may be called for. Here, course objectives are used as a criterion for the assessment of syllabus objectives, which, in turn, can be used as criteria for the assessment of other aspects of instruction. For example, assessment of student achievement following particular lessons or units can be carried out using syllabus objectives as criteria.

Students, too, can make use of information contained in the syllabus for their own purposes. By comparing syllabus plans with their own skills and resources before they take a course, students can judge whether they have adequate resources, such as time, to meet the demands of the course and then decide whether to take the course. By comparing syllabus plans with what they already know about the target language once they are in a course, students can decide where to concentrate their energies. Students must be clearly informed of instructional plans if they are to do this.

Task 2

Describe the language content of a unit or lesson you have taught or might teach.

ORGANIZATION

A course of second language instruction is made up of a sequence of units that is organized in some way — according to, for example, (1) general themes (holidays, transportation), (2) situations (the supermarket, the post office), (3) tasks (preparing research reports, taking lecture notes), (4) communicative functions (inviting, asking for information, greeting), or (5) linguistic structures (prepositions of place, past tense of irregular verbs, direct and indirect pronouns). The organization of the content within a unit of instruction can also be described, often in terms of principles related to language learning or teaching. For example, the instructional plans may specify that whole class activities should precede pairwork so that target language skills can be demonstrated in low risk, whole class situations before students are expected to demonstrate them individually in pairwork. Or the instructional plans may specify that comprehension exercises should precede production exercises on the premise that the former are passive language skills and, therefore, easier than the latter, which require active language use.

The organization of a unit of instruction may be an important factor to consider when trying to understand student learning. On the one hand, failure to respect the organization of a unit may explain poor student achievement; on the other hand, the organization of the unit may have been respected but was somehow flawed. For example, the organization of instructional units could be compared with current theory and research about second language learning, which suggests that students learn language skills more effectively when instruction is planned according to authentic communication needs. Your textbook, however, may organize units around arbitrary notions of simple versus complex grammatical structures that do not map onto your students' needs. There is then a mismatch between instructional plans and current theory about language learning and, therefore, change in the instructional plans is called for.

Task 3

Describe the organization of a unit or lesson you have taught or might teach.

MATERIALS AND EQUIPMENT

Instructional plans can also be described in terms of the materials and equipment needed to carry out the plans. The materials may include textbooks, audiotapes, videotapes, picture sets, language games, flash cards, readers, and realia. Some of the materials may be further characterized as authentic, such as could be found outside the classroom (application forms, commercial advertisements, and announcements), whereas some might be created for use only in the classroom (e.g., worksheets, word games, puzzles). Some of the materials may be included as part of the course or instructional package (e.g., textbook, flash cards). Yet other materials may be brought to class by the students themselves, such as magazines, newspapers, cereal boxes, baseball cards, tourist flyers, and so on. Not all materials need be linguistic in nature. For example, the students may be asked to bring in their favorite food, an unusual toy, or clothing worn in their culture as a method of stimulating classroom discussion.

Equipment might include filmstrip projectors, overhead projectors, tape recorders, audio cassette recorders, videocassette recorders, or television monitors. We would also include in this category paper, pencils, workbooks, mimeograph machines, chalk, and any other equipment or tools the teachers or students might need. Although this kind of equipment is readily available in some areas, it may not be in others. Whether instruction can be implemented as prescribed in the syllabus will depend on the availability of such basic equipment and materials. By comparing the materials and equipment called for in the syllabus with that which is actually available, teachers can determine the feasibility of a course and then decide where to make modifications to the syllabus.

Information about the materials and equipment needed to implement the syllabus is also pertinent to assessing the suitability of a particular syllabus, unit, or lesson to meet instructional objectives. If the objectives indicate that the purpose of the course is for the students to develop conversational skills in English, but most of the planned activities involve written language, then changes in the prescribed materials may be called for – such as the inclusion of audio- and videotapes that depict conversations. Or if the equipment required for implementation of the instructional plans does not match what is available, the teacher may need to make changes to the original plan – alternative activities that do not require such equipment could be incorporated into the plan, or different equipment that is available might be substituted without changing other aspects of the plan.

Task 4

What special or additional materials and/or equipment could you use to teach the unit or lesson you described in Task 3?

ACTIVITIES AND ROLES

Activities refer to the ways in which materials and equipment are used and how the content is to be taught. As with the other aspects of instruction described so far, there is no definitive way in which to describe instructional activities. Activities can be described as: (1) what the students are doing; (2) how the students are grouped; and (3) how the activities are organized in the classroom. Examples of classroom activities are reading, journal writing, oral drills, show-and-tell, conversation, question-response, role play, and so on. Students may be grouped into whole class activities, pairwork, and small group or individual activities. Activities may be teacher-centered or student-centered. All students may work on the same activity, or they might be subdivided and work on various activities according to interest or ability levels.

Student and teacher roles describe the relationship of these individuals to one another and to the content, materials, and activities. A very common role for teachers is to teach the linguistic content, direct and control student learning, and model correct language. The students usually assume a relatively passive or reactive role in response to the active role of the teacher. In student-centered classrooms, students take a much more active role: They decide what activities to do and when, and they consult with the teacher to identify reasonable and worthwhile activities and discuss plans for completing them. In such cases, the teacher acts as a supervisor or resource, advising students about their choices, directing them to relevant materials, and providing feedback on progress. Roles and activities are not independent of one another, obviously. The roles of teachers and students influence the kinds of activities they do, and, conversely, the kinds of activities they do determine their roles. It is the combination of roles and activities that is important to consider.

As with other aspects of instruction, comparisons can be made between activities and roles that are planned and other components of instruction to assess whether they are mutually compatible. Comparing the activities and roles set forth in the syllabus with general course objectives (and with syllabus objectives) can indicate whether the planned roles and activities are likely to lead to attainment of the objectives. For example, objectives that aim for conversational skills would require at least some interactive pairwork that is student-centered using oral material, whereas objectives that aim for reading and writing skills would not require such activities; more individualized, noninteractive activities with written material would be appropriate in this case.

The relation between instructional materials and activities and teacher/ student roles, on the one hand, and language objectives, on the other hand, has especially important implications for evaluation. Where there is a close relationship between objectives and roles, materials, and activities, it is reasonable to use the latter as a basis for assessing whether students have achieved the objectives. Where the relationship between them is remote, alternative activities, materials, and roles need to be used for assessing achievement. In other words, it is advisable to use classroom activities that match instructional objectives and to avoid those that do not match.

To illustrate this point, take a course on survival ESL for adult immi- grants living in an English-speaking country – imagine that the course objectives are described in terms of survival language skills associated with finding a job, using public transportation, and shopping for food. Imagine further that in one case the syllabus includes a number of realistic activities that involve authentic language materials. In one such activity, the students read job want ads from the local newspaper, which they are asked to paraphrase, and then write a letter of application requesting an interview. This particular instructional activity and these materials closely approxi- mate the actual language objective and, therefore, could be used to assess learning of the objective.

In comparison, imagine that the syllabus also includes a number of dictation exercises in which the students transcribe job application letters read to them by the teacher. The use of dictation in this case is not intended to make the students proficient in dictation. Rather, it is used to teach other language skills, such as correct spelling, punctuation, and grammar, that can be used when reading and writing actual job-related material. In this situation, dictation is not a satisfactory basis for assessing the students' attainment of the language objective. Other means of examining achieve- ment need to be devised in this case.

Task 5

Describe alternative roles that teachers and students
can have in second language classrooms and the
advantages and disadvantages of each.

Instructional practices

Instructional practices include the actual strategies, materials, activities,
and tasks used by teachers and students in the classroom. It is necessary to
consider classroom practices separate from plans because what is planned
may not always occur in the classroom. Teachers may not implement
instructional plans as prescribed for a variety of reasons – they do not
understand them well; the plans are poorly described and, therefore, cannot
be implemented unambiguously; teachers do not agree with the pedagogi-
cal, linguistic, or psychological principles underlying them; or they interpret them in ways that were not foreseen by the course-curriculum
designers. Moreover, classroom practice may not proceed according to plan
because the students themselves do not react as expected. It is important
that classroom-based evaluation take into account what actually happens in
class rather than simply what is supposed to happen. It is unfair to assess
student achievement with reference to instructional plans, including objectives, if these do not adequately represent what actually takes place in class.

It is also important to compare instructional practices with instructional
plans in order to determine whether things are going as planned in class and
to decide what changes are needed if they are not. If students are not
responding to instructional activities and materials as anticipated or if they
are not learning what is expected, one needs to determine whether the plan
was not followed or whether it was flawed. If the plans were followed as
prescribed, this would suggest that the plan is inadequate in some respect
and needs changing. However, if the plan was not followed, then this might
explain student performance. There may, of course, be other reasons for
things going awry – students did not understand what was expected of
them; not enough time was devoted to particular activities; or students did
not find the activities interesting.

If a teacher notices that different cohorts of students have difficulty
attaining certain language objectives year after year even though repeated
observation of classroom practice indicates that instructional plans are

being implemented as prescribed and students are responding as expected, then the overall plan, or a particular aspect of the plan, might be to blame and, therefore, should perhaps be changed. Careful and detailed documentation of what teachers and students do in the classroom can ensure that these changes are actually made.

A number of formal schemes for observing and recording observations about classroom practices have been proposed for both subject matter classes and, more recently, second language classes. These observational schemes have been designed for research purposes and cannot be used easily by untrained observers and certainly not by teachers who are occupied with teaching. We will describe a practical method for planning and recording classroom observations in Chapter 5. Suffice it to say at this point that teachers can describe their own classroom practices and their students' responses to activities in the same terms we used to describe instructional plans, namely, (1) content, (2) organization, (3) materials and equipment, and (4) instructional activities and roles.

Input factors

Thus far, we have talked about second language instruction as though it existed independently. Of course, this is an oversimplification. Second language teaching and learning are affected by a variety of factors from outside the classroom itself, which we refer to as *input* factors. Examples of such factors are given in Table 3.

One can regard input factors as prerequisites to the development of

Table 3.   Examples of input factors

- Students' needs
- Students' current level of second language proficiency
- Students' prior educational experiences
- Students' cultural background
- Students' attitudes toward school
- Students' medical status
- Technical resources in the school
- Professional resources in the school
- Teachers' professional training and expertise
- Teachers' attitudes
- Current theories about language teaching and learning
- Class size and composition
- Time for instruction

sound instructional objectives and plans and to the effective implementation of classroom practice. In other words, instructional objectives, plans, and practices should be compatible with input factors. Second language evaluation needs to consider the match, or mismatch, between these prerequisites and instructional objectives, plans and practices for particular teachers working with a particular group of learners in a particular community. For the most part, input factors cannot be changed, so, if there is a mismatch, certain aspects of instruction must be altered to achieve greater compatibility. Let us illustrate how input factors can play an important part in second language evaluation by giving examples concerning each aspect of instruction. Instructional objectives may be inappropriate because they do not match the students' existing second language abilities or their second language learning needs or interests. Objectives that focus on intermediate reading skills would not be appropriate for students with no prior literacy experiences. Objectives that aim for basic interpersonal communication skills would be inappropriate for international businesspeople who need communication skills related to selling electronic equipment to automobile manufacturers. Assuming that these particular groups of learners could not be excluded from the course, the course objectives would need to be modified to better suit the students' actual abilities and needs.

Instructional plans may be judged inadequate because they fail to take into account the resources of the school. For example, plans calling for individualized learning activities using interactive videocomputer labs will not be feasible if the school has only one lab station. Or plans may fall flat because they use interactive teaching techniques that teachers are unfamiliar with. If the course in question is to be implemented soon, alternative activities need to be planned. However, if more time is available, teachers can be given in-service training in the new techniques.

Input factors also need to be taken into account when putting instructional plans into practice. During a unit on reading newspapers, the teacher asks the students to select articles from the entertainment section of an English language newspaper but finds out that most of the students do not have access to English newspapers. An alternative activity or a modified version of this activity is in order. Or a high school teacher asks the students to play the role of patient and to describe a medical ailment to a doctor, but with little success. The teacher learns later that these students are refugees from underdeveloped rural areas and have not had prior experience with doctors, even in their home country. The lesson needs to be modified to enable students to play roles they are already familiar with. Another approach would be to familiarize them with the roles in question before the lesson proceeds.

Task 6

Can you identify any additional input factors not
listed in Table 3?

Summary

In this chapter, we have described various aspects of instructional objectives, plans, and classroom practices to consider in second language evaluation. We have also identified a number of factors (learners' needs and abilities, teachers' abilities, community attitudes, and current thinking about second language pedagogy) that play an important role in second language evaluation. We illustrated how these factors affect second language evaluation and decision making in the classroom.

The examples in this chapter illustrate that second language evaluation involves the comparison of many different but related aspects of teaching and learning. Some of this information is readily available and does not require specialized methods of collection or analysis. Information about instructional objectives and plans is available in course documents; school authorities and records can indicate which technical, material, and professional resources are available; and students' backgrounds (medical history, past education, etc.) may also be illuminated by school records.

Other information relevant to evaluation, however, requires specialized methods of collection and, in some cases, analysis, including details about student achievement or class performance, attitudes toward and perceptions of the course, and language learning needs and interests. In Parts II and III of the book, we turn to these special kinds of information and how to collect them.

Discussion questions

1. Choose a particular theory of language and report on it to your group.
   Discuss whether this particular theory has had an effect on what or how
   you teach. Describe what you think are its strong and weak points.
   Describe how you would evaluate the effectiveness of teaching based on
   this theory.
2. Look at the objectives of the course you are presently teaching. If you
   are a new teacher and not yet teaching, choose a textbook for a class you
   are likely to teach to respond to these questions. Where did these objec-

tives originate? Are they compatible with what and whom you are teaching (or will teach)? If not, what can you do about this?

3. Assess your language teaching objectives in light of the five criteria for judging and preparing objectives outlined in this chapter. Could changes be made that would make your objectives better? Or choose a second language textbook and use the objectives stated in it to answer this question.

4. Are there ways of judging objectives that are better than those described in this chapter? Why are they better?

5. Look at the syllabus or instructional plans for the course you are currently teaching. Do they match the overall objectives for the course? How could they be changed to be a better plan for realizing these objectives? Use the chapters in a second language textbook as a syllabus to answer this question if you are not currently teaching.

6. If you make lesson plans, how do they differ from the general description presented in this chapter? If you have not previously used lesson plans, is there anything in this chapter that might encourage you to do so? What was it that did this?

7. Do you teach your students anything in addition to language? Describe what these other objectives are and how you know whether you have succeeded in teaching them.

Readings

Chamot, A. U., and M. O'Malley. (1987). The cognitive academic language learning approach: A bridge to the mainstream. *TESOL Quarterly, 21*, 227–249.

Coleman, H. (1985). Evaluating teachers' guides: Do teachers' guides guide teachers? In C. J. Alderson (Ed.), *Evaluation* (pp. 83–96). Oxford: Pergamon Press.

Hamayan, E. V., and J. S. Damico. (1991). *Limiting bias in the assessment of bilingual students.* Austin, Tex.: Pro-ed.

Hopkins, C. D., and L. A. Richards. (1990). Instructional objectives. In C. D. Hopkins and L. A. Richards (Eds.), *Classroom measurement and evaluation* (pp. 39–52). Itasca, Ill.: F. E. Peacock.

Mattes, L. J., and D. R. Omark. (1984). *Speech and language assessment for the bilingual handicapped.* San Diego: College Hill Press.

Rea-Dickens, P., and K. Germane. (1993). *Evaluation.* Oxford: Oxford University Press.

Stiggins, R. J., and N. J. Bridgeford. (1985). The ecology of classroom assessment. *Journal of Educational Measurement, 22,* 271–286.

Tierney, R. J., M. A. Carter, and L. E. Desai. (1991). Portfolios and self-assessment by students. In *Portfolio assessment in the reading and writing classroom* (Chapter 7). Norwood, Mass.: Christopher-Gordon.

Wiggins, G. (1989). Teaching to the (authentic) test. *Educational Leadership, 46,* 41–47.

3 *A framework for evaluation*

- Introduction
- The context of classroom-based evaluation
- A strategy for classroom-based evaluation
- Planning evaluation
- Summary

Preview questions

1. When planning instruction for a new group of students, what kind of information about them is useful for your planning? How do you collect this information? Do you consult with parents, other teachers, or the students themselves? What specific topics do you ask each of them about?
2. Who do you provide with assessment information? What kinds of assessment information do you provide them?
3. If you are teaching in a situation where report cards are used, discuss (a) the items covered in the report, and (b) the purposes this information serves.
4. At the end of a course or year's instruction, how do you know if you have attained your instructional objectives? What do you do if you feel you have not?
5. When you give a class test, what do you do if many of the students do poorly? What do you do if only one or two students do poorly?
6. How and when do you assess student achievement? What do you do with the results of these assessments?
7. How do you know that a lesson or unit you are teaching is going well? How do you know when it is not going well? What do you do if it appears to be going poorly? How do you ensure that this does not happen the next time you teach the unit or lesson?
8. Identify reasons why a lesson or unit might not be effective, and then describe what you can do to make it more effective.

Introduction

We have discussed decision making as if this were a straightforward activity. It is not. Even when adequate information is available, there is no automatic procedure to tell you how to use the data you collect in order to reach a sound decision. Sometimes teachers are given decision rules to follow. For example, teachers may be told that a student who misses more than five classes in a term cannot pass the course. Or they may be told that students need a grade of 60 in order to be promoted to the next level. But very often teachers are left to make decisions on their own. For example, the teacher who observes one student who stands out, who is better than the others in a class, must decide whether to recommend the student for placement in a higher class. There is no precise rule for how much better a student must be in order to be advanced. Because we are without precise decision rules, we need a strategy for making decisions. The primary aims of this chapter are to present such a strategy, to illustrate how it can work in the classroom, and to discuss the formulation of plans for effective evaluation.

The context for classroom-based evaluation

As we pointed out in Chapter 1, evaluation is a process that results in decisions about instruction, students, or both. The first step in the decision-making process is to identify the purpose for evaluation – that is, specify the kinds of decisions you want to make as a result of evaluation. Once this has been done, the next step is the collection of information pertinent to these decisions. This aspect of evaluation is referred to as assessment. Assessment information is seldom useful by itself. It must be interpreted – put into context before it is meaningful. This is accomplished by comparing it with some desired state of affairs, goals, or other information that you have that is relevant to your decision. Once this is done, an interpretation of the information is possible, and, finally, a decision can be made about how to proceed.

This four-step process – identifying purposes, collecting information, interpreting it, and making a decision – is characteristic of everyday choices as well as professional decisions teachers make when they are planning instruction and engaged in teaching. In the next section, we present examples to illustrate how decisions are made in the classroom. The examples here are simplified – only two aspects of teaching and learning are discussed at a time. In the following section – A strategy for classroom-based evaluation – we put the pieces together.

Figure 1 summarizes those aspects of teaching and learning that play a role in classroom-based evaluation. The three central components of instruction are purposes, plans, and practice and are highlighted in the center boxes of Figure 1. The purposes identify instructional objectives and shape

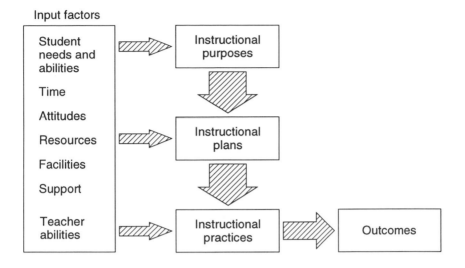

Figure 1   The context of classroom-based evaluation.

instructional plans. The plans present a means for realizing instructional objectives. Classroom practices are how the plans are put into effect; they are what leads to actual outcomes: language learning, new attitudes, or greater cultural awareness. This way of thinking about instruction can apply to segments of instruction as short as a single lesson, several lessons, or an entire unit of instruction; it can also apply to much longer segments of instruction (e.g., an entire year or course of instruction, or related courses that take place over a number of years – that is, a program of instruction).

As noted in Chapter 2, a comprehensive view of evaluation also requires that we consider input factors that can influence teaching and learning in the classroom. These are identified in the box on the left of Figure 1. We have already talked about the relationship between student needs and objectives. Yet other factors, such as students' attitudes, teachers' abilities, and the availability of certain resources and facilities, can also influence instructional practices in the classroom. The importance of input factors notwithstanding, instructional purposes, plans, and practices are the focus of our discussion of classroom-based evaluation because, as we have already seen, it may be necessary or desirable, under certain conditions, to change one or all of these in order to ensure more effective teaching and better learning. Moreover, classroom teachers are seldom able to alter input factors since they fall outside their sphere of influence.

Task 1

Give an example of an input factor that teachers
could modify.

Of course, we must also consider instructional outcomes. Outcomes are
represented on the right side of Figure 1. The main types of outcomes we
are concerned with are those related to language learning, especially the
ability to use language for communication. However, you might want to
consider other language-related outcomes, such as students' attitudes toward the target language or the target language group, or their acquisition of
communication or learning strategies. The kinds of outcomes you consider
depend on your objectives. The ones you consider important may be associated with an entire course of instruction, a unit of instruction, or a single
lesson.

We now present some simple examples of how decisions are made in the
classroom using Figure 1 as a frame of reference.

Example 1: Changing purposes

As noted earlier, second language courses are designed to achieve certain
general objectives. Specific objectives are chosen in accordance with the
anticipated needs of a hypothetical group of students. Unfortunately, often
the students who actually enroll in the course do not have exactly the same
needs or characteristics as the hypothetical group for whom the objectives
were devised. There may be a mismatch between actual student needs and
instructional objectives. If so, then a change is called for. In this case, if the
procedures for selecting the students who are admitted to the course cannot
be modified, then the instructional objectives need to be redesigned to
ensure that they better match student needs.

Example 2: Changing plans

In the previous example, instructional objectives were compared with student needs and then reformulated because they did not match those needs.
Instructional objectives, in turn, can be compared to other aspects of instruction. There are, for example, many second language courses that aim
to teach conversational skills. But let us imagine that an examination of the
instructional plans as set out in the teachers' guide and the students' textbook indicates a mismatch: there are very few activities related to conversa-

tion. Rather, students are expected to read expository texts and write answers to questions about the texts. The few oral activities that are included in the textbook consist primarily of drills that focus on grammatical features of the target language. A mismatch occurs because the instructional objective aims for conversational proficiency but the planned activities emphasize written language. The instructional plans, including the text, need to be revamped if the objective is to be attained.

Objectives can also provide a basis for assessing student achievement. Indeed, the use of objectives to assess student achievement is fundamental to classroom evaluation. In order to compare student achievement with objectives, we need both a clear statement of the objectives and also appropriate ways of assessing student attainment of the objectives. For an individual student, failure to attain objectives is a personal problem; however, when large numbers of students fail to attain the objectives, there is a problem with the course, and revisions must be made. In the latter case, it may be necessary to change the objectives, the instructional plans, the instructional practices, or some combination of these.

Example 3: Changing practices

Imagine a lesson plan in which students, organized in small groups, are supposed to discuss what to take on a three-day camping trip. The teacher explains to the students what they are to do and then goes from group to group to observe and lend assistance as the students begin their assignment. She spends five to ten minutes with each group and observes that, contrary to her plans, the students are speaking in their own language about sports, music, after-school activities, and so on. What is actually happening is clearly not consistent with her plans. It is unlikely that the lesson will achieve its objectives if it continues this way. The teacher must take steps to bring the students back on task. Perhaps they can be better prepared for such activities, or perhaps they need an incentive to stick to the task, such as a reward for the group that finishes first.

In these examples, you can see how each component of instruction can affect evaluation in different ways. Sometimes a specific component is the object of the evaluation. At other times, the same component can itself provide a basis for assessing other aspects of the instructional context. Thus, in example 1, it was the instructional objectives that were being assessed; they were judged against the students' needs. In comparison, in example 2, the objectives were used to assess the instructional plans. Just as objectives are sometimes themselves assessed, at other times they provide a basis for assessing instructional plans. Thus, in example 2, instructional plans were judged against instructional objectives, whereas in example 3, instructional plans provided a basis for judging instructional practices.

Example 4: Students as decision makers

The examples that we have looked at so far have all focused on the teacher as decision maker. Students can be partners in planning instruction and can make some of their own decisions. Just as teachers have in mind goals for student learning, so too students have a sense of what they want to learn. This is certainly true of adult learners. The decisions that teachers make, naturally enough, mostly affect instruction, whereas the choices students make affect the learning strategies they use, their study habits, and even whether they will take a particular second language course. When students observe that they are failing to achieve their own objectives, they must change their ideas about the language, their aspirations, their learning strategies, or the amount of time and effort they devote to studying if they are to succeed. When the objectives of a particular course do not match their needs or wants, they may have to change their mind about which course to take. Effective learning environments provide many opportunities for students to assess their own goals, accomplishments, and ways of studying so that they can make decisions that will advance their second language learning.

Final examinations do not provide useful assessment information for students. When the course is over, it is too late for students to take steps to improve learning. Final exams may provide an incentive to study and may reward students who study hard with high grades. They may even provide teachers with useful information about student advancement and for revising instruction for the next term, but they don't help students learn better.

A strategy for classroom-based evaluation

As you can see from the preceding section, evaluation involves comparison. More specifically, decisions that result from classroom-based evaluation are arrived at by making comparisons between various components of instruction and the larger instructional context (including input factors, purposes, plans, practices, and outcomes) and then taking action to reduce mismatches between the components so that the desired outcome or match is achieved. If there is no mismatch, then instruction can proceed without changing anything. A schematic representation of how this works is presented in Figure 2.

Another way of viewing classroom-based evaluation requires that you look for potential problems and decide on actions to resolve them. Problems take the form of mismatches, incongruities, or inconsistencies between what is actually happening or is likely to happen, on the one hand, and what you would like to happen, on the other. Mismatches indicate that there is a potential problem; decisions about changes that will eliminate or

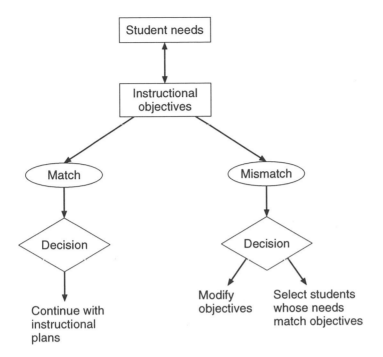

Figure 2   Mismatches and decision making.

reduce the problem are called for. Table 1 presents some sample questions that you can ask to identify problems before they arise.

The double-headed arrows in Figure 3 indicate the various comparisons that can be made when looking for mismatches or potential problems. We explain what these arrows can tell us about instruction and learning now.

A primary concern in education is whether students attain the general objectives of the course of study or the curriculum scope and sequence. Indeed, a common way of thinking about evaluation is in terms of student achievement at the end of a course of instruction in comparison to beginning-of-course objectives. However, evaluation need not wait until instruction has ended. In fact, it is advisable to begin evaluation before instruction actually starts. Waiting until instruction is finished minimizes the beneficial effects of evaluation on instruction and student learning.

Evaluation can even begin prior to the start of instruction with a comparison of instructional objectives and incoming students' needs, goals, previous learning experiences, and present levels of language proficiency; this is represented by Comparison 1 in Figure 3. This comparison can be made only if one has some prior knowledge of students' backgrounds. It is

Table 1.   Identifying potential problems

Some questions for evaluating a course for second language learning:

1. *Question:* Does this course respond to the needs and desires of its clientele?
   Answer: Compare list of needs and desires with general course objectives.
   Source of information: Questionnaire, interview, test, review of course materials and documentation.

2. *Question:* Does the plan for this course seem like a good means for attaining the course objectives?
   Answer: Compare general course objectives with interim objectives to see whether lessons (or parts) should be added or removed; compare materials and activities with interim objectives to see whether all are taught; check whether materials and activities reflect the best current thinking on second language teaching in order to see if anything needs to be altered; check whether instructional requirements can be satisfied by available resources; check whether materials and activities seem appropriate for the intended clientele.
   Source of information: Knowledge of course materials and documentation.

3. *Question:* Is the course working according to the plan?
   Answer: Are the planned activities actually occurring? Are the students performing as expected?
   Source of information: Observation.

4. *Question:* Were the interim objectives met?
   Answer: Check performance and use of language.
   Source of information: Observation, tests (quizzes), assignments, other assessment procedures.

5. *Question:* Were the general course objectives satisfied?
   Answer: Check student use of language.
   Source of information: Tests, "on-the-job performance."

also common practice for teachers to examine the adequacy of their objectives and instructional plans by comparing them with their students' needs, aspirations, and existing skills during the first week or two of class, once they have had a chance to collect background information about their students. Evaluation at these times allows teachers to fine-tune instructional objectives and plans early on. If student characteristics and the instructional objectives are not compatible, then changes to the objectives are warranted. In some cases, it may also be possible to alter the way in which students are

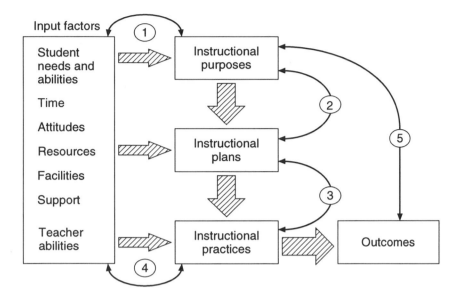

Figure 3   A strategy for classroom-based evaluation.

selected so that students whose needs match the objectives better are admitted to the course or program. If the instructional objectives are compatible with student needs, we can proceed with Comparison 2.

Comparison 2 asks whether the instructional plans are an appropriate and adequate way of attaining the instructional objectives, given the outcomes of Comparison 1. It can entail a comparison of instructional plans with instructional objectives even before teachers have met their new students. If they are not compatible, then changes to the plans will ensure a better match between plans and objectives. If they are congruent, then it is reasonable to put the instructional plans into practice.

Once instruction has begun, Comparison 3 can be made. Comparison 3 asks whether instruction is being implemented as planned. Failure to follow instructional plans may explain why students do not attain instructional objectives. Failure to attain instructional objectives even though the plans have been put into practice as prescribed suggests that the plans are inadequate and need to be modified. As noted earlier, this comparison need not wait until the end of the course. It can occur simultaneously with instruction and periodically during the course of instruction. Classroom practice may be inconsistent with instructional plans because of the influence of input factors, (e.g., time, materials, or other facilities) that make it difficult to implement plans as desired (Comparison 4). If this is indeed the case, the question arises, "Can the input factors responsible for the mismatch be altered so as to reduce their influence?" If not, then a new plan that is less subject to the influence of these factors may have to be devised.

Determining whether students have attained instructional objectives involves a comparison between student outcomes and purposes (Comparison 5 in Figure 3). If a majority of students have succeeded, then instruction can proceed without changes in plans. However, if a number of students have not attained the objectives, changes should be implemented. If the comparison is made during the course of instruction, then instructional plans and practice can be changed immediately with the goal of improving the achievement of current students. If the comparison is made at the end of the course, then changes will benefit future students only; the current group cannot profit from these modifications.

To summarize, evaluation should take place before instruction begins. Systematic and routine assessment of classroom practice and student achievement during the course can improve day-to-day instruction and learning. More specifically, regular monitoring of classroom practice using the evaluation strategy outlined here makes it possible to adjust instructional plans on-line so that the chances for successful learning are enhanced. Furthermore, ongoing assessment of student attainment of lesson and unit objectives, with attendant fine-tuning of instructional plans, will contribute to overall student success. It is a major challenge for busy teachers to evaluate from the beginning to the end of a course, but this is crucial to successful teaching and effective learning. Ensuring useful evaluation requires planning, our next topic.

Task 2

Based on your experiences as a teacher or student, recall a specific mismatch corresponding to each of the five numbered comparisons in Figure 3.

Planning evaluation

To be useful and effective, evaluation requires planning. Preparing for evaluation should be an integral part of planning each lesson or unit as well as general planning at the beginning of the school year or course. Instruction and evaluation should be considered together in order to ensure that instruction lends itself to evaluation and that the results of evaluation can direct ongoing instructional planning. Moreover, if evaluation is not planned along with instruction, the time required for assessment activities will most likely not be available.

When planning evaluation, the following questions are relevant:

1. Who will use the results of assessment and for what purposes?
2. What will I assess?
3. When will I assess?
4. How will I assess?
5. How will I record the results of my assessment?

In the remainder of this chapter, we address the first three questions; discussions of the last two are found in later chapters.

Who will use the results of assessment and for what purposes?

The results of assessment can be used by different people for different purposes. Teachers are certainly the main users of this information, primarily to make decisions about ongoing instruction – about students' current learning needs, instructional activities, the best time to move on to the next unit of instruction, remedial or additional instruction for individual students, and so on. In schools in which students are being educated through a second language (e.g., ESL students in Canada, the United States, or Australia), second language teachers may share the results of their assessments with the students' classroom teachers so that the latter are better able to modify instruction to reflect the students' level of proficiency in the language of instruction.

Although a great deal of second language assessment is normally undertaken and used by teachers, learners themselves can also play an important role in assessing their own language learning. Including self-assessment in your overall plan for evaluation can have a number of general benefits. It can expand responsibility for assessing learning beyond the teacher to include the learners themselves. This can be particularly important in learner-centered classrooms in which instruction is highly individualized and students select and direct their own learning activities. Self-assessment can help do this better. Self-assessment can increase learners' involvement in and responsibility for their own learning and, thereby, ultimately promoting second language achievement. Actively involving learners in assessing their own progress can sensitize them to instructional objectives and assist them in setting realistic goals for themselves. This can be particularly important for adult learners who have practical reasons for learning a second language, such as getting or keeping a job, and, therefore, want to be actively involved in planning and directing their own education.

In some cases, self-assessment can also be advantageous because it expands the basis for evaluation. Whereas teachers can assess learning only within the classroom setting, learners can monitor their own language performance in any and all settings that call for use of the target language, especially outside instructional periods. This information can be valuable to both learners and teachers in tailoring instruction and activities in the classroom. The use of self-assessment is particularly relevant when instructional objectives are based on the performance of tasks normally found outside school settings.

Self-assessment utilizing journals, conferences, and portfolios can assist students and teachers in monitoring student progress once instruction has begun. Self-assessment using questionnaires, rating scales, and interviews can also influence initial placement and screening decisions. Self-assessment can elicit information that is not easily or otherwise available to those making placement and screening decisions. The information garnered from self-assessment should always be used in conjunction with data from other assessment methods.

In the cases discussed so far, the results of assessment are used internally — by second language or regular classroom teachers to plan ongoing instruction and by students to reflect on and plan their learning and study activities. These results can also be used by people outside the classroom. More specifically, teachers are accountable to educational administrators and, in the case of young second language learners, to parents, as well. Although educational authorities may collect the accountability information in some cases, teachers themselves are often responsible for doing so. Second language teachers in elementary and secondary schools also provide parents with feedback about their children — during routine parent-teacher meetings or at special meetings if certain students are having problems. Children who are being schooled in a second language are often regarded as "special" or even "at risk." Consequently, their progress is often monitored carefully, and the educators working with these students are frequently required to account for what they are doing and how the students are progressing.

Deciding who will use assessment information and how it will be used is important because this may affect the method, frequency, and focus of assessment (e.g., achievement versus process), as well as how records of assessment are kept. Evaluation for accountability purposes — for parents and educational authorities — requires systematic and comprehensive evaluation of all students that is related to clearly articulated and well understood instructional objectives. It also necessitates record keeping that is well organized, clear, and concise since that information may be made available to the public. In comparison, assessment for day-to-day instructional planning is largely an internal matter and, therefore, private. In these latter cases, assessment methods may be more informal and include background and process-oriented information as well as achievement results. Record keeping may be more anecdotal since these results will not be shown to others. Evaluation for internal purposes generally occurs more frequently in order to monitor the effectiveness of ongoing instruction as well as that of completed units or lessons.

Task 3

Identify four people who might use assessment information from second language classes. What kinds of decisions might they use the information for?

What will I assess?

Clearly an important focus of classroom-based evaluation, whether for internal or external purposes, is student achievement. Teachers need to know what and how much students have learned in order to monitor the effectiveness of instruction, to plan ongoing instruction, and for accountability purposes. Certainly, all second language teachers will be concerned with their students' achievement. Where students are being schooled through a second language, teachers will also be concerned about monitoring their students' mastery of academic skills and subject matter. This is of primary concern to classroom teachers who teach the academic subjects but may also be of concern to second language teachers who use content-based or integrated approaches to their teaching. Second language teachers in some schools may share responsibility for teaching academic skills to second language students, and, in these cases, they too will be concerned with monitoring their students' understanding of content. The curriculum scope and sequence usually specifies the important content objectives and, therefore, those that should be assessed systematically. Generally speaking, the same content objectives should be used to assess the achievement of second language and native language speakers alike – lower standards of achievement should not be established for second language students.

In order to plan and tailor instruction that is appropriate for individual students or groups of students, it is necessary to understand the factors that influence student performance in class. This means going beyond the assessment of achievement. To illustrate this point, imagine a second language teacher who observes that many of her students' writing skills are not developing as she had planned and hoped for. As a result, she decides that changes in instruction are called for. However, the specific changes she makes will depend on her interpretation of why student performance is below expectation – the students may find the writing activities or materials uninteresting or irrelevant to what they need to be able to do outside class; the students may have been given insufficient time to master the targeted skills; they may have used inappropriate or ineffective learning strategies; or they may lack the background knowledge or skills needed to get involved in the assigned writing activities. If the teacher thinks that it is because she simply spent insufficient time on the development of these skills, she might extend the time devoted to this unit. If, however, she thinks that it is because the students lacked motivation because the writing activities were irrelevant to their out-of-class needs, she might investigate to determine what writing is expected of them outside the classroom and select more appropriate tasks.

In other words, decision making in the classroom is not only about achievement; it is also about the processes and factors that affect student achievement. Some of the factors that influence achievement can be found in the students' backgrounds: their prior educational experiences, medical history, family literacy and education, and so on. Information about such factors can be obtained from students' school records, medical reports, previous teachers, and parents – that is, sources outside the classroom.

Many factors in the classroom itself influence learning, for example, learning strategies used to complete instructional tasks, attitudes toward learning and school, interest in specific instructional activities, and study habits. Information about these influences can be collected in the classroom itself: by observing students while they work, by talking with them about their work, by having them keep journals, or by carefully examining their assignments and classroom performance. We focus on the collection of information in the classroom. Because of space limitations, we do not discuss how to collect background data about students. It is important to recognize, however, that such information is essential for understanding learning processes in the classroom.

The kinds of information we have discussed in this section are not exclusive. There may well be other kinds of information that are useful for individual teachers. The important point is that understanding student achievement and planning appropriate and effective instruction for them require a variety of information.

Task 4

Identify additional kinds of information you might
want to collect for evaluation purposes and discuss
how you could use that information.

When will I assess?

Most teachers assess the effectiveness of instruction informally on a continuous basis. This is sometimes referred to as formative evaluation.
Teachers working with students being educated through the medium of a
second language especially need to assess their language performance at all
times, even when the explicit focus of attention is not on language – during
mathematics as well as language lessons and during formal instructional as
well as noninstructional periods (e.g., at recess and in the hallways). This is
necessary in order to determine whether the students have acquired the
language skills they need to keep up with content instruction and to social-
ize comfortably with native-language-speaking students.

Additional time and attention are occasionally needed for systematic
assessment, such as at the end of instructional units. This makes sense for
teachers who organize and deliver instruction in terms of units. Examining
student progress at the end of major units can help one decide whether the
students are ready to proceed to the next unit and for planning the next unit.
Assessment at the end of each unit of instruction can also provide useful
information about how effective the unit was: Was it too difficult or easy?
Was enough time allotted? Were the materials adequate and interesting?
Did students have the necessary language and conceptual background
skills?

It may also be prudent to examine learning after several units, weeks, or
months in order to ascertain how much students have retained from earlier
instruction and whether they have consolidated or integrated skills, knowledge, or concepts taught over a period of time longer than a single lesson or
unit. Indeed, a developmentally sound curriculum will consist of integrated
and overlapping objectives that aim for cumulative learning.

Summative assessment at the end of the year may be required by the
school district or program director in order to assign grades for purposes of
certification or promoting students to the next level. Regardless of the
specific grading procedures used, it is important that information collected
about students – qualitative as well as quantitative and during as well as at

the end of instructional units – be used to formulate students' final grades. Many of the assessment procedures we discuss later provide qualitative information about student performance.

Although it is a matter of personal choice when to assess and how, we offer the following suggestions:

1. Determine student needs and abilities at the beginning of the course or year as a basis for assessing the appropriateness of general instructional objectives and for planning instruction. Follow-up assessment may be called for in beginner level language courses or other programs in which students' needs may change.
2. Examine student attainment of lesson and unit objectives on a regular basis. This information can be used to make changes in day-to-day instruction and to pace teaching – that is, to "fine-tune" lessons.
3. Provide frequent and regular occasions for informing students about learning success. Students can use feedback on an ongoing basis to guide their own learning.
4. Monitor classroom activities on a regular basis in order to ascertain their effectiveness. Indications that classroom activities are ineffective in promoting instructional objectives should be followed by a search for reasons why they are not working as planned.
5. Examine student attainment of general instructional objectives. In many cases, progress toward attainment of general objectives can be done periodically throughout the year or course. There is no need to wait until the end of the year for the first assessment of general objectives.

Scheduling assessment activities will depend, to some extent, on how the results are to be used and who will use them, as discussed in the preceding section. Assessment at the end of each unit of instruction is probably useful for both internal and external purposes; in other words, it is of interest to teachers for planning instruction, to students for organizing their own learning, to school authorities for accountability, and to parents who are interested in their children's education. Assessment after each lesson is most useful for internal purposes – for teachers as they plan day-to-day instruction and for students as they plan their study activities. Assessment after individual lessons is probably not very useful for external purposes since it provides more detail than is usually necessary. Summative evaluation at the end of the year or course is not particularly useful to teachers because it fails to capture important changes in student learning as they occur and because it cannot be used to affect current student learning; it may, however, be required by local educational authorities. Assessment at the end of the year or course can be useful to teachers when planning future instruction for a new group of learners.

Assessment information is not used only at the time it is collected. For example, information about student achievement during a course may be accumulated and used in assigning grades and making pass or fail decisions at the end of the course. Information about students' previous educational experiences and cultural backgrounds gathered in the opening weeks of instruction may explain why a lesson plan didn't work in the tenth week. It is important, therefore, to make an evaluation plan and to keep good records of the information you collect (see Chapters 5 to 7).

Task 5

What are the differences between summative and formative evaluation, and what is each useful for?

To summarize this section, an evaluation plan should include the following:

1. A list of the people and groups or agencies who will require assessment information. In addition to teachers and students, the list might include other educational professionals, parents, financial sponsors, community agencies, and so forth.
2. A description of the kinds of information each of the individuals or groups identified in item 1 wants and needs.
3. A description of assessment activities.
4. A schedule of when to carry out the assessment activities needed to provide the preceding information.
5. A description of the record-keeping systems to be used.

Summary

In this chapter, we presented a framework for classroom-based evaluation. We stated that evaluation is a process that can guide educational decision making and that there are four aspects to this process:

1. Identifying the purpose(s) for evaluation
2. Collecting information
3. Interpreting information
4. Making decisions

We described a strategy for making decisions that consists of comparing instructional objectives, plans, practices, input factors, and learning outcomes with one another. When there is a discrepancy between them, then decisions are called for that will minimize mismatches, reduce potential problems, and improve chances of attaining instructional objectives. We illustrated this strategy with examples in which instructional purposes, plans, and practices were changed in order to improve the chances of educational success. In these examples, we discusssed the components of evaluation as if they were distinct from one another and happen in linear order. Sometimes this is true, but often it is not – they overlap and are not clearly distinct. Nevertheless, in order to understand better how to do evaluation effectively in the classroom, it is useful to start by viewing these components as discrete and by examining how each component is related to the others.

We also discussed how to plan classroom evaluation and posed five questions to guide evaluation planning. We explored three of these questions in this chapter:

1. Who will use the results of assessment and for what purposes?
2. What will I assess?
3. When will I assess?

The remaining two are discussed in the remainder of the book:

4. How will I assess?
5. How will I record the results of my assessment?

We pointed out that it is important to plan evaluation along with instruction so that the time needed for assessment activities is provided and the results of assessment are useful in instructional planning. We suggested five components of a comprehensive evaluation plan:

1. A list of people who need assessment information
2. A description of the kinds of information they need
3. A description of assessment activities
4. A schedule for conducting assessment
5. A description of record-keeping methods to be used

Discussion questions

1. Who decides what you teach? How are these decisions made? If these decisions are made by someone else, do you have the opportunity to modify them? Why would you want to change them?
2. Are there other purposes for evaluation besides those that have been identified in this chapter?

3. Give as many reasons as you can for a student doing poorly on a test or exam. Then (a) identify those you can change and (b) describe what you can do about them.
4. Do your students (a) participate in self-assessment or (b) provide feedback about instruction? Describe what they do and what you do with the feedback.
5. Do you give final exams? How do you construct these exams? How do you decide what is a passing score? Is this the best way to make this decision?
6. Based on what you have read in this chapter, are there additional kinds of information you would now collect for evaluation purposes in your classroom? What are they and how would you use them?

Readings

Airasian, P. (1991). Assessment for instructional planning. In P. Airasian (Ed.), *Classroom assessment* (pp. 73–120). Chapter 3. New York: McGraw-Hill.

Hopkins, C. D., and L. A. Richards. (1990). *Classroom measurement and evaluation.* Itasca, Ill.: F. E. Peacock.

Hutchison, R. (1991). Reporting progress to students, parents, and administrators. In B. Harp (Ed.), *Assessment and evaluation in whole language programs* (pp. 201–218). Chapter 11. Norwood, Mass.: Christopher-Gordon.

Leblanc, R., and G. Painchaud. (1985). Self-assessment as a second language placement instrument. *TESOL Quarterly, 19,* 673–687.

Lewkowicz, J., and J. Moon. (1985). Evaluation: A way of involving the learner. In C. J. Alderson (Ed.), *Evaluation* (pp. 45–80). Oxford: Pergamon Press.

Murphy, D. F. (1985). Evaluation in language teaching: Assessment, accountability and awareness. In C. J. Alderson (Ed.), *Evaluation* (pp. 1–18). Oxford: Pergamon Press.

Nunan, D. (1988). *The learner-centered curriculum.* Cambridge: Cambridge University Press.

Oskarsson, M. (1978). *Approaches to self-assessment in foreign language learning.* Strasbourg: Council of Europe.

von Elek, T. (1982). A test of Swedish as a second language: An experiment in self-assessment. In Y. P. Lee, A. Fok, R. Lord, and G. Low (Eds.), *New directions in language testing* (pp. 47–57). Oxford: Pergamon Institute of English.

4 Collecting information

Preview questions

1. Have you ever had to plan a new second language course from scratch? If so, how did you decide what to include and what not to include? How did you collect the information you needed to make these decisions?
2. List some extraneous factors that could affect student performance on a test. What, if anything, can be done to minimize the effects of each of these?
3. Sometimes students complain that the way they were evaluated was unfair. What factors can substantiate their claim?
4. When you assign final grades or decide whether to pass or promote a student, what kinds of information do you use? Do you think that your grades are an accurate reflection of what each student has really learned? If not, why not, and what would you do to make your grades more accurate?
5. How do you know that your students are able to use the language skills they are learning in class in authentic situations outside class? How valid are your assessment procedures for predicting how well students can use their new language skills outside the classroom? How could you improve the predictive accuracy of your evaluation procedures?
6. Have you ever had to administer a standardized test that you thought was not valid for your students? If so, why did you think it was invalid?

Introduction

In Chapters 1, 2, and 3, we described our approach to second language evaluation; we described certain aspects of instruction, learning outcomes, and input factors pertinent to second language evaluation; and we presented a strategy for conducting second language evaluation and making evaluation decisions. As you can see, evaluation turns on different facets of teaching, its outcomes, and its context. In this chapter, we discuss characteristics of the information used in evaluation.

Types of information

In making decisions about second language instruction and learners, we use both *qualitative* and *quantitative* information. Qualitative information – that Fanny has an accent when she speaks English, for example – helps in planning special assignments: helping Fanny improve her accent. Quantitative information – for example, that the average reading speed of grade 10 students is 63 words per minute – may assist in selecting reading texts of appropriate average difficulty for grade 10 second language learners.

There is not always a clear distinction between qualitative and quantitative information, but this is not necessarily a drawback. To say that Karl's vocabulary in his second language is nativelike is unquestionably a qualitative statement. And it is clearly a quantitative assertion that Hiroshi scored 604 on the TOEFL. But much evaluation information is expressed in terms that include both qualitative and quantitative aspects: For example, one third of the students in the class speak French as a second language like native speakers, or a majority of the students would prefer to read mystery novels. Second language evaluation involves the collection of both qualitative and quantitative information. In general, having a variety of types of information about teaching and learning can enhance the reliability of your assessments and the validity of your decision making.

All information, whether qualitative or quantitative, refers to characteristics of something: students or teachers, textbooks or videotapes, texts or realia, blackboards or ministries of education. For example, we can have information about a student's reading ability or a teacher's enthusiasm, about the instructional approach of a textbook or the topic of a videotape, about the complexity of a text or the familiarity of an object brought into the classroom, about the size of a blackboard or the political makeup of a department of education. We need to be very clear about our information in order to avoid misunderstandings. Information about a student's knowledge of grammar is not the same thing as information about that student's ability to use the new language, even though teachers, students, and parents often interpret information about the first as if it were about the second.

Qualities of information

Regardless of what methods we use to collect information, we must always be concerned with the quality of the data we use for evaluation. We discuss two technical aspects of quality in this chapter: reliability and validity. In the most general terms, reliability refers to consistency and stability, to freedom from nonsystematic fluctuation. Validity is the extent to which the information is relevant. Reliability and validity are both critical for judging the quality of qualitative information (for example, when observing student behavior in class or assessing their conversational skills) and quantitative information (for example, from tests or rating scales).

At the same time, there are additional matters to be considered when collecting information for evaluation. There is the practical side of gathering data.

Practicality

An obvious practical consideration when planning evaluation is cost. Some procedures, such as standardized tests, can be very expensive, and therefore their use is limited. Closely allied to financial cost is the administrative time required to collect information using certain procedures. Procedures that can be administered to large groups are obviously less time consuming than those that can be used only with individuals. Administration time can be especially important in schools with fixed class periods. Trying to schedule tests, questionnaires, rating scales, and so on, that require more time than a single class period can create major problems. Similar to administrative time is compilation time. We are accustomed to thinking of scoring time for tests, but all procedures for collecting information require time to transform results into a usable form.

Some procedures have demanding administrator qualifications, whereas others require no special talents or training. For most multiple-choice language tests, examiner qualifications pose no problems: Language teachers generally possess the qualities needed to administer such tests. There are some tests, however, such as the U.S. Interagency Roundtable Interview (or FSI Oral Interview), that require special training to enable an examiner to administer the test; most classroom teachers could not administer this test without special training.

A final practical attribute is acceptability. It can be extremely difficult to implement decisions based on information collected using procedures that students, their parents, or the community at large lack confidence in. Before using a particular procedure for making vital decisions, it is wise to determine whether it has community approval. If not, informing the community

Table 1.   Practical aspects of information collection

Cost: Is the method of information collection affordable?

Administrative time: Is there enough time in class to collect information using this method?

*Compilation time:*Is there enough time to score and interpret the information?

Administrator qualifications: Are the teachers qualified to use this method of information collection?

Acceptability: Is this method of collecting information acceptable to students, parents, and the community?

---

about the reasons for your choice may produce the desired approval. If it does not, you may wish to use a more acceptable procedure even though it may not be as desirable otherwise. Acceptability is sometimes called face validity. We prefer to use the term *acceptability,* however, because this practical attribute does not share the technical characteristics associated with other types of validity. Table 1 summarizes these practical aspects of information collection.

You may choose *not* to employ a particular information-gathering procedure because of its practical attributes, but you should never select a procedure or an instrument on the basis of practical qualities alone. The technical attributes of reliability and validity outweigh practicalities, and validity, as we shall see, is the most crucial quality of all. Without validity, gathering information is, at best, a waste of time.

Reliability

Defining reliability

We have stated that reliability is concerned with freedom from nonsystematic fluctuation. Here we amplify that preliminary definition. It is probably easier to understand the notion of reliability from examples of unreliability. Imagine that two teachers observe two ESL students, Charles and Marie, during a conversation together, in order to assess their conversation abilities. The first teacher says that Charles fails to observe turn-taking conventions, and so the conversation falters. The second teacher claims, to the contrary, that it is Marie who fails to observe the conventions. Both teachers listened to and assessed the same conversation and reported different interpretations. There is no way to tell which teacher-observer is correct (if indeed either of them is). We can only say that the information is inconsistent. It is subject to fluctuation, depending on who is observing.

Let us consider another example. On Monday, Elke writes a composition. Her teacher reads it on Monday night and concludes that Elke's main writing problem is in distinguishing major points from supporting details. On Tuesday, Elke writes a letter to her best friend as part of a classroom assignment. Her teacher reads it and concludes this time that her main problem is in use of pronouns and synonyms to increase cohesion. Assuming that Elke has not made any significant improvement in her writing between Monday and Tuesday, we cannot tell what Elke's main problem is because the assignments she wrote do not provide reliable information about her major difficulties in writing the second language.

Here is one more example. Imagine that Victor and Paul are as equal as it is possible to be in their abilities in German, their second language. Next imagine that the two young men take a second language proficiency examination in German that consists of 200 multiple-choice items. Imagine further, since they are so nearly equal, that both know the correct answers to 175 of the 200 items and that they guess randomly at the answers to the 25 items they don't know. Paul is lucky and guesses right 11 times. Victor is not so lucky; he guesses right only 3 times. So Paul scores 186 and Victor, 178. In this example, the information that Paul is more proficient is not reliable. The difference in their scores is attributable to chance. In fact, the results could as well have gone the other way; next time Victor might get a higher score. That information would not be reliable either.

Three general sources of unreliability are exemplified here: The first has to do with instability or nonsystematic fluctuation in the person or among the people collecting the information. This was true in the conversation example. The difference between the two observers is called *assessor-related reliability* or *rater reliability.*

The second source of unreliability concerns the person about whom information is being collected. This was probably the source of unreliability with respect to Elke's writing problems. Depending upon when and what she is writing, different problems show up in quite unpredictable ways. This is called *object-related* or *person-related reliability.*

The third source of unreliability resides in the procedures used for collecting information. Paul appeared more knowledgeable than Victor because the type of examination they took provided opportunity for guessing. This is called *instrument-related reliability.*

Improving reliability

None of the three sources of unreliability is intrinsically better or worse than the others. One always wants to get information that is as reliable as possible; fortunately, there are some very practical ways of doing so. Reliability related to the persons collecting information can be enhanced if they know exactly how to get the desired information and if they are well trained and experienced with the information collection procedures. Whenever possible, it is advisable to use more than a single observer, interviewer, or composition reader. Moreover, they should make their observations or do their interviewing or reading independently. If a number of independent people agree on their assessments, one can have much greater confidence in the reliability of that information.

Person- or object-related reliability can be enhanced by assessing on several occasions. This is especially advisable when human abilities or qualities are the object of assessment, as is the case in second language assessment. If, for example, Elke wrote ten compositions and eight of them indicated that her greatest writing problem involved cohesion, we might then feel that this was reliable information. We could conclude that the two different results obtained earlier were simply reflections of the fact that human beings often differ in their behavior according to transitory moods, momentary distractions, time of day, fatigue, or hundreds of other factors beyond the control or even the recognition of the test taker or the assessor. Using information about a student's performance or achievement collected on different occasions and using different procedures is highly recommended when making decisions about second language learners. It is best to avoid using students' performance on a single occasion (e.g., on a classroom test) as the sole basis for making decisions about them.

Instrument-related reliability can be improved by using a variety of methods of information collection. In this way, the bias or inaccuracy resulting from the use of one method will be offset by other methods; for example, second language learners with particular cultural backgrounds may find it difficult to demonstrate what they have learned if asked to do so in front of other students; they might be more comfortable doing so when alone with their teacher. Using only a method of evaluation that calls for performance in front of the entire class could lead to an unreliable estimate of their achievement. In our example with Victor and Paul, if different procedures had been used to assess their second language proficiency, it is likely that sometimes Paul would have been assessed as superior and an approximately equal number of times Victor would have done better. Sometimes the two would have done virtually the same. Taking all this variation into account, one might accept as reliable information that the two students are for all practical purposes equal.

To give yet another example, one way to find out how much time a student spends on homework assignments is to ask, "On average, how much time do you spend on homework each day?" This procedure is subject to students' forgetting and to various interpretations of the question (average for the days that I do homework, or average across all days, even when I don't do homework?). A more reliable procedure could be to ask students to keep a log of how much they study at home during one week.

A general strategy for thinking about how to enhance reliability is to begin by considering possible sources of unreliability. In other words, identify factors that, if not controlled for, are likely to result in inconsistent or variable estimates of performance. For example, unreliable estimates of performance may result from assessing student performance at times during the day or week when they are not at their best or are ill-prepared or when you are not at your best and cannot give your full and careful attention to assessing their performance. Unreliability can result from poor or inconsistent record keeping so that your assessment of a student's progress and your instructional planning for that student are based on inaccurately recalled information. Improving reliability of information for evaluation often involves reducing or averaging out nonsystematic fluctuations in assessors, objects, and instruments. Some ways of enhancing reliability are summarized in Table 2.

In any given situation, not all sources of unreliability are equally threatening. One does the logical and prudent thing and puts major effort into reducing the greatest source of unreliability. For example, we need not be greatly concerned with rater-reliability when using multiple-choice tests, but we should be very concerned about this kind of reliability when assessing students' oral performance in an interview-type test. We must be concerned about person- and object-related reliability if we want to assess the communicative effectiveness of second language learners because their per-

Table 2.   Types of reliability and ways of enhancing reliability

Type of reliability	*Ways of enhancing reliability*
Rater reliability	Use experienced, trained raters Use more than one rater Raters should carry out their assessments independently
Person-related reliability	Assess on several occasions Assess when person is prepared and best able to perform well Ensure that person understands what is expected (that is, that instructions are clear)
Instrument-related reliability	Use different methods of assessment Use optimal assessment conditions, free from extraneous distractions Keep assessment conditions constant

formance might fluctuate according to the time of day or their state of mind. In contrast, if we are assessing the linguistic complexity of a written text, object-related reliability is of little concern; that is, we need not be concerned that the text will change from moment to moment or from day to day.

In summary, the effects of unreliability on the quality of information you collect and the decisions you make can be serious, and, therefore, the reliability of your information should always be given careful attention.

Task 1

Think about some information you would like to have about a group of students (e.g., their reasons for wanting to learn a language). Make a plan to collect that information using all the ways of enhancing reliability presented in Table 2.

Estimating reliability

Up to this point, we have talked about reliability as if it were an all-or-none quality. Reliability is actually a matter of degree. We cannot obtain information with perfect reliability, yet there is seldom information that is completely unreliable. Thus reliability ranges from zero to total without ever quite reaching either of those extremes.

The idea of reliability as a continuous quality rather than a dichotomous one becomes clearer when we consider the sort of information evaluators are usually interested in. In one of the preceding examples, information was provided that one student, Paul, was superior to another student, Victor. Usually, however, an evaluator is not interested in the scores of just two students. Typically tests are administered to entire classes or to all students in a given grade. In our example, one – and only one – comparison was possible. If 20 students were to take the test instead of just 2, 190 comparisons between pairs of students could be made. If we assume that no two students are equal, one could guess randomly which student in each comparison was the better. Chance alone would yield half of the guesses (95/190) correct. And, by the same token, half would be wrong.

Suppose that you actually knew which student in each comparison was the better one. Then a test that made 140 correct identifications would be considered more reliable than one that made 125 correct identifications. And 150 correct would be more reliable than 140 correct, and so forth. The test that makes 150 correct identifications would improve the accuracy of assessment by 55 over what you could achieve by guessing. That is an improvement of 58 percent (55/95). This figure of 58 percent can be interpreted as an index of reliability.

Unfortunately, it is not actually possible to compute the true reliability of information or of the procedures used to collect data because we do not know the true state of affairs about the people or objects we are assessing. In practice, we can only estimate the reliability of our information or procedures. There are a number of different ways of doing this. Most of them yield indices that range from .00 for no reliability at all to 1.00 for perfect reliability. This is called a coefficient of reliability. In Chapter 13, we discuss a number of different indices of reliability and how to use them to judge the quality of standardized tests.

For the moment, it is enough to know that:

- Reliability is a matter of degree and is usually expressed by indices ranging from .00 to 1.00
- Reliability can only be estimated and not truly calculated
- High reliability is desirable for any information used for evaluation purposes
- There are practical ways of enhancing reliability in classroom evaluation

Validity

Defining validity

Validity is the extent to which the information you collect actually reflects the characteristic or attribute you want to know about. This is a rather straightforward definition of the term, but there are some rather subtle implications to be aware of. First of all, the question of exactly what you want to know about is not always an easy question to answer, especially when it comes to second language learning. For example, just what is communicative competence? What is second language learning aptitude? What is knowledge of basic sentence patterns? What is appropriate turn taking in dyadic conversations? What is authenticity of texts? What are authentic contexts? All of these questions have been subject to debate among language teachers and applied linguists, and they will surely continue to be.

The second subtlety concerns the matter of extent. For example, you might be interested in your adult ESL students' prior exposure to English. Thus, you might ask your students, "How long have you been in the United States?" Your Japanese student, Yuriko, tells you, "five years." You might initially think that this report is either accurate or it is not. However, it might be argued that some inaccurate responses are more inaccurate and, therefore, less valid than others. If the accurate response is five and a half years, is Yuriko's response of five years less inaccurate than a response of four years?

In a related vein, evaluators are often concerned with information about a large number of students. This also has implications for validity. For example, a question during a background interview with prospective second language students may elicit accurate information from most students in a group, but a few might give inaccurate answers. Some people in this situation may be inclined to overestimate, whereas others may underestimate their prior exposure, possibly in order to enhance or diminish, respectively, the interviewers' judgment of their second language proficiency or simply because they cannot remember very well. The proportion of responses that accurately indicates how long each respondent has been exposed to the second language can be interpreted as an index of validity.

As with reliability, validity is generally reported as an index that ranges from .00 to 1.00. Perfect validity is indicated by a value of 1.0, and zero validity by a value of .00. Also, as with reliability, these numbers represent theoretical limits. In practice, we can never know with complete certainty the validity of our assessment procedures; we can only estimate. Moreover, in the realm of human assessment, we cannot expect assessment procedures that are perfectly valid.

There is an important relation between reliability and validity that you should be aware of – an assessment instrument or procedure (such as a test) can be only as valid as it is reliable. Worded differently, inconsistency in a measurement procedure reduces validity. We stated earlier that an unreliable procedure or test is one that contains a lot of nonsystematic variation. In other words, the results of the procedure are influenced by sources of influence that are not those that the procedure or test is trying to assess. As a result, it produces inconsistent, erroneous, or unreliable results. Such nonsystematic variation is like noise: it masks what you are really trying to measure. Since validity is the extent to which the information you get is the information you want, validity can be no greater than reliability. In fact, it will always be less. In short, a "noisy" instrument reduces validity.

Recall the question about students' prior exposure to the second language. Perhaps one of the students did not include visits to the United States prior to moving there permanently because he did not consider this experience important. And perhaps another student misunderstood the question and thought you had asked how many ESL courses she had taken in the United States. These nonsystematic effects on the answers reduce the validity of the information. If only 90 percent of your students answer your question the way you intended, then you can know the amount of time spent in the United States for only 90 percent of them.

There are additional sources of unreliability that reduce validity. For example, we said earlier that attitudes toward age might also influence some students' responses to questionnaires. For example, answers to a question about one's age might be influenced by the fact that some people want to be regarded as older than they are, whereas others want to be taken as younger. If such attitudes are operating, the validity of people's answers to a question about age is reduced by whatever amount reflects the influence of attitudes toward age reporting as compared with the influence of the desire to be truthful.

Finally, a test can be reliable without being valid for its intended purpose. Take, for example, a question on a student evaluation form that asks students their impressions of their instructors. On separate occasions, students might consistently rate their teachers very favorably. However, they might respond this way because they feel that that is the socially appropriate way to respond or they are afraid their instructor will see their evaluations and downgrade them as a result. Their true feelings of their instructor may be quite different, but their responses are nevertheless consistent.

Task 2

Describe other possible cases in which measurement might be reliable but invalid for its intended purpose.

Estimating validity

Validity, like reliability, cannot be assessed directly. The reason why it cannot is the same. To assess the validity of information directly, you would have to be certain of the true state of affairs in order to compare it with the information you have collected. In the realm of human assessment, most of the qualities and attributes evaluators are interested in are not themselves subject to direct assessment. Thus, there is no direct way to know the true level of most human qualities or abilities that we are interested in. We have only indicators that allow us to make inferences about attributes of interest.

Since we cannot assess the validity of information about most human characteristics directly, we are forced to use indirect approaches to estimate the validity of our data and collection procedures. In the context of evaluation, in general assessment information is collected so that we can make sound educational decisions about students and instruction. If the information we have collected helps us to do so, we conclude that the information and the procedure for obtaining it have validity. Depending upon the kind of decisions we want to make, we employ different procedures to determine the validity of our assessment information and our methods of collecting it. We describe the three main procedures for doing this now.

CONTENT RELEVANCE

Content relevance is assessed logically by carefully and systematically examining whether the method and content of the assessment procedure are representative of the kinds of language skills you want to assess. Content relevance is important for classroom-based assessment because second language teachers often want to judge how students can perform in a range of situations or in certain types of situations when, in fact, it is not possible to assess student performance directly in the situations in question. Therefore, it is necessary to assess student performance in a restricted range of situations or in situations that are not exactly the ones we are interested in and then to generalize the results of this assessment to those situations we are most interested in. For example, an objective may be that students be able to converse with native speakers of the target language in situations outside of class that are typical for the age level of the students. Because the teacher cannot observe students conversing with native speakers of the same age in nonclass situations of the sort she is interested in, she might set up simulated conversations between her students and a native speaker that consist of prerecorded messages from a native speaker. The second language students' responses to these messages are tape-recorded and later assessed by the teacher. In effect, the teacher uses the information from these student conversations to infer how well they could actually converse with native speakers in authentic situations.

The teacher in this example could argue for the *content relevance* of her assessment procedure if she could demonstrate that the kinds of language skills called for in the simulated conversation are the same as those called for in authentic conversations involving native speakers. In other words, she should be able to show that the situations she observed her students in are representative of situations in which conversations could take place with native speakers.

Content relevance is important when devising classroom tests. It is also important when using standardized tests. In these cases, it is a question of whether the content of the test is representative of the kinds of language skills the teacher has taught and is interested in assessing. Let us take a placement example: students may be misplaced in specific classes because of a lack of content relevance in the placement test. If the content of the placement test does not accurately reflect the content of the classes that are offered, student performance on the test will not accurately predict their performance in those classes. Another way of saying this is that if there is little or no correspondence between the language skills required on the placement test and those needed to succeed in the available classes, we cannot accurately judge students' readiness for those classes.

The procedure for determining content relevance is not mathematical. Rather, it is logical and calls for good judgment. Content relevance can be characterized as high, moderate, or low, but it cannot be quantified.

CRITERION-RELATEDNESS

Criterion-relatedness is the extent to which information about some attribute or quality assessed by one method correlates with or is related to information about the same or a related quality assessed by a different method. For example, a teacher may want to use interesting texts in class because he is convinced that students learn more when the texts are intrinsically interesting. He collects information about students' preferences by showing them titles of texts and asking them to judge whether the passages that go with those titles are "very interesting," "somewhat interesting," "a bit dull," or "tedious." He records the interest categories selected by the students. Later he makes a record of the time that students spend, on average, working with each of the texts. Then he compares interest ratings with work times. If high interest ratings are associated with longer study times, the teacher may accept this as evidence for the validity of his procedure for assessing the interest value of texts for his students.

Another example of criterion-relatedness concerns testing. Let us return to our earlier placement example. On the basis of their performance on a placement test, students are placed in beginning, intermediate, or advanced second language classes. Often, however, despite this procedure, it turns out that the students do not fit into the assigned class very well. Teachers find that they have a group of students with widely varying kinds and levels of second language ability and they do not do as well as expected. In these cases, the placement test clearly lacks criterion-relatedness: the ability to identify students with second language skills suitable for different levels of classroom instruction. The test was unable to predict the students' ability to handle instruction in specific classes.

Criterion-related validity can be determined using statistical procedures that quantify the degree of agreement between one type of assessment and a criterion. It is usually expressed as a correlation coefficient that ranges from .00 (no correlation) to ±1.00 (perfect correlation). There is more discussion of validity in Chapter 13.

CONSTRUCT VALIDITY

Construct validity is probably the most difficult to understand and the least useful for classroom-based evaluation although it can play an important role in judging the quality of standardized tests. A relatively uncomplicated example may help to explain what it is. Suppose a teacher of Chinese wants to know how important each of her students considers the learning of Chinese to be. She has them rate the importance to themselves on a scale ranging from "very important" to "no importance at all." Later, she compares the students' self-ratings with their achievement in the course. She finds, not surprisingly, that most of the students who indicated that knowing the language was important to them were among the best learners in the class. She concluded that the ratings were valid because students who are more motivated should in general be better learners.

This illustrates the elements of construct validation:

1. You have information you want to validate.
2. You have a theory about how that information should relate to other data.
3. You can verify the predictions of your theory.

Let us now consider a more complex example. Suppose you want to assess the validity of a computer program that estimates the readability of written texts. You do not know how the program works, but you can get readability scores for a number of texts. You also have a theory about readability that states that readability is enhanced by explicit cohesion markers, lexical diversity, familiarity with the lexical items in the text, and familiarity with the content schemata. The theory also states that readability is unrelated to the number of clauses per sentence or the complexity of verb phrases in the text.

It would be relatively easy, although time consuming, to calculate indices of these linguistic variables for each of the texts. For example, you might construct an index of familiarity with schemata by letting students read the first half of the texts and then try to complete them. The amount of second-half content the students could guess would be an indication of familiarity with schemata. The last step would be to compare your information about the variables in the theory with the readability scores generated by the computer. The strongest evidence of construct validity would be afforded if the readability scores were positively related to indices of all the variables except density of clauses and complexity of verb phrases.

Construct validation is most useful when you do not know the exact content of the quality or attribute you want to assess, thereby ruling out the use of content validity. It is also useful when you have no well-defined or generally accepted criterion that could establish the criterion-relatedness of the assessment procedure.

Like reliability, the validity of assessment procedures can often be judged by identifying the possible factors that can invalidate them; in the case of test scores, for example, other factors besides second language ability might explain student performance. If there are a lot of other factors that could explain performance, especially poor performance, then the evaluation procedure probably has low validity as an indicator of second language proficiency. Improving validity is often a matter of eliminating, reducing, or otherwise taking into account these other factors. For example, poor performance may be due to a lack of understanding of what is expected, insufficient time to carry out the task, lack of interest in the activity, or the possibility of performing the task in different ways that are equally valid but unforeseen by the evaluator. These possibilities can be reduced substantially if they are first seen as possible sources of contamination.

Table 3 summarizes these three approaches to assessing validity as applied to tests. The same notions of validity apply to other methods of collecting information.

Methods of information collection

As you can see, second language assessment entails the collection of a great variety of information about instruction (objectives, plans, and practices), students (e.g., their needs, goals, personal background, language experiences, achievement, and attitudes and feelings), teachers (e.g., their language experiences, language skills, and attitudes), and about schools (such as the school's physical and personnel resources). Different techniques are available for gathering these kinds of information. Tests, considered later in this book, are useful for collecting information about student achievement but cannot be used for collecting any of the other types of information, however. Other methods of data collection are appropriate for these. For example, classroom observation and student conferences can garner information about the strategies students might be using to read or write in the second language; dialogue journals can shed light on students' attitudes toward their learning experiences in class. School records, curriculum documents, or other instructional materials reveal facts about the physical and personnel resources of the school system as well as about the course of instruction itself.

Some procedures for collecting information for evaluation purposes are straightforward and require no special preparation, for example, examining school records or instructional materials. In these cases, one simply locates the relevant sources of information and becomes familiar with their contents. Other methods, such as portfolios, conferences, or questionnaires, require advanced preparation and somewhat specialized procedures. We devote our attention to these in the following chapters. The methods we consider in detail are listed on page 70.

Table 3. Three approaches to validity

	Question	Method	Common use	Example
Content relevance	How well does the content of the instrument sample the kinds of things about which conclusions are to be drawn?	Logically conclude whether the content of the instrument comprises an adequate definition of what it claims to assess.	Achievement tests.	A course examination analyzed to see if the contents relate to the course objectives.
Criterion-relatedness	How does the information from this instrument compare with information from more direct measures of the attribute being assessed?	Administer the instrument and compare results with information from direct measures obtained concurrently or in the future.	Instrument used to select and classify people.	Results of a placement test are compared with performance of students in class.
Construct validity	To what extent do certain explanatory concepts account for the information provided by this instrument?	Set up hypotheses regarding people with much or little of the attribute based upon underlying theory. Test the hypotheses.	Instruments used for description or in scientific research.	A test of learning styles is studied to see how well types account for learning by different teaching methods.

Source: Adapted, with permission of the publisher, from *Handbook in research and evaluation*, 3d ed., by S. Isaac and W. B. Michael, 1995, p. 125. San Diego: Robert K. Knapp.

Observation (Chapter 5)
Conferences (Chapter 6)
Portfolios (Chapter 6)
Questionnaires and interviews (Chapter 7)
Dialogue journals (Chapter 7)
Tests (Chapters 8–13)

We do not intend that all of these methods be used at all times. Rather, one determines which method or combination of methods is most appropriate for making a particular decision at a given time. Moreover, not all methods are suitable for collecting all types of information that you might need for evaluation purposes, as we noted earlier. Some of the methods under consideration (for example, conferences and journals) can be used for instructional as well as evaluation purposes. Teachers will, therefore, want to use a variety of procedures as part of their total evaluation activities, and the methods they use will vary depending on their assessment purposes.

In the chapters that follow, we describe each method and compare them to one another. Some of these may be more similar to one another than you might imagine. We discuss the advantages and disadvantages of each and briefly describe the conditions under which they can or cannot be used practically. We also suggest guidelines for devising and using each method. We illustrate ways in which each can be used in decision making at different times and for different purposes. These are merely suggestions, and you should consider ways to adapt each method to better suit your purposes.

Task 3

Imagine that you are the director of a large English language institute that trains students in an English language university. Imagine further that for two years now the performance of many of the students at the end of the year has been very poor. You suspect this is due to low motivation on the part of the students, and you decide to administer a questionnaire to examine this possibility.

Wishing to ensure that your questionnaire results are reliable and valid, you use CLEVER (Checklist to Enhance Validity and Enhance Reliability) as you devise your questionnaire.

Indicate the steps you would take to devise a questionnaire that is reliable and valid according to CLEVER.

We have done the first one to illustrate how to proceed.

CLEVER

1. *Instrument-related reliability:* Use more than one type of assessment; for example, interview a number of the students who have completed the questionnaire to see how their oral responses match their questionnaire responses.

2. *Person-related reliability:*

_____

_____

_____

3. *Rater reliability:*

_____

_____

_____

4. *Content validity:*

_____

_____

_____

5. *Criterion-related validity:*

_____

_____

_____

6. *Construct validity:*

_____

_____

_____

Other considerations (practical constraints: cost, time, acceptability, etc.):

_____

_____

_____

Summary

In this chapter, we discussed three characteristics of information: practicality, reliability, and validity. We pointed out that:

- These characteristics of information are vital for judging the quality of both quantitative and qualitative information
- Reliable and valid procedures for collecting information are essential for sound educational decision making
- Validity is the most important quality of information; furthermore, in classroom-based evaluation, content and criterion validity are particularly desirable
- Validity is related to (in fact, limited by) reliability
- Validity and reliability are relative qualities, not absolute
- Reliability and certain types of validity can be estimated statistically by an index that ranges from .00 to 1.0
- Classroom teachers need to consider factors that can reduce the reliability or validity of an evaluation procedure
- There are practical ways of enhancing the reliability and validity of evaluation procedures that involve minimizing sources of unreliability or invalidity

In this chapter, we also identified the methods of collecting information that we discuss in the remaining chapters. We begin in the next chapter with observation.

Discussion questions

1. Make a list of the qualitative information you use to make decisions in your classroom. Now make a list of quantitative information you use. How do you keep records of this information? Which record-keeping methods work well and which do not?
2. How do you ensure that your decisions about student grades are reliable? Do you use any of the suggestions discussed in this chapter? If not, would you consider using them in the future? Are there other methods for improving reliability that have not been mentioned in this chapter?
3. Imagine that you are going to listen to tape-recorded language samples of ESL speakers to assess their proficiency. Before doing so, decide (a) what qualities or abilities you will listen for and (b) how you will record your assessments of these qualities. If you can actually listen to some tapes with a group of other students, compare each student's assessments with those of the rest of the group. Consider areas of agreement and disagreement, and discuss ways to reduce the disagreements if you

were to repeat the exercise. What does this activity tell you about reliability?

4. Listen to tape-recorded samples of anonymous native and nonnative speakers of English reading the same short text. As you listen, decide who is native and who is not and why you thought so. Devise a rating scale for recording your judgments. Share your opinions and rating scales with someone else, and note the similarities and dissimilarities. What does this tell you about rater reliability?

5. Select a standardized second language test that is used in your school or university. Read the instruction manual and then evaluate how practical this test would be for use in your setting. Using the technical manual for the test, assess the validity of the test for your students.

6. If you were devising a new second language course, what kinds of information about your prospective students would you want in order to make the course as effective as possible? How would you collect that information? Who would collect it? How would you ensure its reliability and validity?

Readings

Airasian, P. (1991). Using assessment information. In P. Airasian (Ed.), *Classroom assessment* (pp. 409–424). New York: McGraw-Hill.

Bachman, L. F. (1990). Reliability. In L. F. Bachman (Ed.), *Fundamental considerations in language testing* (pp. 160–235). Oxford: Oxford University Press.

Bachman, L. F. (1990). Validation. In L. F. Bachman (Ed.), *Fundamental considerations in language testing* (pp. 236–295). Oxford: Oxford University Press.

Henning, G. (1987). *A guide to language testing.* Cambridge, Mass.: Newbury House.

Popham, W. J. (1978). *Criterion-referenced measurement.* Englewood Cliffs, N.J.: Prentice-Hall.

PART II:
EVALUATING WITHOUT TESTS

5 *Observation in the classroom*

- Introduction
- Observation in the classroom
- A framework for classroom observation
- Recording classroom observations
- Preparing report forms
- Summary

Preview questions

1. Besides using tests, how do you know that your students are making progress in language learning?
2. List classroom events or teacher and student behaviors that could be helpful in reflecting the effectiveness of teaching and learning in your class. Explain how they could be helpful and how you could use them to create more effective instruction.
3. How do you keep track of important observations about your teaching? What have you found to be obstacles in using these techniques?
4. What do you look for when presenting a lesson to determine if it is going well?
5. What do you look for in order to decide if a student is having trouble in class?
6. Have you ever observed yourself or another teacher teaching? What stood out?

Introduction

The following three chapters are devoted to so-called alternative assessment methods, including observation, portfolios, conferences, and dialogue journals; we also discuss the use of interviews and questionnaires. Before proceeding with the topic of this chapter – observation – we briefly discuss alternative assessment in relation to grading. The popularity and usefulness of alternative assessment methods, especially portfolios, conferences, and dialogue journals, have led to the incorporation of the results they provide into students' grades. For example, at least one state in the United States has mandated student portfolio assessment as the basis for grading students.

We do not favor this use of alternative assessment methods because, in our opinion, it subverts the numerous distinct advantages of alternative assessment that are possible when grading is not an issue. We favor the use of these assessment methods for purposes of individualization of instructional planning. Thus, in Chapters 5, 6, and 7, we focus on the use of portfolios, conferences, journals, questionnaires, and interviews for instructional planning and not for student grading. We return to this topic in more detail at the end of Chapter 7.

Observation is basic to assessing human skills and behaviors. In fact, all methods of collecting information for second language assessment can be thought of as specialized methods for eliciting behavior, attitudes, or skills to be observed under specific circumstances. In fact much of the material in this section can be applied to the methods of collecting information that we discuss later. In this chapter, we focus on observation of events, activities, and interactions in the classroom, independent of the methods to be discussed later.

Researchers have devised sophisticated formal methods of observing teacher-student interaction in order to describe and understand second language teaching and learning better (see Figure 1 for Part B of the Communicative Orientation of Language Teaching (COLT) observation scheme). Real-time observation of second language classrooms by trained observers permits the compilation of detailed and complex information about language use by teachers and students that is difficult for the participants themselves to collect. Observation by trained observers is thus an important aspect of second language research and is also used in some teacher-training programs. For example, in some cases, trained supervisors or credentialed experts systematically observe teachers-in-training while they practice teach. In these situations, the student-teachers' grades and ultimate certification can depend on what the supervisor observes. In other cases, teachers-in-training are videotaped while practice teaching and later view and analyze themselves. In these instances, observation facilitates self-assessment by the new teachers and does not usually figure directly in grading.

Observation in the classroom

Classroom teachers seldom use formal observational procedures, such as the COLT, because they are too complex to use while attending to everything else going on in the classroom. Yet informal observation is an integral part of everyday teaching: teachers continuously observe their students' language use during formal instruction or while the students are

COLT Part B Communicative Features

Communicative Orientation of Language Teaching Observation Scheme

School ______________________ Date of visit ______________________

Teacher ______________________ Subject ______________________ Coder ______________________

			Teacher Verbal Interaction																		Student Verbal Interaction																					
				Target language		Information gap				Sustained speech		Reaction to form/ message		Incorporation of student utterances								Target language		Information gap				Sustained speech			Form restriction			Reaction to form/ message		Incorporation of student/teacher utterances						
						Giving Info.		Request. Info.																Giving Info.		Request. Info.																
A	E	M	Off task	L1	L2	Predict.	Unpred.	Pseudo requ.	Genuine requ.	Minimal	Sustained	Form	Message	Correction	Repetition	Paraphase	Comment	Expansion	Clarif. request	Elab. request	Discourse initiation	L1	L2	Predict.	Unpred.	Pseudo Requ.	Genuine Requ.	Ultra-minimal	Minimal	Sustained	Choral	Restricted	Unrestricted	Form	Message	Correction	Repetition	Paraphase	Comment	Expansion	Clarif. request	Elab. request
			1	2	3	4	5	6	7	8	9	10	11	12	13	14	15	16	17	18	19	20	21	22	23	24	25	26	27	28	29	30	31	32	33	34	35	36	37	38	39	40

Figure 1 COLT observation scheme, part B. [Reprinted with permission of the publisher, from N. Spada and M. Frolich (1995), The communicative orientation of language teaching (COLT) observation scheme: Coding conventions and applications, *App. 2. Sydney: National Centre for English Language Teaching and Research.]*

working individually at their desks; teachers may arrange individual "conference times" during which they observe students carefully on a one-to-one basis; teachers observe how students respond to and use instructional materials and how they interact during group work; teachers observe how effectively they themselves are presenting particular lessons, units; and so on.

On the basis of their observations, teachers assess what students have and have not learned; they infer the learning strategies students may be using that are facilitating or impeding learning; they assess the effectiveness of particular teaching strategies; they determine which instructional activities and materials the students enjoy; and so on. Information derived from such observations is fundamental to the day-to-day functioning of the classroom because it provides a basis for understanding what is happening and for making decisions about what should follow. For example, based on a number of observations, a teacher may judge that a particular student has not learned what was being taught in class that week, whereas the other students have. Alternatively, the teacher may judge that quite a few students have not learned the target structure. The observation that only one student has failed to learn a target structure will lead to very different decisions by the teacher than the observation that most of the students have not learned it.

Teachers also seek to understand how their students are learning and, in particular, to explain those instances when learning does not occur as planned. Their explanations of these situations can be used to plan instruction that will promote learning. In seeking to explain failure to learn, teachers use observation to make inferences about instructional or learning *processes* or *strategies.* Observation of student behavior when a particular unit is taught might lead the teacher to infer that the students were using strategies that might be effective in their first language but lead to mistakes in the second language. For example, the students may use discourse patterns from their first language that are inappropriate in the second language. Or the teacher may infer that the students did not find the materials and activities interesting and, therefore, they were not motivated to learn. Teachers' observations of themselves may lead them to infer that they are using instructional strategies that are not working: perhaps they had not been very clear when explaining an assignment or they did not model a new grammatical pattern sufficiently before having the students try using it.

Inferences concerning learning and teaching *processes* are much more difficult to make than inferences concerning learning *outcomes,* yet they are equally important for effective teaching. Inferences about language learning outcomes can be made on the basis of observations of concrete instances of the students' actual language use. For example, does the student use the past tense correctly and appropriately when speaking and/or writing? In comparison, inferences about processes related to teaching and learning are based on observations of a wider range of behaviors and events and their interrelationships. For example, a teacher's understanding of student errors when writing and what to do about them might follow from observations directed at answering the following kinds of questions: What kinds of errors do the students make? Can their mistakes be traced to a particular source, such as the first language? Do they tend to make certain errors under some circumstances more than others? Do they avoid the use of certain structures or communicative functions altogether? It is evident from this single example that it is not the observation of discrete instances of language use that provides evidence about learning processes; rather, it is the observation of categories of events (such as errors) or fairly complex interrelationships among events (for example, the linguistic or communicative contexts within which errors tend to occur more frequently) that are the bases for inferences about learning processes. The same can be said about processes related to teaching.

Inferences about learning and instructional processes are important because they affect significantly the ways in which teachers respond to their students. For example, the inference that students are using strategies derived from the first language when using their second language might lead the teacher to explain to the students the difference between the first and second language with regard to the grammatical structure or communicative function in question. Of course, this would work only if the students were old enough and had acquired sufficient linguistic sophistication to understand such an explanation. In comparison, the inference that the teacher did not provide ample demonstration of a particular linguistic structure or communicative function might lead the teacher to provide more time for practice using it in whole group activities.

Classroom observation and any associated inferences about teaching and learning are important for planning instruction of the same unit, lesson, or course in the future. Observation of how particular units worked with the current group of students may lead to decisions to retain, drop, or modify them with future groups of learners. Units may be dropped because they were too easy, too difficult, uninteresting, or not useful. Certain units may be modified because observation of their effectiveness with the current students suggested deficiencies or areas for improvement. Observations that a course did not work effectively in general with the current students might lead to decisions to revise the way in which students are placed in the course to ensure greater compatibility between the course and the characteristics of the learners in the course.

Task 1

Review the COLT observation scheme carefully.
What aspects of it could you use in your classroom?
What aspects would not be useful? Could it be
adapted to be more useful for you?

A framework for classroom observation

That teachers make use of classroom observation in some way during day-to-day instruction is indisputable. That social interactions and language use in second language classrooms is extremely complex and variable is also indisputable – a quick glance at any scientific observational scheme (such as the COLT) gives a hint of the complexity of classroom life. Classroom teachers, unlike researchers, are engaged in teaching and classroom management while simultaneously trying to observe and make sense of their students' learning and their own teaching. Thus, the challenges facing classroom teachers as observers are how to organize observations in a systematic and manageable way, how to record the resulting information and inferences, and how to make use of this information in planning effective instruction.

The purpose of this section is to provide a strategy for organizing classroom observation that is manageable, systematic, and effective. Without a coherent strategy, teachers' observations and the inferences that they derive from them run the risk of being fragmented and disorganized and, consequently, ineffective. Our strategy for organizing classroom observation is based on the framework for classroom-based second language evaluation discussed in the opening chapters.

Accordingly, classroom observation should be concerned primarily with those language skills that are specified in the objectives. By comparing observations of student learning with instructional objectives, teachers can assess the extent to which student learning is progressing as planned. This does not mean that teachers should ignore all other aspects of teaching and learning, but rather that their observations should be organized primarily with reference to specified language objectives. Focusing initial observations in this way will make classroom observation manageable and systematic because it defines and delimits what is to be observed. Otherwise, it can be difficult to know which of the many classroom events and student behaviors to focus on. In addition, this strategy will increase the instructional usefulness of classroom observations and inferences because it focuses attention on language learning that is relevant to instruction, assuming, that is, that the teacher's actual instruction is organized according to objectives.

In the event that student achievement does not match your objectives or expectations, observation of classroom practices might help explain why. Once again, our general strategy for evaluation can be useful. Accordingly, observation of classroom practices should be organized according to your instructional plans and focus specifically on instructional content, organization, materials and equipment, and activities. A discrepancy between observed classroom practices and your instructional plans may provide an explanation for student attainment – the students may not have achieved certain objectives because instruction was not implemented according to plans. One might also be on the lookout for signs that assumptions about input factors (student attitudes and needs, teacher qualifications, etc.) were inaccurate.

In contrast, observation that classroom practices *do* conform to instructional plans would suggest at least two possibilities: (1) The plan does not work as intended even when implemented as recommended, and (2) it would be useful to look for factors not specified by the plan that might help to explain inadequacies in student achievement. For example, observation of students' work habits, their involvement in instructional activities, their patterns of errors, their strategies for communicating with limited linguistic knowledge, and the questions they ask about the content could provide insight into problems with instructional plans. Observation of these aspects of learning can lead to changes in instructional purposes and/or plans so as to make instruction better suited to the students you have.

Use of the evaluation strategy in this way provides both a focus for classroom observation and a logic for making inferences about learning. At the same time, it does not preclude the teacher from organizing observations and using observational information in other ways. In particular, it does not preclude observing unexpected events that appear to be important and meaningful with respect to your objectives. Indeed, teachers should always be prepared to take note of such unexpected events.

Planning classroom observation

A number of decisions need to be made when planning observation. They are summarized in Table 1. First, it is important to identify why you want to observe and, more specifically, what kinds of decisions you want to be able to make based on your observations. Some reasons for systematically observing your students are as follows:

- To determine whether students are progressing as planned and are ready to move on to the next unit.
- To identify difficulties that particular students are having so that appropriate instruction can be planned for them.
- To assess a new student's language skills in order to identify specific needs and plan appropriate instruction.
- To assess whether students find a unit of instruction interesting, worthwhile, and useful with a view to deciding whether to repeat it with the next group of students.
- To assess the appropriateness and usefulness of a new textbook.

The reasons for carrying out observation will determine what you observe. Deciding whether to move on to the next unit would call for observation of the students' performance with respect to the learning objectives set out in the current unit. Decisions about how to tailor instruction for new students would call for observation of the students' language proficiency upon joining to the class. Identifying the difficulties of individual students who need additional attention would suggest observation of such students focusing on problem areas of performance. Assessing a new textbook would call for observation of student involvement with the book.

Once you have identified why and what to observe, you can decide how to observe. Observation can focus on individual students or groups of students. Observing individual students can provide detailed diagnostic information about those who are experiencing difficulty or have just joined the class, for example. Observation of individual students can also provide detailed information to be shared with parents, other teachers, or educational professionals who are concerned with the student's progress. It can be useful for grading purposes, provided it is done systematically and with

Table 1.   Planning classroom observation

1. Why do you want to observe and what decisions do you want to make as a result of your observations?
2. What aspects of teaching or learning that are appropriate to these decisions do you want to observe?
3. Do you want to observe individual students, small groups of students, or the whole class?
4. Will you observe students engaged in specific, pre-arranged activities or during routine classroom activities?
5. Will you observe on one occasion or repeatedly?
6. Will you incorporate non-linguistic content from the students' other classes or from outside class?
7. How will you record your observations?

all students. It can provide insights about learning strategies that individual students are employing that might be counterproductive.

Observing individual students, however, can be time consuming and, in second language classrooms, new students with different cultural backgrounds may feel uncomfortable being singled out. In comparison, observing groups of students takes less time, can give the teacher a general sense of student learning, and can reveal how students work or interact together. Furthermore, individual students will not feel singled out and self-conscious. Observing groups of students is useful primarily to ascertain whether things are generally on track – in other words, diagnosing whether things are working for the whole class as intended.

Observation can focus on student performance during a single prearranged activity that has been structured to elicit targeted language skills or other kinds of performance. For example, the teacher may arrange individual reading conferences at the end of a unit during which each student reads to the teacher and/or answers a set of questions on a text the student has chosen. Such individualized conferences give teachers opportunities to observe carefully a wide range of reading-related skills. Or teachers can plan to have students play roles that require certain kinds of language skills, or to demonstrate and explain projects they have been working on so that their expository language skills can be observed and assessed.

Alternatively, teachers may decide to observe students during routine classroom activities – indeed, teachers do this as a matter of course. Observing routine activities, such as cooperative learning tasks, helps to monitor how students are responding to particular instructional activities. In the case of students who are being educated through a second language, teachers may want to observe their second language students outside the classroom, when they are with other students at lunch or in the playground, in order to assess their social language skills.

There is also the question of whether to observe students on one specific occasion or on a number of occasions. Monitoring students repeatedly makes it possible to detect changes in student achievement. Furthermore, repeated observation can increase the reliability of the information you obtain because student performance on any particular occasion may be subject to momentary extraneous influences and does not necessarily reflect accurately what they have really learned. It may be safe to assume that performance of any new skill is unstable and variable and, therefore, only multiple observations can lead to confidence in one's observations. Clearly, if important decisions about individual students are to be made, there should be repeated observation of these learners – this will increase the reliability of your judgments.

Depending on your own instructional situation, there may be yet other questions to answer. For example, if you are teaching English as a second language (ESL) to immigrant children who need to learn English in order to benefit from instruction in English in content areas (such as math and science), you may want to consider incorporating content from some of their other school subjects. Doing this will permit you to decide whether they are able to talk about, or demonstrate through language, knowledge of a nonlinguistic nature that they are learning in their other classes – a form of performance assessment. In a related vein, if you are teaching second language skills to adults who have recently immigrated and need to learn the language to get a job or fit in socially, you may want to incorporate content from job-related or day-to-day events (e.g., banking or using public transportation).

Finally, having decided all of these questions, you will want to plan how to record your observations. We turn to these next. Before doing so, however, we want to emphasize that, notwithstanding the usefulness of focused observations and a plan to carry them out, observation does not have to be planned to be useful. One of the distinct values of observation is the possibility it affords of noting spontaneous, unexpected, and vital information about teaching and learning in your classroom. Teachers must always be vigilant to unexpected events that provide insights into and understanding of their students and their own teaching.

Recording classroom observations

Deciding how to record observations and concomitant interpretations is as important as deciding why, what, how, and when to observe. Good record keeping is essential for effective classroom evaluation. Records of classroom observations must be systematic, complete, and explicit if they are to be useful. Observations that are not recorded in writing or some other permanent way are likely to be forgotten or distorted with time. It is unreasonable for teachers to think that they can remember the numerous important details of classroom life over time without recording them for later reference. Good record keeping helps teachers:

1. Keep track of important information about student learning and the effectiveness of instruction.
2. Form sound impressions of student achievement and progress.
3. Accurately identify persistent difficulties experienced by individual students.
4. Report student progress to other educational professionals and parents.
5. Assign grades to students, if and when required to do so.
6. Monitor, evaluate, and redesign instructional plans.

Like information collection itself, record keeping is an ongoing process that takes time – not only after each unit or chapter, but every day, after specific lessons, and even during lessons. Effective evaluation requires a combination of record keeping techniques: some for daily recording and some that are periodic; some that focus on students and others that focus on instruction; and some that are general and some that are specific. In this section, we discuss three ways of recording classroom observations:

1. Anecdotal records
2. Checklists
3. Rating scales

Anecdotal records

Anecdotal records (or notes) can be made on file cards, adhesive labels, or clipboards with notepaper that are left in strategic locations around the classroom so that you can record your observations quickly and easily no matter where you are or what you are doing. Alternatively, they can be recorded in a book or journal kept especially for this purpose. It is important to date each entry and describe briefly the context in which the observation was recorded. Organize your comments according to student name or instructional unit or activity in order to facilitate retrieval of information at a later time. Commonly, teachers organize their notes in filefolders or a notebook organized according to student names and instructional activities. Anecdotal records that are not identified and stored systematically quickly become simply pieces of paper with random notes on them. If you keep records of students on file cards or adhesive labels, take the time to organize them according to student name or instructional unit or activity shortly after you have recorded your observation. Otherwise, their significance and relationship to other relevant information will be forgotten.

Anecdotal records can be as structured or open-ended as desired, although they are particularly suited for open-ended recording of information. Open-ended reports are especially useful for recording observations and inferences that are unique and unexpected and that might be difficult to record using other methods. As we noted earlier, unplanned observations are an important part of classroom-based evaluation. They provide an unobtrusive way of recording observations about instruction and about students at all times of the day, even during recess or lunch time.

Anecdotal records are most useful for internal purposes, that is, by teachers as they evaluate and tailor instruction for their students. They can be particularly helpful for beginning teachers who have not yet developed systematic ways of observing their students. Over time, use of anecdotal records can assist new teachers in sharpening and focusing their observational skills. Once teachers develop more precise categories for observing their students, then other, more specific, methods of record keeping (such as checklists) can be used. Anecdotal records are useful for all teachers, no matter how much experience they have had, for recording observations of unexpected events during instruction, when it is sometimes difficult to know exactly what to expect. Because of their informality, they are not well suited for sharing information with parents or other teachers.

If anecdotal records are to furnish a coherent record of student performance and/or instructional effectiveness for sharing with others, then the recorded observations must be focused and organized in some systematic fashion. Our discussion of the context of second language evaluation provides a minimum set of guidelines for deciding what aspects of teaching and learning to focus on. More specifically, we recommend focusing on those aspects of instruction (including objectives, content, organization, materials, and activities) that are part of your instructional plans. Teachers should include notes about what works and what does not work as planned so that their record is complete.

Anecdotal records that are made after each lesson, at the end of each day, or, minimally, at the end of each unit can provide a useful record of what worked and what did not for future planning. Reports that are recorded infrequently may not be representative and detailed and, therefore, are less useful than reports that are recorded more frequently. Once again, entries should be dated, identified, and organized around aspects of instruction that are specified in your instructional plans or that are otherwise important to you. For completeness, observational records of students should include notes about what students can do or what progress they have made along with areas of difficulty.

Anecdotal records of student performance need not be limited to recording classroom observations – they can also be used in conjunction with other methods of collecting information, for example, during student conferences or while marking tests or reading students' journals. In addition, anecdotal reports by teachers or by students themselves can be included in students' portfolios of their work. In this way, a cumulative record of student performance is created that can be referred to for instructional planning and/or grading purposes.

Checklists and rating scales

Checklists and *rating scales* are tools for recording observations. Because they are very similar in form and use, they are discussed together here. They consist of lists of items that describe specific aspects of learning and teaching. In comparison with anecdotal records, they consist of predesignated categories for recording your observations. Thus, they require precise and well-articulated categories and criteria for observing and assessing student performance or instructional activities. Because they yield system-

The following checklists are designed to assess students' receptive and productive oral language skills. Assess only those items that are pertinent to your instructional objectives or are otherwise relevant. You can include additional aspects of oral language.

If you want more precise assessments, you could respond to each item using a rating scale based on criteria that are suitable for your purposes (for example, unsatisfactory, satisfactory, excellent).

Receptive oral skills

_____ 1. Understands simple directions.
_____ 2. Understands simple sentences.
_____ 3. Understands simple yes/no questions.
_____ 4. Understands plurals.
_____ 5. Understands vocabulary appropriate to age.
_____ 6. Understands adjectives appropriate to age.
_____ 7. Understands several related sentences.
_____ 8. Understands contractions, common shortened forms, and so forth.
_____ 9. Understands tense indicators.
_____ 10. Distinguishes tones and understands their meaning.
_____ 11. Understands meaning of different intonation patterns.
_____ 12. Understands more complex directions.
_____ 13. Understands rapid speech.
_____ 14. Understands language in classroom situation.
_____ 15. Understands language of peers.

Productive oral skills

_____ 1. Pronounces vowel sounds correctly.
_____ 2. Pronounces consonant sounds well.
_____ 3. Pronounces blends correctly.
_____ 4. Uses word stress correctly.
_____ 5. Uses phrase/sentence stress well.
_____ 6. Uses tone correctly.
_____ 7. Uses intonation correctly.
_____ 8. Gives one-word responses.
_____ 9. Produces simple sentences.
_____ 10. Produces simple questions.
_____ 11. Gives simple directions.
_____ 12. Uses tense markers correctly.
_____ 13. Uses prepositions correctly.
_____ 14. Forms complex sentences.
_____ 15. Uses several continuous sentences.
_____ 16. Gives descriptions.
_____ 17. Uses vocabulary appropriate to age.
_____ 18. Speaks fluently.
_____ 19. Uses classroom language easily.

Figure 2   Sample language skills checklist.

atic and specific information in a uniform manner, checklists and rating scales can be instrumental in sharing information with parents, other teachers, or specialists, as well as in formal grading. In the case of checklists, you simply check off or select those items that correspond to what you have observed or inferred from your observations; see Figures 2 and 3 for

Content

5 = excellent	Main ideas stated clearly and accurately; change of opinion very clear
4 = good	Main ideas stated fairly and accurately; change of opinion relatively clear
3 = average	Main ideas somewhat unclear or inaccurate; change of opinion statement somewhat weak
2 = poor	Main ideas not clear or accurate; change of opinion statement weak
1 = very poor	Main ideas not all clear or accurate; change of opinion statement very weak

Organization

5 = excellent	Well organized and perfectly coherent
4 = good	Fairly well organized and generally coherent
3 = average	Loosely organized but main ideas clear; logical but incomplete sequencing
2 = poor	Ideas disconnected; lacks logical sequencing
1 = very poor	No organization; incoherent

Vocabulary

5 = excellent	Very effective choice of words and use of idioms and word forms
4 = good	Effective choice of words and use of idioms and word forms
3 = average	Adequate choice of words but some misuse of words, idioms, and word forms
2 = poor	Limited range; confused use of words, idioms, and word forms
1 = very poor	Very limited range; very poor knowledge of words, idioms, and word forms

Grammar

5 = excellent	No errors; full control of complex structure
4 = good	Almost no errors; good control of structure
3 = average	Some errors; fair control of structure
2 = poor	Many errors; poor control of structure
1 = very poor	Dominated by errors; no control of structure

Mechanisms

5 = excellent	Mastery of spelling and punctuation
4 = good	Few errors in spelling and punctuation
3 = average	Fair number of spelling and punctuation errors
2 = poor	Frequent errors in spelling and punctuation
1 = very poor	No control over spelling and punctuation

Figure 3 Sample observation rating scale for writing. [From A. Cohen (1994), Assessing language ability in the classroom. *Boston, Mass.: Heinle and Heinle.]*

examples that focus on language use. In effect, a checklist is like a multiple-choice question with two response alternatives: Yes or No.

The only difference between a checklist and a rating scale is that the latter provides more than a yes or no response choice. Rating scales can take two basic forms. In one, only the end points of the scale are described (e.g., "never" and "always") whereas the intermediate responses are labeled simply by a number or letter:

The student works cooperatively with other students.

always   1   2   3   4   5   never

In another case, each point along the scale may be described:

always   frequently   sometimes   rarely   never

1   2   3   4   5

In either case, you select the response alternative for each item that best corresponds to what you have observed.

In addition to assessing student language acquisition, checklists and rating scales can serve a variety of purposes – for example, by teachers to assess their plans, including instructional activities and materials (see Figure 4) and by students to report their learning preferences (see Figure 5 on page 92).

The items in a checklist or rating scale can refer to relatively observable behavior, such as specific aspects of language use (e.g., uses capital letters correctly, uses correct auxiliary verbs, uses pronouns appropriately), work habits (e.g., student is punctual, follows instructions well, meets goals, prepares for class assignments, seeks assistance when needed), or social behavior (e.g., works cooperatively, socializes with peers, participates in class discussion). Or they may refer to aspects of learning and teaching that are more inferential, such as:

1. Learning strategies (for example, takes risks, improvises, focuses on meaning/form, self-corrects, uses first language strategies)
2. Affective and personality styles (for example, enthusiastic, self-reliant, resourceful, passive)
3. Reactions to the course (for example, student participates actively in class activities, requires extra guidance, shows initiative)

In comparison with anecdotal records, checklists and rating scales are relatively structured and close ended and, therefore, require less time and effort to complete. However, they take considerably more time to construct initially. They are particularly useful for recording observations of specific classroom events and specific aspects of student performance. Indeed, they are generally designed with these purposes in mind. Because they are relatively easy to use, once they have been constructed, they are a particularly advantageous form of record keeping when every student is asked to do the same thing, such as presenting an oral report of a current event or a book they have read. Because they are highly specific, existing checklists

The following list of questions can help you assess and modify your instructional materials and activities. You do not have to respond to every question. Select those questions that are of most interest to you. You can also include additional questions that reflect concerns of yours that are not included in this set.

_____ Do these materials/activities match your instruction objectives?

_____ Do the materials/activities make clear the communicative uses of the language?

_____ Is the language in the materials/activity meaningful to these students?

_____ Is it clear to the students how to use the materials?

_____ Do the students clearly understand the purpose of the activity?

_____ Do the materials/activities accommodate different learning styles and preferences?

_____ Is the activity structured so that students can complete it in different ways?

_____ Do the materials/activities encourage active student use of the language?

_____ Are students given opportunities to assess their performance? Can they assess the activities/materials?

_____ Do the materials/activities include cultural content appropriate to the target culture?

_____ Are the materials/activities relevant to the students' needs?

_____ Are the activities/materials authentic and age appropriate?

_____ Did the students have enough time to complete the activity?

_____ Did the students find the activities/materials interesting?

_____ Is the activity/material of appropriate difficulty?

_____ Did the students have the language skills needed to participate in this activity or use these materials?

_____ Was the activity effective in getting students to use and practice the language skills they were intended for?

Figure 4   Sample checklist for assessing activities and materials.

and rating scales are not appropriate, without modification, for use in your classroom. Whether the content of existing checklists and rating scales is useful will depend on your particular instructional plans and objectives. When devising your own record-keeping system, you might consult existing checklists or rating scales, but they should never be used without careful scrutiny first.

As in the case of anecdotal records, checklists and rating scales are most helpful when used regularly and systematically to record observations so that the information contained in them is comprehensive and detailed. The same suggestions that were offered for keeping anecdotal records apply here: date, identify, and briefly describe them. Whereas anecdotal records can be made immediately after a particular instructional event or some time later, checklists and rating scales are best used as soon after a particular

Read the sentence and circle the response that is appropriate for you.

Example:

I like to learn by listening to songs   no   a little   good   best

1. In English class, I like to learn by reading.	no	a little	good	best
2. In class, I like to listen to cassettes.	no	a little	good	best
3. In class, I like to learn by playing games.	no	a little	good	best
4. In class, I like to learn by conversations.	no	a little	good	best
5. In class I like to learn by pictures, films, video.	no	a little	good	best
6. I want to write everything in my notebook.	no	a little	good	best
7. I like to have my own textbook.	no	a little	good	best
8. I like the teacher to explain *everything* to us.	no	a little	good	best
9. I like the teacher to give us problems to work on.	no	a little	good	best
10. I like the teacher to help me talk about my interests.	no	a little	good	best
11. I like the teacher to tell me all my mistakes.	no	a little	good	best
12. I like the teacher to let me find my mistakes.	no	a little	good	best
13. I like to study English by myself (alone).	no	a little	good	best
14. I like to learn English by talking in pairs.	no	a little	good	best
15. I like to learn English in a small group.	no	a little	good	best
16. I like to learn English with the whole class.	no	a little	good	best
17. I like to go out with the class and practice English.	no	a little	good	best
18. I like to study grammar.	no	a little	good	best
19. I like to learn many new words.	no	a little	good	best
20. I like to practice the sounds and pronunciation.	no	a little	good	best
21. I like to learn English words by *seeing* them.	no	a little	good	best
22. I like to learn English words by *hearing* them.	no	a little	good	best
23. I like to learn English words by *doing* something.	no	a little	good	best
24. At home, I like to learn by reading newspapers and magazines.	no	a little	good	best
25. At home, I like to learn by watching TV in English.	no	a little	good	best
26. At home, I like to learn by using cassettes.	no	a little	good	best
27. At home, I like to learn by studying English books.	no	a little	good	best
28. I like to learn by talking to friends in English.	no	a little	good	best
29. I like to learn by watching and listening to Australians.	no	a little	good	best
30. I like to learn by using English in stores, on the bus, etc.	no	a little	good	best

Figure 5   Sample student learning styles rating scale. [Adapted from K. Willing (1988), Learning styles in adult migrant education. *Adelaide, Australia: National Curriculum Resource Centre.]*

event as possible so that your exact impressions are recorded accurately. As with any of the other techniques discussed in this chapter, you must be prepared to experiment with each method in order to devise a system that suits you and works well for you.

These methods of record keeping are not limited to recording observations of classroom events, activities, and interactions. They can also be employed with the other methods of collecting information that we discuss. For example, anecdotal records or checklists can be used to record information while grading tests, when reading students' journals, or when reviewing student portfolios. Rating scales can similarly be used to record information while grading tests or during student conferences. In fact, all methods of collecting information, with the possible exception of tests, require some method of recording your observations, impressions, and judgments of student performance.

So far we have discussed the use of checklists for recording information about individual students. There is an additional use for them: to record observations of a group or an entire class of students. For example, using a checklist such as the COLT (referred to in the introduction to this chapter), it is possible to record how often students use particular kinds of utterances in class (e.g., single word, phrase or clause, complete sentence, nonverbal gesture), the frequency of occurrence of particular kinds of errors (e.g., phonological, lexical, grammatical), or the types of questions teachers ask of students (e.g., yes or no, display, cognitive). In this case, the observer simply checks off each category of utterance, error, or question type included in the list whenever it occurs. Such information can describe general patterns of language use or the social climate in a classroom. This can aid in understanding and explaining overall patterns of language learning.

Task 2

Compare anecdotal records, checklists, and rating scales with respect to both their structure and uses.

Preparing report forms

Anecdotal records

Special forms are not required for anecdotal records. However, if you have identified specific kinds of observations that you wish to report in this narrative form, then report forms can be prepared with headings for each item or aspect of teaching and learning to be observed followed by space for comments. For example, when observing instructional units, you may decide to record your observations of (1) students' use of the materials, (2) their interactions with one another, (3) their level of enjoyment and involvement, (d) whether sufficient time was allocated for the unit, and so on. As noted earlier, systematizing your observations in this way allows you to monitor each instructional unit comprehensively and in ways that will facilitate future instructional planning. If no forethought is given to what you want to observe and record, you may overlook issues that pertain to assessing the unit and planning to use the unit in the future. Similarly, when reporting observations of your students, if the nature of the observations you record changes considerably from one report to another, it may be difficult to discern trends or patterns in student performance that influence student progress.

It may take some trial and error to identify what to focus on consistently in order to identify relevant categories. With practice, anecdotal reporting becomes easier to do and of more utility. One suggestion is to refer to preceding reports on individual students or on particular lessons in order to identify what was of concern last time and, therefore, worthy of attention this time.

Checklists and rating scales

The preparation of checklists and rating scales requires time and special attention. The following suggestions are offered:

1. Identify specific behaviors, events, or aspects of teaching and learning to be observed. What you select to record will reflect your purposes and the categories of useful information you identified when planning your observations.
2. Select items for the checklist or rating scale that are relatively observable and related to your instructional plans so that the information you record can direct your ongoing instructional planning.
3. Select categories that are nonoverlapping to avoid redundancy; categories that overlap are difficult to differentiate and rate or check off.
4. Prepare descriptions of each item above; the descriptions should be clear, concise, and meaningful.
5. Select response formats for each item; that is, will each item be responded to in checklist format or in rating scale format? If the latter is chosen, prepare descriptors of response choices.
6. Pilot test the form and revise it accordingly.
7. Be prepared to continuously revise the form until it works efficiently and effectively for you.

Summary

As we noted at the beginning of this chapter, classroom observation is fundamental to all forms of evaluation and is a routine part of every teacher's day. The challenge is to plan observation and record keeping of observations in a manner that will benefit instruction and ultimately student learning. In a general sense, classroom observation consists of a set of observational categories that directs teachers in their search for information, inferences, and explanations of teaching and learning. Observation can take a relatively open-ended form (anecdotal records) or a focused form with predetermined response categories (i.e., observational checklists or rating scales). The open-ended form is most appropriate for capturing important but unexpected classroom events and for examining instruction when the essential observational categories are not known. This type of classroom observation allows teachers to explore further an interesting or important observation that was not expected. The focused form can be used only when all or most of the important observational categories are already known. Even then, it is advisable to allow for unknown or unexpected observations. In other words, use a hybrid method of recording that includes both focused and open-ended possibilities.

Here are suggestions for conducting classroom observation:

1. Identify the purposes for which the observational information will be used (e.g., to assess student attainment; to individualize instruction; to adapt instruction to student attainment; to assess the effectiveness of a unit, lesson, or activity; or to explain student learning, or lack thereof).
2. Identify the kinds of observational information that would be useful for these purposes: student language use, work habits, learning strategies, reactions to instructional materials and activities, classroom interactions, and so on.
3. Decide how you will observe in order to collect the desired information. Decide (a) *whom* to observe: individual students or groups of students; (b) *how often* to observe them: once or more than once; and (c) *when:* during which specific lessons or occasions.
4. Select a method (or methods) for recording your observations: anecdotal records, checklists, or rating scales.
5. Prepare the necessary reporting forms.

Discussion questions

1. If you use any system for keeping track of classroom events and information, would you modify how you use it based on what you have read in this chapter? Explain how you would change it.

2. If you are reading this book as part of a class, have other students in your class make an oral presentation of Chapter 4. Prior to doing this, as a group, identify aspects of each presentation that would be important to observe were the presentations being graded. Then discuss how these observations could be recorded. Devise a record-keeping technique to carry out your observations, and then use it while each student makes his or her presentation.

3. Based on a lesson plan that you have used or are currently using, identify an important aspect (or aspects) of student behavior that is supposed to occur if the plan works as expected. Then devise a record-keeping technique for observing and recording the occurrence of these behaviors.

4. If you are teaching a second language class, select a learning objective that you are currently working on. Then plan an activity for students that would call for performance of the new skills; describe what you would look for that would indicate attainment of the objective; and devise a way of recording your observations. Try it out and then examine it critically.

5. If you are reading this book as part of a course, select another student in the class or a colleague who is currently teaching and arrange to observe him or her while teaching. Beforehand, discuss (a) what you think would be useful to observe, (b) the specific behaviors that you would observe, (c) how you would record your observations (consider the advantages and disadvantages of different record-keeping techniques), and (d) how this information could be useful for modifying instruction.

6. Describe any other record-keeping methods that you could use to record classroom observations not mentioned in this chapter. Compare these with those that are described in this chapter.

Readings

Barrs, M. S., S. Ellis, H. Hester, and A. Thomas. (1988). *The primary language record: Handbook for teachers.* Portsmouth, N.H.: Heinemann.

Baskwill, J., and P. Whitman. (1988). *Evaluation: Whole language, whole child.* New York: Scholastic.

Butler, F. A. (1992). *Some thoughts on assessing the oral language skills of students K-6.* Los Angeles: National Center for Research on Evaluation, Standards, and Student Testing.

Church, J. (1991). Record keeping in whole language classrooms. In B. Harp (Ed.), *Assessment and evaluation in whole language programs* (pp. 177–200). Norwood, Mass.: Christopher-Gordon.

Damico, J. (1991). Descriptive assessment of communicative ability of limited-English-proficient students. In E. V. Hamayan, and J. S. Damico

(Eds.), *Limiting bias in the assessment of bilingual students* (pp. 157–218). Austin, Tex.: Pro-ed.

Genishi, C., and A. Haas Dyson. (1987). *Language assessment in the early years.* Norwood, N.J.: Ablex.

Goodman, Y. M. (1985). Kidwatching: Observing children in the classroom. In A. Jagger and M. R. Smith-Burke (Eds.), *Observing the language learner* (pp. 9–18). Newark, Del.: International Reading Association.

Goodman, K. S., Y. M. Goodman, and W. J. Hood. (1989). *The whole language evaluation book.* Portsmouth, N.H.: Heinemann.

Graves, D. H. (1983). *Writing: Teachers and children at work.* Portsmouth, N.H.: Heinemann.

Harp, B. (Ed.) (1991). *Assessment and evaluation in whole language programs.* Norwood, Mass.: Christopher-Gordon.

Hopkins, C. D., and L. A. Richards. (1990). Using observation in the classroom. In C. D. Hopkins and L. A. Richards (Eds.), *Classroom measurement and evaluation* (pp. 69–99). Itasca, Ill.: F. E. Peacock.

Jagger, A., and M. R. Smith-Burke. (Eds.) (1985). *Observing the language learner.* Newark, Del.: International Reading Association.

Porter, W. R. (1983). Toward more effective record-keeping. *School Organization, 3,* 85–95.

Taylor, D. (1991). From a child's point of view: Alternate approaches to assessment. In J. A. Roderick (Ed.), *Context-responsive approaches to assessing children's language.* Urbana, Ill.: National Council of Teachers of English.

6 *Portfolios and conferences*

- Introduction
- Portfolios
- General guidelines for using portfolios
- Guidelines for using portfolios interactively
- Portfolios and student self-reflection
- Guidelines for using portfolios to plan instruction
- Conferences
- Guidelines for conducting conferences
- Record keeping
- Summary

Preview questions

1. How can students tell whether they are making progress in learning a second language?
2. Do you ever sit with individual students and discuss their schoolwork with them? What kinds of things do you discuss? What questions do you ask? How do you use the information elicited in these discussions?
3. Do you ever ask students what difficulties they are having in class? Do you ask them what they expect to learn or want to learn while in your class? Do you ever modify what you do in response to their feedback?
4. What is your understanding of portfolios and how they can be used in class? Do you currently use portfolios? If so, how? What are their advantages? Have you encountered any problems using portfolios? Discuss them.
5. Do you think that students should have an opportunity to provide feedback to teachers about the course or their teaching? How should such feedback be solicited?
6. How do you know if you are meeting students' expectations about second language learning? Is it even important to know this?
7. How do you know what strategies students are using to tackle and master new language skills?

Introduction

In this chapter, we discuss the use of portfolios and conferences in second language assessment, and we suggest methods of recording information that results from the use of these procedures. We discuss portfolios and conferences together because, unlike other forms of assessment in which the learner is the object of evaluation, portfolios and conferences involve learners as active collaborators in documenting and monitoring their own progress and in identifying learning goals. Portfolios and conferences provide excellent opportunities for student self-assessment. Conferences are often used in conjunction with portfolios as teachers review the contents of students' portfolios with them. We begin with portfolios.

Portfolios

Introduction

A portfolio is a purposeful collection of students' work that demonstrates to students and others their efforts, progress, and achievements in given areas. Student portfolios have been inspired by professionals such as photographers and architects as a means of keeping a record of their accomplishments to show to others. Second language portfolios can have a very specific focus, such as writing, or a broad focus that includes examples of all aspects of language development. Students should have their own portfolios, which can be a conventional file folder, a small cardboard box, a section of a file drawer, or some other such receptacle. Portfolios should be kept in readily accessible places so that students can review or update them easily or show them to others without the teacher's assistance.

The primary value of portfolios is in the assessment of student achievement. They are particularly useful in this respect because they provide a continuous record of students' language development that can be shared with others. If portfolios are reviewed routinely by teachers and students in conference together, then they can also provide information about students' views of their own language learning and the strategies they apply in reading and writing, for example. This in turn can enhance student involvement in and ownership of their own learning. Indeed, classrooms in which portfolio assessment plays a major role are often quite different from classrooms that use only tests or more conventional forms of assessment; they are generally more student-centered, collaborative, and holistic. Some of the benefits of using portfolios are summarized in Table 1.

The positive effects of portfolios on student learning arise from the opportunities they afford students to become actively involved in assessment and learning. This does not happen automatically, however, simply by having students keep portfolios of their work. Rather, it depends critically on teachers' conscientious efforts to use portfolios as a collaborative assessment process. They must be used actively and interactively, and they must be an integral part of instruction and instructional planning.

Table 1.   Benefits of portfolios

Portfolios provide:

- A continuous, cumulative record of language development
- A holistic view of student learning
- Insights about progress of individual students
- Opportunities for collaborative assessment and goal-setting with students
- Tangible evidence of student learning to be shared with parents, other educators, and other students
- Opportunities to use metalanguage to talk about language

Portfolios promote:

- Student involvement in assessment
- Responsibility for self-assessment
- Interaction with teachers, parents, and students about learning
- Student ownership of and responsibility for their own learning
- Excitement about learning
- Students' ability to think critically about schoolwork
- Collaborative, sharing classrooms

Portfolios need not be limited to language-related work, however. In the case of students who are being educated through the medium of a second language or who are learning language for specific purposes, you can broaden the range of work samples in the portfolio to reflect their second language goals; for example, include math work sheets or science reports (in the case of ESL students in English-medium schools) or business and financial reports (in the case of adult students learning a second language for business).

General guidelines for using portfolios

Getting started

Teachers must take the lead in starting this activity off on the right track. They must ensure that the portfolios are used actively and interactively. As with any new evaluation procedure, the implementation of portfolios takes time and a willingness to explore alternatives before the optimal strategy emerges. In the beginning, it is vital that you negotiate with students how you will jointly implement portfolios in your classroom. This is equally true for students who have used portfolios in the past and for students who have never used them before. For those who have used them before, negotiating their implementation is essential in order to reestablish ownership and consensus on how to use them in your classroom. Those who have never used them will clearly need guidance in setting them up; more importantly, negotiating this procedure will give them a sense of ownership and engagement that is critical for their success. It can be helpful to invite someone who has used portfolios in their work to visit your class to show and explain the entire process.

What are portfolios?

A file folder, box, or any durable and expandable container can serve as a portfolio. If everyone uses the same type of folder, the folders can be stored more easily. Folders should be clearly marked with each student's name, and they can also be decorated to each student's tastes, if desired, to enhance students' feeling of ownership.

What kinds of work are kept in portfolios?

Samples of writing, lists of books that have been read, book reports, tape-recordings of speaking samples, favorite short stories, and so on can all be included in a portfolio. Portfolios have most frequently been associated with written language, but they can also be used effectively with oral language. In this case, students keep audio recordings of speaking samples in their portfolios.

Some educators suggest that anything the student chooses be kept in the portfolio. We do not favor the inclusion of simply anything the student wishes to add because of the danger that they will merely become "junk drawers" of students' work. More important, it is difficult to assess a broad range of work that draws on different skills and knowledge (for example, science projects along with language arts projects).

Task 1

Discuss the advantages and disadvantages of portfolios with (1) a narrow focus and (2) a broad focus.

Students need not have a single portfolio: they can have a writing portfolio, a reading portfolio, a science portfolio, or whatever. Moreover, students can have one portfolio for their best work and one for work in progress. The best work portfolio might be used to show parents and visitors and for grading purposes, whereas the work-in-progress portfolio might be used by teachers and students themselves to monitor their progress and set learning goals.

Each piece of work in the portfolio should be dated clearly and, often, annotated with a short description of why it is included, what the student likes about it, or other pertinent comments.

How much work should be kept in portfolios?

The number of pieces in a portfolio should be limited for practical reasons. Portfolios that are constantly expanding and never cleaned out become difficult to store and, more important, difficult to review and assess. Students may choose to keep a portfolio of current work and one of completed work – the former would be more up to date and reflect current accomplishments whereas the latter would reflect previous accomplishments and the progress they have made.

If the number of pieces is to be limited, then it is necessary to review and update the portfolio periodically. In this case, decisions need to be made concerning the number of pieces (or range) to keep and the criteria for inclusion and exclusion. These decisions should be shared by teachers and students so that the students maintain ownership of and responsibility for their portfolios.

When and how often is work put in portfolios?

Students should have access to their portfolios at all times in order to add or take out pieces. Systematic review and analysis of each student's portfolio should be carried out by teachers on a regular basis – time permitting, once every four to six weeks. Systematic review of portfolios is also advisable at the end of significant instructional periods, such as at the end of the semester or a major unit and at the end of a grading period. At times, teachers may want to review the portfolios collaboratively with their students and at other times without them. Reviewing portfolios with students is important for a variety of reasons, including joint goal setting. Reviewing portfolios without students is useful for monitoring the effectiveness of instruction and for instructional planning.

Who has access to portfolios?

Clearly, students should have access to their own portfolios at all times. Teachers also need to have easy access to them; whether teachers seek permission from or inform students before reviewing their portfolios probably should be negotiated with the students as a whole. Sharing the contents of portfolios with parents and other teachers and educational professionals enhances their beneficial effects. Portfolios that are not shared are mere collections of school work.

There are occasions when it is not possible or desirable to include students in reviewing their portfolios, however. For example, sharing students' portfolios with administrators may be undertaken as part of a review procedure to examine student placement in particular programs or to revise grades based on standardized testing procedures. Furthermore, students' portfolios may be shared with teachers at the next level or grade so that they know the qualifications and skills of their incoming students in advance and can plan appropriate instruction. Student involvement in these cases may not be practicable or useful.

Where to keep portfolios

Keep the portfolios in a common, readily accessible area to which students have easy access. Storing them in the students' or teacher's desk is not a good idea because it disconnects them from students and from the general life of the classroom. If you are teaching part-time students who do not have their own classroom, it is not possible to store them in a common fixed area. In this instance, students need to keep their own portfolios.

Guidelines for using portfolios interactively

Responsibility and excitement for learning come from sharing one's accomplishments with others who are supportive and collaborative. Thus, the sense of responsibility and excitement for learning that can result from the use of portfolios is critically dependent on (1) their being used interactively, (2) students' assuming ownership of them, and (3) students' controlling the review process. Using portfolios interactively and collaboratively does not happen automatically but requires conscious and systematic planning by teachers. What follows are suggestions for making portfolios interactive vehicles for promoting student involvement in learning:

- Include students in all or as much decision making about portfolios as possible; ways in which this can be accomplished have already been discussed.
- It is particularly important that students choose the pieces to be included in their portfolios.
- Negotiate with students to determine how the work will be assessed, what criteria will be used for assessment, and how the assessment will be used.

- Plan portfolio conferences periodically so that students can review their work with their teachers and jointly set individualized goals; portfolio conferences are discussed in a later section of this chapter.
- With school-aged students, include parents in reviewing portfolios; this can be done by inviting parents to the school to discuss their children's portfolios with them or by sending pieces from student portfolios home for parental review and comment. In the latter case, it is important to give parents guidelines for reviewing the work (see Table 2).
- Encourage students to review and share their portfolios with other students.
- Organize reviews of individual student portfolios by small groups of students or the whole class; it is important in this case that all students' portfolios be reviewed in this way and that students be taught how to provide positive, constructive feedback to one another.
- Ensure that discussions of student portfolios are positive, collaborative, and under the control of the students whose portfolios are being reviewed; otherwise, the process will take on the characteristics of more conventional evaluation and grading procedures without the beneficial spin-off effects.
- Always adopt a positive, collaborative, and supportive attitude.

Table 2.   Guidelines for reviewing portfolios

Dos

- Build on what students have done and help them recognize what they have accomplished.
- Praise students for specific techniques or strategies they have used (in writing, for example) and point out the positive effects of those strategies.
- Listen and respond carefully to students' concerns about their progress or difficulties; offer reasonable suggestions in response to these concerns.
- In writing portfolios, reinforce students' use of appropriate terminology and metalinguistic references.
- Discuss processes and strategies as well as products
- Be realistic in setting goals.
- Be positive and supportive at all times.

Don'ts

- Focus on what has not been done or what is wrong with what has been done.
- Be judgmental about student work.
- Make too many suggestions or goals.
- Take over discussion of students' work.

The following questionnaire can be used by students to reflect on work they include in their portfolios. It can be adapted for specific kinds of work, such as writing assignments, book reviews, or a project related to schoolwork or their general interests. Students do not need to respond to all questions, and additional questions can be added to make the questionnaire more relevant.

1. What makes this a good or an interesting project?
2. What is the most interesting part of this project?
3. What was the most difficult part of this project?
4. What did you learn from doing this project?
5. What skills did you practice when doing this project?
6. How is this project different from or better than other projects in your portfolio?
7. What is the best part of this project? Why?
8. What is the weakest part of this project? Why?
9. How would you make this project better?
10. What assistance or resources did you use to complete this project?

Figure 1   Sample self-report form for student portfolios.

Portfolios and student self-reflection

Many methods of assessment treat students as objects of evaluation and place the responsibility and task of assessment in the hands of teachers or other adults. There is little opportunity provided by these methods for students to assume positions of responsibility and control. In comparison, portfolios make students the agents of reflection and decision making and thus give them control of their own learning. They encourage students to reflect on their own learning, to assess their own strengths and weaknesses, and to identify their own goals for learning. Teachers do this by asking students to reflect on their work and by being supportive and attentive during such reflections.

Here are some specific ways of accomplishing this:

1. Have students include a brief note describing why each piece is included in their portfolio; what they like about it; what they learned when they did it; and where there could be improvement. An example of a checklist to be completed for specific pieces of writing is presented in Figure 1.
2. During portfolio conferences, allow students to control the review process; ask them to describe their current strengths and weaknesses and to indicate where they have made progress; ask them to give evidence of this progress.

3. Ask students to compare pieces of work in their portfolios and to identify what makes one piece better than another and what they might do differently if they were to redo a piece.
4. Ask students to select their best work, or their most improved work, or their most difficult work, and explain why each was selected.
5. Be interested, supportive, and constructive when providing responses to or feedback about portfolio pieces and students' reflections on their work.
6. Ask students how they think they can strengthen weaknesses and what the teacher can do to help.
7. Collaborate with students to set goals for language development.
8. Encourage students to reflect on their work in the presence of other students so that they see this as an integral aspect of classroom teaching and learning and so that they become comfortable with self-assessment and adept at giving supportive feedback to their peers; it is important when students share their portfolios that the interaction be noncompetitive and student-centered.
9. Ask students to comment on or write about keeping portfolios and how portfolios help them learn better.

Students' initial reflections on their work might be somewhat simple and superficial and perhaps repetitive from one occasion to the next. Allow time for students to become comfortable with using portfolios and to develop insights and provide details about their work.

Guidelines for using portfolios to plan instruction

As well as using portfolios to boost student involvement in learning, teachers can use them to plan instruction that is responsive to students' needs. This is largely an issue of reviewing evidence of student achievement in their portfolios (with the students or privately) and keeping a record of areas that require additional attention. More specifically,

- Plan regular conferences with students to review the contents of their portfolios.
- Review students' portfolios after major units or periods of instruction to monitor the impact of instruction.
- Look for recurrent and persistent difficulties experienced by students and keep a record of them (checklists or anecdotal notes can be helpful here); make provisions for keeping track of observations across time and of a number of students so that you can identify frequent and common difficulties.
- Listen carefully to students' comments about the difficulties they are experiencing or the areas they feel are important to improve and build

these into your lessons; otherwise, students will not believe that their comments make a difference.

- Engage students in joint goal setting and instructional planning, and ensure that these goals and plans are incorporated into your instruction.

Reviewing and responding to portfolios is time consuming. It may not fit neatly into your classroom routine as it is currently organized. You may find it necessary to reconceptualize your role as a teacher to become that of facilitator and listener; and you may need to reorganize your way of doing things in class to make time for portfolio activities. Portfolios should become an integral part of your teaching if they are to lead to the benefits described earlier.

Task 2

Re-do the rating scale for writing portfolios presented in Figure 1 so that each question takes the form of a closed-ended question. What are the advantages of this format?

Task 3

Divide the class into groups of four or five students. Each group discusses one of the following topics for five or ten minutes and then reports to the entire class.

Group 1: Implementation of portfolios

Group 2: Using portfolios to assess language achievement

Group 3: Using portfolios to promote student self-reflection

Group 4: Using portfolios to plan instruction

Conferences

Introduction

In the preceding section, we referred to portfolio conferences. These conferences are often used to review the contents of portfolios; examples of

Conference about a single piece of writing

- Why did you select this piece of writing?
- What do you see as its strengths?
- What was especially important to you when you were writing this piece?
- What things did you have difficulty with?
- If you could work on it further, what would you do?
- How is this piece the same as or different from other pieces?

Conference about a reading selection

- Why did you select this story?
- What do you particularly like about this story?
- How do you think others would react to this story?
- How was this the same as or different from other things you have read and responded to?
- How will this influence what you read in the future?

Conference about a portfolio

- What kinds of materials have you included in your portfolio?
- In what ways are they the same? Different?
- What does your portfolio reveal about you as a reader? (A writer? A person?)
- What does your portfolio suggest your strengths are?
- How does your portfolio reveal how you have changed?
- What do you think people will learn from your portfolio?
- How do you plan to use your portfolio?

Figure 2   Sample portfolio conference protocols. [Adapted from R. Tierney, M. Carter, and L. Desai (1991). Portfolio assessment in the reading-writing classroom. *Norwood, Mass.: Christopher-Gordon Publishers, Inc.]*

questions that can be used in conferences for reviewing portfolios are presented in Figure 2. Conferences can be used more widely as part of evaluation, and generally take the form of a conversation or discussion between teachers and students about school work. Conferences can include individual students, several students, or even the whole class; they can be conversations about completed work (as in the case of portfolio conferences) or about work in progress (for example, during a reading or writing activity); and they often focus on activities the teacher has set up expressly to observe and discuss. Although conferences have been widely used for understanding students' reading and writing, they can also be used in conjunction with oral language skills (such as comprehending class lectures) and with other areas of the curriculum or program of study (such as mathematics and science). We focus on their use with language.

In comparison with portfolios, whose primary benefits are related to the assessment of achievement, conferences are advantageous for understand-

Table 3.   Conferences and instructional planning

Conferences improve instructional planning because they help teachers:

- Identify successful and problematic learning strategies or styles that students are using
- Identify aspects of instruction that students have and have not successfully mastered
- Identify problematic aspects of language performance for individual students
- Understand students' motivations and interests

---

ing the processes, strategies, and approaches students use in the performance of school work and language-related tasks. During conferences, teachers direct questions to their students to gain insights about:

- Their application of skills and knowledge taught in class
- Specific difficulties they have when doing schoolwork and how they resolve them
- The processes or strategies they use in the performance of certain language-based tasks
- Their understanding of or beliefs about certain aspects of language, such as reading and writing
- Their interests and goals with respect to language
- Their understanding of and responses to instructional activities

Like portfolios when used interactively, conferences have additional benefits. They provide opportunities for students:

- To be self-reflective
- To assume responsibility for their own learning
- To collaboratively set individual learning goals
- To assume ownership of learning
- To recognize and enjoy their accomplishments
- To communicate orally in one-to-one conversations with their teachers about schoolwork in ways that are important to them

It is their focus on process that makes conferences distinct from other methods of assessment and, therefore, distinctly useful in instructional planning (see Table 3). They are especially helpful for teachers who may be unfamiliar with the diversity of learning strategies and performance styles that students from different cultural and linguistic backgrounds bring to the classroom. These insights can be difficult to gain during whole class activities because some students are reluctant to participate fully in such public activities. Conferences can give these students an opportunity to talk to the teacher in private. Moreover, routine classroom activities generally focus on the products of learning and leave issues related to process unexplored. The heavy reliance on verbal communication in conferences makes it difficult for students at the very beginning levels of proficiency to participate fully and meaningfully; alternative assessment strategies may have to be used in these cases.

Guidelines for conducting conferences

In this section we set forth general guidelines for conducting conferences with individual students about a piece of completed work from a portfolio or class assignment. References at the end of this chapter provide more detail about conducting other types of conferences.

At all times, students must feel that the conference is under their control and for their benefit. Begin by having students review the work for you; permit them to comment on whatever is important from their point of view even though it might not seem so to you. To facilitate discussion, the following kinds of questions can be asked of students:

- What do you like about this work?
- What do you think you did well?
- How does it show improvement from previous work? Can you show me the improvement?
- Did you have any difficulties with this piece of work? Can you show me where you had difficulty? What did you do to overcome it?
- What strategies did you use to figure out the meaning of words you could not read? or What did you do when you did not know a word that you wanted to write?
- Are there things about this work you do not like? Are there things you would like to improve?
- When you are reading and come across a word or something you do not understand, what do you do? or When you are writing and you have difficulty writing what you want, what do you do?

Because they are focused on student concerns and views, these questions can give students a sense of ownership and involvement in assessment and learning that are difficult to achieve otherwise. Responses to these sorts of questions provide teachers with insights about students' learning strategies that can promote understanding of student achievement and progress. They can serve as the basis for individualizing instruction or for modifying instructional plans to be better attuned to all students' needs. An example of a conference protocol for writing is presented in Figure 3, and one for reading is presented in Figure 4.

- Tell me about your writing.
- What is the part you like best?
- Does it say what you want it to say?
- Where does your story take place?
- What do you mean by . . .?
- I don't understand the part about . . .
- How could the order of your ideas be changed to be clearer?
- Does your beginning encourage the reader to read on? Explain why.
- Do you like the ending? Could it be improved?

Figure 3   Sample writing conference protocol. [Reprinted with permission from S. Schwartz (1987). All write. *Toronto: OISE Press.]*

Name: _____ Age: _____ Date: _____
Grade: _____ Sex: _____ Level/Placement _____

Directions: Ask the following questions in a comfortable one-on-one interview setting. The student should be assured that you are interested only in learning his/her thoughts on reading. Ask the student to elaborate on answers by using such prompts as "Can you tell me more about that?" "What else do you do?" The more you get the students to talk, the more insight you will gain about their reading process.

1. When you are reading and you come to something you don't know, what do you do? Do you do anything else?
2. Who do you think is a good reader?
3. What makes this person a good reader?
4. Do you think this person ever comes to something that she/he doesn't know while reading?   Yes   No

If Yes: What do you think this person does when he/she comes to something he/she does not know?

If No: Suppose this person did come to something she/he didn't know, what do think she/he would do?

5. During your reading group, what do you spend most of your time doing?
6. If you knew that someone was having difficulty reading, how would you help that person?
7. What would your teacher do to help a person having trouble with reading?
8. How did you learn to read? What was done to help you learn to read?
9. Do you think you are a good reader?   Yes   No
10. What would you like to do better in reading?

Figure 4   The Burke reading interview.

Conferences can also focus directly on instructional issues. The following questions can be useful in this regard:

- What do I (i.e., teacher) do that helps you be a better reader (or writer)?
- What do I do that does not help you be a better reader (or writer)?

- What do you want me to help you with next?
- What do you want to learn next?
- What is something important that you learned today (or this week) about reading or writing?

Questions during conferences can also focus on young students' image of themselves as language learners and users:

- Who is a good reader (or writer) in the class? What makes him a good reader (or writer)?
- Are you a good reader (or writer)? What makes you a good reader (or writer)?
- What can good readers (or writers) do?
- What do you need (or want) to learn in order to become a good reader (or writer)?

Responses to such questions can provide teachers with valuable insights about young students' views of what reading, writing, or other language skills entail so that they can tailor their interventions to match those of their students or to move students beyond what might be limiting or inappropriate perceptions.

As we have already noted, conferences can be used to discuss work that has been completed. At other times, teachers can ask students to perform a task while they look on – for example, read a passage from a book of the student's choosing, write a short piece, or describe a story they have read or television program they have seen. Teachers can then observe student performance directly and discern use of specific strategies. Teacher and student can then discuss the student's performance using modifications of the questions suggested earlier.

Students may at first be awkward, uncomfortable, and confused about what is expected during conferences, and they may provide little meaningful feedback at first. As with other alternative assessment activities, however, students usually become comfortable over time and indeed enthusiastic and eventually provide teachers with much valuable insight about their learning.

When to conference

Conduct your conferences with each student on a regular basis throughout the year or course in order to monitor progress and difficulties that might be impeding progress and to plan lessons or instruction that is responsive to students' ongoing needs. Conferencing is particularly valuable for providing timely feedback that can enhance fine-tuning of instruction. When used at the end of a major unit, conferencing can help assess learning with respect to major instructional objectives. Conferences that are conducted irregularly and infrequently are not useful for instructional planning, nor does this allow students to become familiar with the exercise so that it is maximally beneficial. Since it can be time consuming to conduct individual conferences, you may want to set aside time each day during which three or four conferences are conducted with individual students while other students in the class work on their own or in small groups. Routine conferencing of this sort is most frequently organized around common activities or pieces of work that all students are asked to engage in.

Special conferences with individual students who are experiencing difficulty and require additional attention are also recommended. It can be difficult to understand the real problem(s) individual students are having during routine instructional periods when there are many other things and students to attend to. In these cases, conferences should be planned around an activity, such as reading, that is pertinent to the individual student's area of difficulty.

Conferencing and grading

We do not recommend using conferences for grading purposes because grading generally focuses on learning outcomes or achievement, whereas the primary focus of conferences is process. Moreover, there are better, more direct, methods of assessing language achievement for grading purposes, such as tests and portfolios. However, if conferences are to be used for grading, the following guidelines are offered; these suggestions contrast with our previous recommendations that encourage individualization and student control.

1. The teacher should direct the conference and retain control of it at all times in order to ensure uniformity of the procedure.
2. All students should participate to ensure the collection of the same kind of information to be applied to grading all students.
3. The conference protocol should be the same for all students so that individual differences in student performance are not due to variations in protocol.
4. Use assessment information from conferences along with information collected from other assessment procedures, such as testing.
5. It is essential to keep detailed notes of conferences if they are to be used for grading in case you are called on to back up your grade with reference to information collected during the conference.

Record keeping

By their very nature, portfolios provide an ongoing record of student development. It is also useful to record observations and insights arising from the review of portfolios and include these in the portfolios themselves or in a file or book dedicated to this purpose. Recording comments about conferences is especially useful and important because the conferences do not provide a written record. Students' willingness to collaborate in the use of these procedures and their confidence in the value of these activities is critically dependent on using information emanating from them to plan instruction. Detailed record keeping of student performance demonstrated during conferences or in portfolios can also facilitate the planning of individualized instruction and the assessment of individual development. Such detailed records are also necessary if conferences and portfolios are to be used systematically in assigning grades. A variety of record-keeping methods can be useful.

Conference and portfolio notes

Keep your notes about student performance emanating from portfolios and conferences in a separate loose-leaf notebook or filefolder with a section for each student. Make your notes as soon as possible after reviewing portfolios or conducting conferences; any delay in recording your comments should be minimized so that records are accurate. Such notes should be dated and accompanied by a brief description of the activity or work. The following kinds of questions can guide note taking:

- What knowledge or skill did the student demonstrate?
- Where did the student demonstrate growth or improvement?
- Where did the student appear to have difficulty?
- What strategies did the student use to cope with difficulties?
- How did the student organize his work? Did the student have a strategy for planning writing or reading assignments?
- Does the student know her strengths and weaknesses?
- What likes and dislikes did the student express?
- What goals are appropriate for this student?

Teacher journals

We recommend recording insights and feedback pertinent to instruction that arise from portfolios and conferences in a separate notebook. Such notes might be about activities or materials that students did not like; things they do that facilitate or hinder learning; or sequencing or timing of activities or objectives. It would not be appropriate to keep such notes in students' records. A journal devoted to notes about instructional matters can be set up for this purpose. Observations about students during a conference or portfolio review can be recorded using anecdotal notes that are entered in a journal later.

Checklists

Checklists with predesignated categories can be used to record observations during conferences and about portfolios if these activities are organized around instructional objectives and if they are conducted with all students at roughly the same stage of instruction. Instructional objectives can serve to define the categories. Checklists cannot be used if there is no predesignated focus for the conference.

Rating scales

Rating scales designed to reflect instructional objectives can provide even more precise records of student performance as revealed during conferences and portfolio reviews. This kind of precision is most useful when the record may be shown to others (school administrators, other teachers, or parents). What is gained in precision by using rating scales is lost in nuance, however. Rating scales, like checklists, are useful only if you have a clear and precise knowledge of what to look for or expect.

Student anecdotal records

Students can also be asked to keep records of portfolio reviews and conferences to assist them in reflecting on the results of these activities and any strengths or weaknesses they encountered during them. Such records also serve to remind students of any goals they set following the activity. Learning logs, journals, or a folder especially for conference or portfolio notes can be established for this purpose.

Task 4

Using the questions presented in Figure 2, add questions to each conference protocol that you think would be useful, and describe what additional useful information each question would elicit from students.

Summary

Portfolios and conferences are innovative and valuable methods of collecting information for evaluation. They give students opportunities to use language with teachers in ways that rarely occur during regular class time. When used interactively, portfolios and conferences give students a sense of involvement in, control over, and enthusiasm for learning. These exercises shift the emphasis from students as objects of evaluation to agents of evaluation. Special care must be taken by teachers to ensure that these activities are used in student-centered, interactive ways; otherwise, the unique benefits of these methods will not be realized.

Discussion questions

1. What are some of the difficulties students might experience when initially using portfolios or participating in a conference? What are some techniques for responding to these difficulties?
2. What are some problems teachers might experience when first using portfolios or conferences? What would you recommend to alleviate or remedy these difficulties?
3. Can you suggest strategies for using portfolios interactively in addition to those suggested in this chapter?
4. If you are currently using portfolios, identify ways you might modify them based on suggestions presented in this chapter. If you have never used portfolios, (a) identify a general instructional objective you have used or are currently using that would lend itself to portfolio assessment, (b) describe the kinds of information student portfolios would provide, and (c) indicate how you could use that information to monitor teaching or learning.
5. List some processes associated with writing (or speaking) that would be useful to observe in order to assess students' developing language skills, and identify ways that you could observe these in a student conference. Devise a method for recording observations during the conference.
6. If you are reading this book as part of a course on second language evaluation, identify ways that portfolios could be employed in your course and describe how they could help you evaluate your progress in the course.
7. What are questions that could be asked of students during a conference about reading (or writing) in addition to those suggested in this chapter that could help you better understand the strategies your students use?
8. If you work with young second language learners, devise a set of guidelines for parents to use when reviewing their children's portfolios. Iden-

tify what parents should and should not do to encourage student ownership of, pride in, and enthusiasm for language learning.

9. In what ways could group conferences be useful for revealing important aspects of language learning? How could you record observations of important information revealed during such a conference?

Readings

Barrs, M., E. Ellis, H. Hester, and A. Thomas. (1988). *The primary language record.* Portsmouth, N.H.: Heinemann.

Belanoff, P., and M. Dickson. (1991). *Portfolios: Process and product.* Portsmouth, N.H.: Heinemann.

Cambourne, B., and J. Turbill. (1990). Assessment in whole language classrooms: Theory into practice. *The Elementary School Journal, 90,* 337–349.

Goodman, K. S., Y. M. Goodman, and W. J. Hood. (1989). *The whole language evaluation book.* Portsmouth, N.H.: Heinemann.

Graves, D. (1983). *Writing: Teachers and children at work.* Portsmouth, N.H.: Heinemann.

Hamp-Lyons, L. (1991). *Assessing second language writing in academic contexts.* Norwood, N.J.: Ablex.

Jongsma, K. (1989). Questions and answers: Portfolio assessment. *The Reading Teacher, 43,* 264.

Short, D. (1993). Assessing integrated language and content. *TESOL Quarterly, 27,* 627–656.

Taylor, D. (1990). Teaching without testing: Assessing the complexity of children's literacy learning. *English Education, 22,* 4–74.

Tierney, R. J., M. A. Carter, and L. E. Desai. (1991). *Portfolio assessment in the reading and writing classroom.* Norwood, Mass.: Christopher-Gordon.

Valencia, S. (1990). A portfolio approach to classroom reading assessment: The whys, whats and hows. *The Reading Teacher, 43,* 338–340.

Watson, D., and J. Henson. (1991). Reading evaluation: Miscue analysis. In B. Harp (Ed.), *Assessment and evaluation in whole language programs* (pp. 51–72). Norwood, Mass.: Christopher-Gordon.

Woolfolk, A. (1993). *Educational psychology.* Boston: Allyn and Bacon.

7 *Journals, questionnaires, and interviews*

- Introduction
- Journals
- Guidelines for using dialogue journals
- Record keeping
- Interviews and questionnaires
- Guidelines for constructing questionnaires and interviews
- Summary

Preview questions

1. Do you keep a personal diary or journal? How often do you write in it? What kinds of things do you write about? Why do you keep a journal? If you were advising someone else about how to keep a journal, what would you suggest to them?

2. Do students in your class have ways of providing feedback about their learning experiences in class? Describe them and tell how they are useful.

3. Do your students now keep or have they ever kept journals in your classroom? What do you find useful about them? In particular, what kinds of assessment information did they provide that you might not otherwise have? What do you find is not useful or is difficult about them?

4. How do you or how would you find out about important aspects of your students' backgrounds, such as their prior education or language learning experiences? How satisfactory are the methods you use for collecting this kind of information? What are their strong and weak points?

5. Have you ever been annoyed by a questionnaire you were asked to complete? What was wrong with it?

6. Have you ever been interviewed? What aspects of the interview bothered you and why? What aspects worked well in your opinion? If you had to interview students (or their parents) in order to determine whether the course you teach is appropriate for them: (a) what kinds of questions do you think you would ask, (b) how do you think you would explain the purpose of the interview to them, and (c) how would you put them at ease?

7. Have you ever had to interview your students in order to collect background information about them prior to teaching them? What kinds of questions did you ask? What did you find to be the major difficulties in doing the interviews? If you work with young second language learners, answer these questions about interviewing their parents.

Introduction

The methods of collecting information discussed in this chapter include journals (also referred to as interactive diaries or dialogue journals), interviews, and questionnaires. We discuss interviews and questionnaires together because of their overall similarity in form and function. We have included a discussion of journals because we regard them – like the other two – as methods of collecting information for evaluation purposes that can be likened to conversations between learners and teachers. It is important to recognize that this pairing is arbitrary: each method has its unique features as well as similarities to other methods of information collection.

The primary use of journals, interviews, and questionnaires is in the collection of information about students' backgrounds and about teaching and learning processes: for example, information about students' goals or expectations about second language learning; their feelings or attitudes about themselves, the classroom, and other instructional matters; their work habits, interests, and preferences; and so on. These methods can also be used to collect information about second language proficiency: writing in the case of journals and questionnaires and speaking in the case of interviews. However, if your primary concern is to document student language achievement, there are other, better methods for doing this. These methods of collecting information can also be useful for student self-assessment.

Journals

Why?

Journals are written conversations between students and teachers. Dialogue journals have a number of important benefits (Table 1). They provide opportunities for students to provide feedback about their learning experiences. Are they able to keep up in class? Did they understand particular lessons? Do they enjoy working by themselves or with other students? It may be helpful and, indeed, necessary to explicitly let students know that it is all right to comment on such classroom matters in their journals and to openly express feelings about their teachers, classmates, and classroom activities. Some second language students may feel reluctant to express themselves openly during regular classroom activities for linguistic or cul-

Table 1.   Benefits of dialogue journals

---

1. They provide useful information for individualizing instruction, for example:

   - writing skills
   - writing strategies
   - students' experiences in and outside of school
   - learning processes
   - attitudes and feeling about themselves, their teachers, schooling
   - their interests, expectations, goals

2. They increase opportunities for functional communication between students and teachers.
3. They give students opportunities to use language for genuine communication and personalized reading.
4. They permit teachers to individualize language teaching by modeling writing skills in their responses to student journals.
5. They promote the development of certain writing skills.
6. They enhance student involvement in and ownership of learning.

---

tural reasons. For second language learners who are being educated in the second language, keeping a journal can help them express and deal with issues related to integration into mainstream classes. These kinds of information can enhance one's understanding of individual students and can be useful for individualizing instruction. Candid, spontaneous feedback from students in their journals demands acceptance and openness on the part of teachers.

Journals can also be used to gain insights about students' writing skills in the second language and the strategies they use when writing, if their entries are spontaneous and free flowing, including any or all errors, corrections, and editing. Students should not feel that their language must be correct or perfect. If they feel they lack certain methods of written expression, they should be encouraged to ask for help from their teachers or fellow students and to use whatever means of expression they have, even pictures. Evidence in students' journals of recurrent or specific writing difficulties can be used to plan writing activities or lessons of a more formal nature at another time. If regular entries are made, journals can provide a continuous record of students' writing development.

Because of their personal, student-centered nature, journals have the added advantage that they allow students opportunities to express themselves personally about their interests, goals, and desires using the second language. Table 2 identifies certain writing skills whose development can be promoted by dialogue journal conversations; these are particularly relevant to second language learners in the elementary and secondary grades.

Table 2.   Literacy skills promoted by journal conversations

Topic initiation
Topic variety
Elaboration of topics
Metacommunication about reading and writing
Audience awareness
Awareness and use of print
Creativity and independence in writing
Grammar
Language functions

Source: Staton (1990) and Peyton (1992).

Journals provide teachers with opportunities to assess their students' ability to express themselves personally in writing using the second language without the pressures that students may feel during whole class activities.

How?

To be useful for evaluation purposes, journals must be used interactively: they should be shared with teachers, and teachers should share their ideas in writing with their students. One can think of dialogue journals as written conversations between students and their teachers. Some teachers collect student journals and return them with written comments, feedback, or advice on a daily basis; other teachers do this on a weekly basis. In some cases, to make the task more manageable, teachers use a rotation system so that they do not have to read all students' journals all the time. In any case, it is advisable to set aside regular times for students to write in their journals and for teachers to collect, read, and respond to their entries. The feedback provided by students in their journals is particularly useful for on-line instructional planning that responds to students' current and changing needs. If they are not shared in a regular and timely fashion, the useful information they contain remains unavailable to teachers for planning purposes. When used in these ways, journals have some of the same advantages as conferences (as discussed in the previous chapter) – they are personal, individualized, private, and instructional, and they encourage student involvement in and ownership of learning and the assessment process itself.

To ensure that journals are truly interactive or conversational and that they do not become like other classroom writing assignments such as essays or reports, it is important that they not be highly structured or that limits not be put on what students write about; one exception to this is learning logs. In addition, in order to ensure spontaneity and sincerity in journal writing, teachers should avoid direct evaluative feedback to students about their writing skills or the substance of their writing. Comments that teachers might make regarding the linguistic forms used by students should focus on meaningful communication and be supportive and only indirectly evaluative (for example, "I am not sure what you mean by this; can you say it in another way?" Or provide a corrected paraphrase of a student's entry and ask if this is what the student means). Some educators recommend that no evaluative feedback of any type be given in response to students' journal entries. However, this is a matter of personal choice and depends, in part, on what the students themselves want. In fact, some second language learners, especially older ones, may explicitly seek feedback about the form of their language in their journals. Indeed, such private, individualized feedback may be welcomed by students who are uncomfortable when teachers make public comments about them.

Much of the information contained in journals can be collected using other methods. For example, interviews and questionnaires can be employed to elicit learners' judgments of their language skills, their attitudes toward activities in a course or lesson, their impressions of course content and its organization, and so on. Journals, however, are unique as methods for collecting information for evaluation because they are largely under the control of students. The other methods we discuss are largely under the control of teachers. In comparison, students can write whatever they want and however they want in their journals. They will probably need some guidance and encouragement when beginning to use journals interactively in order to become familiar and at ease with them. Teachers themselves need time to become comfortable using interactive journals and to arrive at a way of maximizing their benefits.

Learning logs

Student journals need not always be open ended. They can be structured somewhat so that students focus their entries in specific ways. A special use of student journals that utilizes some structuring is the learning log. In learning logs, students describe their learning experiences in specific classes (e.g., mathematics or science); the difficulties they had; what they enjoyed learning; whether they had the language skills needed to follow instruction; and so on. Learning logs are particularly useful for teachers working with students who are being educated through the medium of a second language, that is, students who need to learn the second language in order to benefit from academic instruction in the second language (e.g., non-English-speaking immigrant children in Australia).

Here are some prompts that can help students think about what they want to write in their learning logs; these prompts could also be used for language classes:

- This week I studied . . .
- This week I learned . . .
- My difficulties are . . .
- I would like to know . . .
- I would like help with . . .
- My learning and practicing plans are . . .

Learning logs that are used to monitor students' progress in their school subjects are a way for second language teachers to stay in touch with how their students are doing in their other classes without actually being there. As well as providing general information about students' learning experiences in their other classes, learning logs can also indicate to second language teachers whether their students' second language skills are adequate for full participation in these other classes and where they might be having specific difficulties. They can reveal whether students are making connections within subject areas and, where appropriate, between subject areas; in other words, whether they are actually progressing in their other school subjects. Such information can help teachers plan instruction that incorporates the language skills their students need in other academic domains and/or the actual content from these domains into their language teaching.

Students themselves can use learning logs for self-assessment – to monitor their progress toward achieving their personal goals or the objectives of other content areas and to identify areas of difficulty, linguistic or nonlinguistic, that may be interfering with their language or general academic progress. Even though learning logs call for some structure and focus, they remain largely student centered and, therefore, contribute to student involvement in the assessment process. Consequently, they have an important role to play in an overall classroom-based evaluation plan.

Guidelines for using dialogue journals

The following guidelines for using journals are suggested:

1. Students should have separate books for journal writing. Students with access to computers may want to keep electronic journals.
2. Set aside regular times – at the end of class or at the beginning or end of the day – when students can write in their journals. It is preferable that time be devoted in class for journals but, alternatively, students can write in their journals at home on their own time. Journal writing should be routine.

3. Collect students' journals on a regular basis and read them carefully before returning them. Reading journals is time consuming, so it is important to find a method of keeping track of them that works for you. Keep the interval between readings as brief as possible; otherwise, students may perceive the feedback contained in their journals as unimportant and merely a writing exercise.

4. Writing journals is not easy in the beginning. Students will probably need some direction in order to know what you are looking for. More specifically, it can be helpful to guide them through a series of stages, progressing initially from writing about impersonal, factual matters to more personal, factual subjects, and finally to interpersonal as well as personal feelings and opinions. Or give students topics, issues, or themes concerning their classroom experiences to write about to get them started.

5. Encourage students to write about their successes as well as their difficulties and hardships. Similarly, encourage them to write about classroom activities and events that they found useful, effective, and fun as well as those they found to be confusing, useless, uninteresting, or frustrating.

6. Be patient and allow students time to develop confidence in the process of sharing their personal impressions. If this is the first time students have written journals, they may be cautious and circumspect. It will take time for them to develop insights about what is important for effective learning and teaching.

7. Avoid the use of evaluative or judgmental comments to ensure students' confidence and candor. Candor is essential for the effective use of dialogue journals.

8. Help students interpret their own feedback and decide on actions take in response to it.

Ethical concerns

Students' journals may contain descriptions of feelings or references to events in their lives that are upsetting and even highly disturbing. As professionals entrusted with the care of second language learners, teachers are obliged to take such feedback seriously. A sympathetic and supportive response from the teacher may be effective and sufficient in some instances, as in the case illustrated in Figure 1. In other instances, what constitutes an adequate response may not be so straightforward – for example, in cases where laws appear to have been broken or the physical well-being of a student appears to have been seriously jeopardized. It is advisable for teachers who use dialogue journals to ascertain the policy of their school or school district with respect to the use of confidential or personal

Student: March 24
thes mone I look at
a car hit a cat the
little cat die

Teacher: That is so sad. Did you
cry when the car hit the
cat? I know I would have
cried— The poor little cat.

Ravi, 12th Grade

*Today is Wednesday the 10th who is
that teacher anyway I hate that teacher
why does she always come in our class.
I am sick and tired of school. I don't
know why because they don't have a
cooler in our school. It is always hot in
this school. Sometimes I think of
quitting the school. I think that the
school is boring. Mrs. B why is it very
hot in this school. I hate hot wether any
way.*

*Figure 1   Sample excerpts from students' journals. [Reprinted, with
permission from the publisher, from* Dialogue journal writing with
nonnative English speakers *(p. 88) by J. Peyton and J. Staton, 1992,
Alexandria, Va.: TESOL.]*

information in students' journals and with respect to alleged cases of misdemeanor and abuse. In the absence of an official school or district policy, it is prudent to establish a policy at the outset so that guidelines are in place to direct a response if the need arises.

Task 1

(a) Discuss issues related to the limits of teachers' responsibility to respond to personal information contained in students' journals and (b) describe alternative policies with respect to confidentiality and personal revelations in students' journals.

Record keeping

Journals themselves are a record of student writing skills. At the same time, it is important for teachers to keep records of important observations and insights that they glean from reading the journals that can be used for instructional planning. Although any of the previous methods of record keeping we have discussed could be used, anecdotal records and teachers' journals are likely to be the most useful because they are the most open ended. It is probably best to record your observations about individual students in a record book in which a section has been reserved for each student; in this way, you have easy access to information about particular students.

Summary

Because they are student centered and student driven, dialogue journals have a number of potential advantages that recommend their use as part of a comprehensive approach to evaluation:

- Student journals can reveal important aspects and useful insights about second language teaching and learning that might not be revealed by other feedback techniques.
- Having students keep journals about their learning experiences can increase their involvement in the teaching-learning process and make them more responsible for their own learning, including joint goal setting and collaborative establishment of assessment criteria with teachers.

- Learners can become more aware of the criteria on which assessment is based; they may gradually internalize these criteria and thus be in a better position to monitor and judge their own learning.
- Students' journal entries can raise teachers' consciousness about those aspects of teaching and learning that are important to their students and, therefore, allow them to make more informed, student-centered decisions about instruction.
- They provide valuable insights about students' writing skills.
- They can promote the development of certain writing skills.
- They give students opportunities for real, functional written communication.
- They allow teachers to get to know their students better.

Task 2

Discuss how journals, conferences, and portfolios can be used together for student self-assessment.

Interviews and questionnaires

Introduction

Interviews and questionnaires are discussed together in this section because they are very similar: Both consist of a set of questions or statements the student is expected to respond to.

Why and when to use questionnaires and interviews

Interviews and questionnaires are relatively structured and formal. Therefore, they are most useful with older learners who have acquired more than beginning levels of proficiency in the second language, that is, unless the questionnaire or interview is in the students' native language. In addition, they require considerable planning and preparation time. Therefore, they are most useful when employed periodically and when relatively systematic and uniform feedback is desired from students, parents, or teachers — for example, before instruction begins and at the end of major units of instruction or an entire course of instruction. At these times, the information they provide is valuable for planning and assessing whole courses or units.

How is your English? This self-evaluation questionnaire allows you to describe your own level of proficiency in English. The statements below describe specific language use situations. They are designed to help you evaluate what you can do in English in relation to the content of this course.

Use the following ratings to answer each question:

1. Never
2. Rarely
3. Half of the time
4. Often
5. Always

Listening

I can listen to the news or the weather forecast on the radio and pick out specific information.

I can follow and understand movies, shows, or other kinds of entertainment on television.

Reading

I can read an article and pick out specific items of information.

I can skim an article and get the gist, or main idea, of the text.

Writing

I can write a letter expressing my interests and experiences.

I can summarize the information contained in a short newspaper article.

Speaking

I can make social introductions.

I can tell people about myself, my education, and my family in some detail.

Figure 2   Sample items for a student self-evaluation questionnaire.

More specifically, before instruction, questionnaires or interviews can be used with students (or their parents, in the case of young learners) to collect information about input factors that might influence instructional planning, including, for example, information about incoming students' social, cultural, and personal backgrounds, their previous educational and language experiences (including literacy), their current language skills (Figure 2 presents sample items for a student self-evaluation questionnaire), their second language needs and goals, and so on. By comparing such information with instructional objectives and plans, teachers can assess the appropriateness of both for their incoming students. They can also be used with teachers before instruction begins to collect information about their qualifications for and interest in teaching specific courses.

Questionnaires and interviews can be used after instruction to gather

How do you know when you have taught an effective foreign language lesson? Ask yourself the following questions:

1. Are all students actively participating in the foreign language, either individually, in small groups, or in whole-class activities?
2. Are the youngsters given the opportunity to use the foreign language in functional situations during the lesson?
3. Are students able to use the language (depending on the goals of the program) in all four skills of listening, speaking, reading, and writing? and for higher-order thinking skills activities?
4. Is there ongoing evaluation for purposes of diagnosis of problems as well as for grouping?
5. Are cultural topics woven into each foreign language lesson?
6. Is the textbook adapted to suit the curriculum and the ability of the students?

Figure 3   Sample self-evaluation checklist for elementary school foreign language teacher. [Excerpted, with permission of the publisher, from G. C. Lipton (1988). Practical handbook to elementary foreign language programs. *Chicago: National Textbook Company.]*

information about the effectiveness of a unit or an entire course – information such as students' general impressions of the course or unit and its various components (content, organization, materials or equipment, and activities), and their satisfaction with their achievements in the language as a result of the course or unit. Teacher questionnaires and interviews can also provide valuable information for assessing the effectiveness of instruction. Figure 3 presents excerpts from a questionnaire for foreign language teachers working in elementary schools. Evaluative information collected at the end of a course can be used to revise instructional plans for subsequent groups of students; it cannot be used to modify instruction for current students. Using questionnaires to collect assessment information at the end of instruction can be particularly beneficial because they are efficient and provide permanent, systematic records of feedback from all students. Feedback from questionnaires has the added advantage that it can be easily quantified if structured, multiple-choice questions are used.

Questionnaires and interviews are much less useful for collecting information during instruction for day-to-day planning and assessment of instruction. If questionnaires or interviews are used during instruction, they are likely to be relatively simple and informal. During the course of instruction, conferences and dialogue journals can provide much the same kinds of information as questionnaires and interviews; at the same time, they have a number of other benefits and uses, discussed earlier, that questionnaires and interviews do not have.

One might assume that questionnaires and interviews could be used to collect samples of students' writing and speaking skills, respectively. However, with a few exceptions, the language skills called for in responding to interviews and questionnaires are not authentic and, therefore, not generalizable to most other domains in which the second language is likely to be used. The exceptions are questionnaires and interviews that simulate authentic language situations, such as job interviews or application forms. The use of interviews and questionnaires for such purposes is better viewed as a form of performance testing.

Organization of interviews and questionnaires

The organization of questions in interviews and questionnaires can be linear or nonlinear. In a linear arrangement, all students respond to all questions in the same sequence. In a nonlinear arrangement, some students may skip certain questions or may be asked to respond to additional questions depending upon their specific response pattern. For example, students who respond "No" to the question "Are you happy with your language course?" may be required to respond to additional questions concerning their reasons for being unhappy, whereas students who respond "Yes" to this question may skip these additional questions.

Responses to questions in interviews and questionnaires can take several forms. They can be open-ended, for example:

Why do you want to learn English as a second language?

_____

_____

_____

_____

Alternatively, they can require checking or endorsing one or several multiple-choice alternatives. In the two following examples, each response alternative is described in words, and students choose the one or ones that best correspond to their answer to the question. Note that the second question would definitely have to be written in the first language of the students.

Why do you want to learn English as a second language?

Check two of the following answers as the most important reasons:

_____ a. To be admitted to an English language university.
_____ b. To travel to English-speaking countries.
_____ c. To get a job in an English-speaking company.
_____ d. To make friends with English-speaking people.
_____ e. To read English language books and magazines.

Put a check mark next to the description that best corresponds to your level of proficiency.

_____ I read and understand English as well as a well-educated native.

_____ I understand nearly everything written in English in non-specialized fields. There may be words I do not understand in difficult texts.

_____ I understand simple written instructions; I can understand the essential points in simple text dealing with familiar topics.

_____ I can understand words and simple sentences written in English.

_____ I cannot read English at all.

In another type of multiple-choice format, students indicate their responses to questions or statements by choosing a point along a scale that best corresponds to their feelings or impressions. Only the extreme response alternatives are described; the intervening alternatives are represented simply by numbers. In this case, the response alternatives are like rating scales that form a continuum varying from a little to a lot. The exact descriptors used to anchor the end points depend on the wording of the question or statement. This type of format is usually used to elicit self-assessments about language skills or information about attitudes and feelings – in other words, about nonfactual information. Here are three examples:

- How well do you understand English that you hear on television?

I understand nothing.				I understand everything.
1	2	3	4	5

- It is important for me to learn English as a second language in order to receive my college diploma.

Disagree strongly				Agree strongly
1	2	3	4	5

- Imagine that you were asked to write a letter of application for a job. The employer wants you to describe your qualifications and experience. How well do you think you could do this?

I would not be able to write anything.				I would have no problem writing a detailed and correct letter.
1	2	3	4	5

Multiple-choice answer formats can be used only when most of the possible and important types of responses to a given question are known and when those responses can be grouped into nonoverlapping and meaningful categories. In contrast, open-ended response formats can be used when one does not know what the response possibilities are or when they cannot be presented in discrete categories. It is common for open-ended questionnaires and interviews to be used as a preliminary step in the development of a multiple-choice format in order to identify categories of responses that can be presented.

Multiple-choice questions are generally easier and faster to answer than open-ended questions because they indicate clearly the nature of the response called for, and students simply have to select their answers. This increases the chances that every student will respond to every question. Multiple-choice formats are also easier to analyze because they require little interpretation of the answers. Multiple-choice questionnaires and interviews are very helpful when there is a large number of respondents because responses can be tabulated easily: one simply has to count up the number of times each response choice is selected. In comparison, open-ended questions are more difficult and time consuming to answer because they require that students compose responses rather than simply selecting one. Moreover, respondents may have to think about the nature of the desired response because it may not be clear from the question what is expected.

Open-ended response formats are also more difficult to analyze because each respondent's wording will be different. As a result, the analysis of open-ended responses calls for a great deal of interpretation. Thus, use of this format is practical only if there is a limited number of respondents.

Questionnaires versus interviews

Questionnaires can be used only with respondents who are literate. Interviews do not require reading and writing skills and, therefore, can be used with a wide range of respondents. In some cases, a questionnaire may be administered orally to respondents who lack reading and writing skills. However, a questionnaire does not always lend itself well to an oral interview because the wording of its questions may be more formal and complex than the wording of interview questions.

An advantage of questionnaires over interviews is that they can be administered simultaneously to many respondents and require only one person for administration. In comparison, interviews require considerable personnel time because each respondent must be interviewed individually.

An additional advantage of questionnaires is that they provide permanent and exact records of respondents' answers. Permanent records of responses to interviews can be made by audiotaping them. Alternatively, each response can be recorded in writing by the teacher or interviewer after each question. This procedure can be difficult and time consuming. Detailed, verbatim recording of interviews is probably necessary if the information being solicited is factual and if it is to be used to make important screening or placement decisions. Interviews in class with individual students or groups of students (i.e., class discussions) about their learning experiences can be done impressionistically using narrative or anecdotal records. They can also be recorded using checklists or rating scales. (These methods of recording were described in some detail in Chapter 5.)

An advantage of interviews over questionnaires is that they permit the interviewer to probe the respondents for additional information in response to interesting or important answers that arise unexpectedly from the planned questions. Questionnaires, in contrast, do not allow for spontaneous probing because the questions are fixed.

Task 3

Discuss similarities and differences in the structure and use of interviews and conferences.

Guidelines for constructing questionnaires and interviews

Constructing questionnaires and interviews

The quality and usefulness of interviews and questionnaires depends on the amount of thought and time that is put into them: Useful questionnaires and interviews require considerable thought and time to construct. Those that are not well constructed can result in ambiguous and incomplete information of questionable usefulness. Even questions that seek to collect what appears to be simple, straightforward information require careful preparation. Take the following question about immigration, for example: "When did you arrive in the United States?" It is not clear from the wording of this question whether the answer calls for the date of the respondent's arrival or her age. Or the question: "What language(s) do you know?" Unless provisions are made for respondents to list each language they know, what skills they have in each language (e.g., speaking, listening, reading, and writing), and what level of skill they have in each, there is no single way in which answers to this question can be given. The investment in time and thought needed to develop clear, concise questions will pay off in comprehensive, relatively unambiguous, and useful information.

The amount of time devoted to the construction of questionnaires and interviews depends on the importance of the decisions or actions to be taken following analysis of responses to them. On the one hand, if decisions that affect many individuals or an entire course or program are to be made (e.g., whether to adopt a particular textbook for an entire school system) or if decisive action is to be taken about individual students (e.g., whether to accept a student or teacher into a program), then construction of the questionnaire or interview warrants as much attention as possible.

Planning questionnaires and interviews

In this section, we suggest a general procedure for the planning and construction of formal questionnaires and interviews. Such a thorough procedure is not necessary for devising questionnaires and interviews during a course to solicit student feedback about teaching and learning. The procedure suggested below can be streamlined to be more suitable for constructing questionnaires and interviews for use in such contexts.

1. Identify the decisions you want to make using the information that will be collected.
2. Identify the general and specific information that will help make these decisions. It is useful here to, first of all, identify general types of information that you would like and then specific information within general categories. It is also helpful to write down everything that comes to mind at first. You can always delete redundant or unimportant items during revision.
3. If possible, review other questionnaires or interviews that have been used to make the same kinds of decisions. They can provide guidance with respect to the types of information to collect, types of questions, wording of questions, response formats, the organization of questions, and instructions.
4. Draft questions pertaining to the information you are seeking. Again, it is advisable to be overinclusive at this point; redundant or useless questions can be deleted afterward. If you are using multiple-choice answer formats, draft versions of alternative answers.
5. Organize the questions according to some logical or otherwise meaningful order and then revise them accordingly. The arrangement of the items should make sense to respondents. Questionnaires and interviews that are organized in haphazard ways will confuse respondents.
6. Prepare a set of instructions. These should explain as thoroughly and honestly as possible the purposes of the questionnaire or interview (e.g., to make decisions about admission to a program) and how the

respondents' answers will be treated (e.g., confidentially and anonymously). The instructions should also indicate clearly how respondents should proceed in answering questions.

7. Ask colleagues who are familiar with the purpose of the interview or questionnaire to review it.
8. Make revisions based on your colleagues' comments.
9. Try the questionnaire or interview out with respondents who are similar to those you will ultimately use it with. Seek both written and oral feedback from these respondents; ask them to make comments while they are responding as well as after they have completed the activity.
10. Make final revisions.

Devising questionnaire and interview items

In this section, we suggest guidelines for devising interview and questionnaire items.

GENERAL

1. Avoid items that may be interpreted in more than one way.
2. Avoid items that are irrelevant to your interests.
3. Keep the language of the items simple, clear, and direct. Avoid the use of negative and double-negative wording; most people, especially second language learners, have difficulty interpreting such questions. For example, avoid this kind of question: "When do you not like to speak your second language?"
4. Whenever possible, items should be worded as simple sentences rather than as compound or complex sentences.
5. Each item should usually include only one question or idea. This is especially important if the response options are "true" and "false" or another single response format. For example, avoid this kind of item: "I speak and read English fluently."
6. Whenever possible, provide multiple-choice response alternatives rather than open-ended responses.
7. Make sure that multiple-choice response alternatives are logically related to the question or statement.
8. When using a multiple-choice response format, make sure that all important response possibilities are provided for.
9. Wherever possible, include the response category "other" or "do not know" so that respondents can provide unexpected responses or indicate that they do not possess the knowledge needed to answer an item. Respondents can be frustrated if they feel they are forced to make choices they do not like.

The following suggestions are specific to oral (i.e., interview) and written (i.e., questionnaire) items.

QUESTIONNAIRE ITEMS

10. Use numbers to identify questions and letters to identify response alternatives.
11. Leave ample blank space so that questions are distinguishable from one another and from their corresponding response alternatives.
12. Make sure that it is clear where and how respondents should report their answers.

INTERVIEW ITEMS

13. Start off the interview with a few simple items that call for factual, impersonal information that is not threatening to respondents. Items of a more difficult or personal nature should follow later.
14. Similarly, end the interview with items that are easy to answer and likely to leave respondents with positive feelings about themselves.
15. Keep interview questions simple at all times. It is more difficult to process information presented orally than in writing.
16. Be prepared to withdraw a question or discontinue the interview if the respondent is threatened by or uncomfortable with an item or the interview in general.

Summary

Journals, interviews, and questionnaires can all be thought of as conversations between students (or parents, if they are asked to fill out a questionnaire or do an interview) and teachers. These methods are useful primarily for collecting information about students' linguistic, cultural, and educational backgrounds and experiences; their attitudes, goals, likes and dislikes; and other qualitative information. They provide secondary information about writing and speaking skills, although, as pointed out earlier, the language skills needed to respond to interviews and questionnaires are not highly generalizable to many authentic language situations. In contrast to interviews and questionnaires, journals are informal, individualized, student driven, student centered, and open ended. In addition, whereas interviews and questionnaires are generally useful before and after instruction, journals are clearly useful during instruction. Journals can be used with learners of any age and proficiency level, whereas interviews and questionnaires are of most value with older and more proficient learners. Journals along with conferences are particularly valuable as part of a comprehensive evaluation plan because they are interactive; they can give learners a sense of control and responsibility over learning; they also provide opportunities for students to be partners in assessment. Questionnaires and interviews are most useful when uniform feedback or information from many individuals is desired for planning and assessing instruction.

Discussion questions

1. If you are reading this book as part of a formal course on evaluation, keep a journal of your experiences in this course. As well as making notes in the journal about the course, make notes about keeping a journal. Share your journal with other students in the course, and make a list of suggestions for using journals.
2. If you are currently using journals in your class, are there ways you would modify them, based on what you have read in this chapter? Are there suggestions you have for using student journals in addition to those suggested in this chapter?
3. If you are reading this book as part of a course, work with other students in the course to construct a questionnaire to collect information about the students that is pertinent to this course. Include questions about students' prior education, training in testing and evaluation, and any other information that might be pertinent for determining the match between this course and the students in it.
4. Try using the questionnaire in item 3 in an interview format. Devise a system for recording students' responses if the questionnaire answer format is inadequate. What are the problems, if any, you encounter when using the questionnaire as an interview?
5. Suggest ways of extending the use of journals for assessment and instructional purposes in addition to those suggested in this chapter. How could you use journals with beginning second language learners in view of their limited writing skills?
6. How and for what purpose could you use interviews?
7. Select a questionnaire that you have been asked to fill out and critically examine it from the point of view of the guidelines suggested in this chapter.
8. If you are reading this book as part of a course, imagine that all the students in the course are about to enter a second language course in Italian. Devise an interview to collect information that would be pertinent for planning a course (or courses) appropriate for all students. Before constructing and doing the interview, as a group decide what kinds of information are needed, and then individually construct questions to solicit the relevant information. Then compare the questions you

have prepared. How do they differ? What are the strengths and weaknesses of the questions that have been prepared? Make a list of guidelines for preparing interview questions.

Readings

Atwell, N. (1987). *In the middle: Writing, reading, and learning with adolescents.* Portsmouth, N.H.: Heinemann.

Davis, F. (1983). Why you call me emigrant?: Dialogue journal writing with migrant youth. *Childhood Education,* November/December.

Larson V. L., and N. L. McKinley. (1987). *Communicative assessment and intervention strategies for adolescents.* Eau Claire, Wis.: Thinking Publications.

LeBlanc, R., and G. Painchaud. (1985). Self-assessment as a second language placement instrument. *TESOL Quarterly, 19,* 673–687.

Matsumoto, K. (1987). Diary studies of second language acquisition: A critical review. *JALT Journal, 9,* 17–34.

Murphy-O'Dwyer, L. (1985). Diary studies as a method for evaluating teacher training. In C. J. Alderson (Ed.), *Evaluation* (pp. 97–128). Oxford: Pergamon Press.

Peyton, J. K. (1987). *Dialogue journal writing with limited-English proficient students.* Washington, D.C.: ERIC.

Peyton, J. K. (1990). Beginning at the beginning: First grade ESL students learn to write. In A. M. Padilla, H. H. Fairchild, and C. M. Valdez (Eds.), *Bilingual education: Issues and strategies* (pp. 195–218). Newbury Park, Calif.: Sage.

Peyton, J. K., and L. Reed. (1990). *Dialogue journal writing with non-native English speakers: A handbook for teachers.* Alexandria, Va.: TESOL.

Staton, J., R. W. Shuy, J. K. Peyton, and L. Reed. (1987). *Dialogue journal communication: Classroom, linguistic, social and cognitive views.* Norwood, N.J.: Ablex.

PART III:
EVALUATING WITH TESTS

8 Testing

- Introduction
- What is a test?
- Types of measurement
- Classification of second language tests
- Summary

Preview questions

1. What kinds of decisions do you make based on the results of students' test performance?
2. Do you tell students, before they take a test, how you will judge their test performance? If not, why not? How do you report students' test results, and how do you use those results?
3. How do you decide when and how often to test?
4. Many people believe that tests undermine the value of education. Do you share this view? Explain your thinking. If you disagree with this view, explain what value you see in testing.
5. What are some of the advantages of tests? What are some of their shortcomings? Are there ways of overcoming the shortcomings?
6. Are standardized tests superior to teacher-made ones? Explain.
7. Have you ever had a student or a group of students who just couldn't do well on tests? What is your explanation of their difficulty? What did you or could you do about it?
8. Do you personally like taking tests? Explain.

Introduction

We have already defined evaluation as an activity of gathering information to be used in making educational decisions. Sometimes these decisions are about students, but more often they are about instruction. There are many methods for collecting information for evaluation purposes. Testing – along with questionnaires, interviews, observation, examination of documents, and portfolios – is just one of those methods. In Chapters 8 to 13, we review testing methods, both classroom based and standardized. In this chapter, we present a general overview of testing and important aspects to consider when making and using tests. We also describe a variety of second language tests that have been discussed by others.

We consider as tests what some teachers variously refer to as exams, tests, and quizzes. In doing so, we do not suggest that exams and quizzes are identical. They often differ with respect to their scope, importance, function, and the care with which they have been prepared. Nonetheless, they are alike in so many other respects that it is useful to consider them all as tests. Typically, they all consist of a set of standard tasks that are attempted by a group of students (not necessarily all at the same time, however) in order to demonstrate their knowledge or ability.

In this introductory chapter on testing, we consider three general topics: (1) What is a test? (2) What do test scores refer to? and (3) What are the different kinds of second language tests?

What is a test?

We have already characterized a test as one method for collecting information. Ideally, it would also be possible to identify what makes a test uniquely different from other methods of collecting information. However, it turns out that this is very difficult to do. The other methods of information collection that we discuss in this book have something in common with tests. In fact, most alternative methods of collecting information that we have talked about could, under certain circumstances, serve as tests. For example, an individual reading conference with a student could be structured like a reading test. Because it is so difficult to distinguish tests from other methods of information collection, we describe certain important aspects to consider when devising and using them.

A test is, first of all, about something. That is, it is about intelligence, or European history, or second language proficiency. In educational terms, tests have subject matter or *content*. Second, a test is a task or set of tasks that elicits observable behavior from the test taker. The test may consist of only one task, such as writing a composition, or a set of tasks, such as in a lengthy multiple-choice examination in which each question can be thought of as a separate task. Different test tasks represent different *methods* of eliciting performance so that, taken together, tests are not a single method of collecting information. Third, tests yield scores that represent attributes or characteristics of individuals. In order to be meaningful, test scores must have a frame of reference. Test scores along with the frame of reference used to interpret them is referred to as measurement. Thus, tests are a form of *measurement*.

We discuss each of these aspects of tests now: content, method, and measurement.

Test content

The content of a test is what the test is about – to use our earlier examples, it can be about intelligence, European history, or second language proficiency. Generally speaking, the content of educational tests is about academic subjects, knowledge, and skills. The content of second or foreign languages tests is about second or foreign language skills and usage. It is important to understand that the actual content of a test is generally narrower than the subject matter, skills, or knowledge it seeks to assess. An intelligence test, for example, does not require test takers to answer all questions and solve all problems that pertain to intelligence. Nor does a high school test of European history pose all possible questions about European history as presented in the students' textbook. And a second language test does not examine every aspect of second language proficiency. The content of tests is virtually always only a sample of the subject matter, skills, or knowledge being assessed.

The quality of classroom tests, like all tests, therefore, depends on whether the content of the test is a good sample of the relevant subject matter. If the content of a test is a poor reflection of what has been taught or what is supposed to be learned, then performance on the test will not provide a good indication of achievement in that subject area. Moreover, if the content of a test reflects more than one subject matter, set of skills, or knowledge, then test performance will reflect achievement in more than one area. For example, a mathematics test that includes computational problems and word problems assesses both types of skills. Performance on the test cannot be interpreted in a simple way to reflect achievement in only one of these areas of mathematics. A listening comprehension test with written multiple-choice answers calls for both listening and reading comprehension skills. The significance of test content is this: An individual's performance on a test is a reflection of subject matter, knowledge, and skills because the content of the test is a sample of subject matter. Moreover, because the content of tests is a sample of a larger set of abilities or skills, interpreting test scores in terms of those abilities is a matter of inference – that is, we infer test takers' levels of general reading proficiency, for example, on the basis of a sample of their performance on a reading test. This point is illustrated schematically in Figure 1.

Test methods

Content by itself is an abstraction. It needs to be operationalized, instantiated, or expressed in some way. Test methods give form to test content. Test methods are the kinds of tasks that test takers are asked to perform. We are

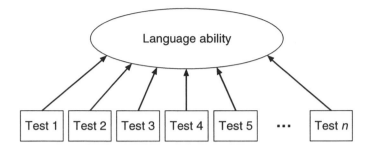

Figure 1   Making inferences about language from tests.

all familiar with such methods as reading texts accompanied by questions that require written or multiple-choice answers among which test takers must choose. We also know about performance test methods. For example, typing speed is often measured by having the test taker actually type a standard passage as fast and carefully as possible. The same testing method can be applied to different kinds of content. Multiple-choice methods can be used to test such diverse attributes as the ability to repair watches, knowledge of traffic safety regulations, and the acquisition of certain grammatical rules in a second language. Likewise, performance tests can be used to assess the physical fitness of military personnel or the ability to respond appropriately and correctly in a simulated job interview conducted in a second language.

Testing methods can have an effect on test takers' scores because they call for certain kinds of skill or knowledge that is independent of the content itself. Responding successfully to multiple-choice tests, for example, draws on test-taking skills that are different from those required for responses to other kinds of test tasks. Test takers who are experienced with or skilled at certain kinds of testing methods tend to do better on those kinds of tests than do test takers who lack such experience, all other factors remaining constant. It follows that two tests that employ the same method are, to a degree, measuring the same thing because the task demands are the same — no matter how different their content may otherwise be. Conversely, tests that employ different methods are measuring somewhat different skills, no matter how similar their content. The significance of test methods is this: What a test is measuring is a reflection of not only its content but also the method it employs. It is important in classroom-based testing to choose test tasks (or methods) that call for the kinds of skills that are compatible with instructional objectives and practices in the classroom. In addition, where possible, use tasks that minimize and balance out the effects of abilities or task demands that are extraneous to the skills you are interested in assessing.

Task 1

Imagine a test of listening comprehension in which
students must listen to a tape-recorded conversation
between two people and then either (a) respond to
multiple-choice questions about the conversation or
(b) write short answers to open-ended questions
about the conversation. Compare the task demands
of each test method, and consider when each would
be appropriate.

Another important point about testing methods is that there is no universal agreement about how to assess language proficiency or a specific aspect of language proficiency. Take vocabulary as an example: vocabulary knowledge could be measured by asking learners to provide equivalents of target language words in their first language, or by asking for definitions or synonyms in the target language, or by asking students to supply appropriate words to complete sentences in which certain words have been deleted. No single test method or combination of methods can be claimed to be a direct measure of word knowledge. Ideally, one would use multiple methods that together would provide an optimal estimate of vocabulary skills. However, this is impractical. One is usually limited to using one method of assessment. Thus, we must infer word knowledge from whatever testing method we use. The same is true of all aspects of language. We suggest how to choose appropriate test tasks (or methods) for classroom testing later in this chapter and in the next chapter.

Task 2

Select a language skill, such as note taking, and then
(a) identify as many ways as you can to test it and
(b) discuss how these different methods influence
your inferences about this language skill.

Tests as measurement

Tests are like other measurement devices that you are familiar with in your day-to-day lives – they describe attributes or qualities of things and individuals by assigning numbers (or scores) to them. Thermometers measure temperature; rulers measure distance; and scales measure weight. Measurement includes the assignment of numbers to qualities or characteristics according to some standard and rational method and the interpretation of those scores with respect to some frame of reference; we discuss frames of reference in the next section. Generally speaking, there are two kinds of measuring devices, those that measure differences in kind and those that measure differences in degree. Testing serum for blood type and testing chromosomes for gender are examples of measuring differences in kind because they result in categorical descriptions of the quality in question: blood type A or female, for example. When measuring differences in kind, there are no variations in degree within a category. Tests for differences in kind are common in the physical sciences. In education and, therefore, in this book, we are usually interested in tests that measure differences in degree – tests that describe how proficiently students can read a second language or how appropriately they speak in particular social situations, for example.

Measuring educational achievement is difficult because it calls for tests that are sensitive to differences in degree within the same kinds. This requires that test items measure how much of a particular ability or attribute the test taker has and not simply whether the test taker has it. Moreover, it requires that all of the items that make up a test measure only one attribute or quality; otherwise, the test is measuring different qualities, and the score or measurement is not pure. To illustrate this point, imagine that the following three items were part of the same test:

1. Change the spark plug in a gasoline-powered lawnmower.
2. Piece a diamond-in-the-square patterned quilt.
3. Play the piano part of the Concerto for Piano and Orchestra no. 21 in C major by Mozart.

Imagine further that test taker A achieves a score of 2 by getting items 1 and 2 "correct," and test taker B gets a score of 1 by getting item 3 "correct." In what sense can we say that the two test takers are different in degree but not in kind? What is the skill or ability that test taker A has more of? Similarly, if two test takers achieve the same score on this test but have different items correct, in what sense can we say that they differ neither in degree nor in kind?

We have chosen an unlikely combination of divergent items to include in our example test. Consider these three language-related items:

1. A sentence completion task in which one word has been deleted from each sentence, and the test taker must supply the missing words.

2. A five-part multiple-choice set of questions on a short newspaper article about a recent political event.
3. A paraphrase task in which the test taker must write a one-sentence summary of a brief radio broadcast.

Once again, imagine that test taker A achieves a score of 2 by getting items 1 and 2 "correct," and test taker B gets a score of 1 by getting item 3 "correct." In what sense can we say that the two test takers are different in degree but not in kind? What is the skill or ability that test taker A has more of? Similarly, if two test takers achieve the same score on this test but have different items correct, in what sense can we say that they differ neither in degree nor in kind? Our earlier point remains – not all tests allow for measurement of degree or kind, just by adding up the number of correct items.

Task 3

Imagine that you are asked to assess a book review written by ESL students. Identify as many aspects of these reviews as you can that could be scored for differences in level (degree) of writing skill. Can you identify any ways of scoring these reviews that would measure differences in kind?

Types of measurement

We are all familiar with reference in measurement because it is part of our everyday life. Temperature is measured with reference to the freezing and boiling of water. The temperature at which water freezes is taken as 0° C; boiling temperature is assigned a temperature of 100° C. Time (or duration) is measured with reference to the movements of celestial bodies in our solar system: one day is a rotation of the earth, and a year is one revolution of the earth around the sun. Old measures of length were referenced to parts of the human body, for example, the foot and the hand.

In the measurement of educational qualities and abilities, the frame of reference generally used is the knowledge and ability of known groups of people or explicit definitions of the knowledge or ability being measured. Reference to a known group is called *norm referencing*. Reference to defined knowledge or ability is known under various names: domain referencing, criterion referencing, and objectives referencing. Because the term *criterion reference* has been used with very different meanings by different writers, we will use *domain reference* and *objectives reference.*

Norm reference

The logic of norm reference is quite simple. Imagine that you are told someone's score on a reading test is 43 items correct. By itself this score is uninterpretable. If, however, you know that the same test was taken by a thousand first-grade students, a thousand second-grade students, and the same number of third- and fourth-grade students, and if you also know how each of those groups did on the test, then you would have a basis for interpreting the score of 43. Let us say that the average scores for the first-through fourth-graders were 28, 36, 44, and 51, respectively. You can now interpret the 43 as "just barely below the score achieved by the average third grader." Figure 2 presents examples of two norm conversion tables. In the top table, scaled scores for vocabulary (VOCAB) and reading comprehension (COMPRE) subtests of a hypothetical foreign language achievement test can be converted to percentiles (%ile RANK), standard scores, or stanines (STA); in the bottom table, raw scores on a test of listening comprehension in French as a second language can be converted to percentile form.

Stanines (*standard nine*) range in value from a low of 1 to a high of 9. A stanine is not a single score, but rather includes a band of scores; for example, a stanine of 1 includes the lowest 4.01 percent of raw scores; whereas a stanine of 9 includes the top 4.01 percent of the raw scores. The percentage of raw scores that are included in each stanine is summarized in Figure 3. These percentages are related to the standard deviation of the raw scores obtained by the test takers who made up the norming group. Thus, any student who gets a stanine of 9 on a standardized test can be said to have scored as well as the top 4 percent of the norming group; this is equivalent to a percentile score of 96 percent.

In order for norm referencing to work, tests must be constructed in certain ways. To continue with our reading test example, suppose that you make up a number of test items that you believe test reading ability in primary school children. Then you try out these items with groups of students who differ from each other in their reading ability. If the students at all levels of ability perform approximately the same on one of your items, you would probably conclude that it is not a very good item for measuring the differences that you know exist among the groups. In contrast, if students in successive grades do progressively better on an item, you conclude that the item is a good one for measuring these differences, and you would probably include it in your test.

Hypothetical foreign language achievement test				
Reading comprehension	Vocabulary	Percentile	Standard score	Stanine
75–80	80	99	73	
—	79	99	72	
74	78	98	71	9
73	—	98	70	
—	77	97	69	
72	—	96	68	
71	76	96	67	
70	75	95	66	
—	—	93	65	8
69	74	92	64	
68	73	90	63	
67	—	88	62	
66	72	86	61	
65	71	84	60	7
64	—	82	59	
—	70	79	58	
63	69	76	57	
62	68	73	56	
61	—	69	55	6
59–60	67	66	54	
58	66	62	53	
57	65	58	52	
56	64	54	51	
55	63	50	50	5
53–54	62	46	49	
52	61	42	48	
51	60	38	47	
50	59	34	46	
49	58	31	45	4
48	57	27	44	
47	56	24	43	
46	55	21	42	
45	54	18	41	
44	53	16	40	3
—	52	14	39	
43	51	12	38	
42	50	10	37	
41	49	8	36	
40	48	7	35	2
39	47	5	34	
38	46	4	33	
—	44–45	4	32	
37	43	3	31	
36	42	2	30	1
35	41	2	29	
34	40	1	28	
0–33	0–39	1	27	

Figure 2 continues on next page

| French comprehension test (level 1) | | | | | |
Raw score	Percentile	Raw score	Percentile	Raw score	Percentile
41+	99	31	62	21	13
40	98	30	56	20	11
38	97	29	50	19	8
37	95	28	44	18	7
36	92	27	38	17	5
35	88	26	33	16	4
34	84	25	29	15	3
33	79	24	24	14	3
32	73	23	19	13	2
	67	22	16		1

Figure 2   Sample norm conversion tables. [The French comprehension test is reprinted, by permission of the publisher, from H. Barik, The French Comprehension Test, Level 1 *(1976). Toronto: OISE.]*

Stanine	1	2	3	4	5	6	7	8	9
	4.01%	6.55%	12.10%	17.47%	19.74%	17.47%	12.10%	6.55%	4.01%

Figure 3   Stanine scale.

It follows from this method of test construction that items that assess skills that all students have or have not mastered will not be included because they do not differentiate among students with different levels of ability. You can include only items that differentiate among groups or individuals. But this can be a problem in classroom settings if you want to identify those skills that all students have mastered (or have not).

You may have noted another problem in a norm-referenced approach to test construction. In our reading test example, we include items that show differences among students at different grade levels because we suppose that students in successively higher grades will read better; this is the logic of norm referencing. However, we know that many developmental changes take place in children during their primary school years. Items that we select on the basis of norm-referencing procedures may be sensitive to any of these developmental changes; they may not be indicative of changes in reading ability only (or at all). Norm-referenced testing can be advantageous in some cases and under certain circumstances, but it should not be used to the exclusion of the other considerations about test content and method that we discussed earlier. We describe norm-referenced standardized tests and their application in greater detail in Chapter 12.

Some people believe that norm referencing is the same thing as "grading on the curve," a practice in which a predetermined number of students in a group will be given As, Bs, and so on. As you can see from the preceding discussion, this practice has nothing to do with norm referencing.

Domain reference

Test scores can also be interpreted with reference to domains of skill or knowledge. In education, a domain is like an area of study – in other words, like an academic discipline such as mathematics or science. Use of domains for test construction purposes requires consensus on what knowledge or skills comprise the discipline or domain of interest. If the domain can be described comprehensively and precisely, then test tasks that provide an accurate reflection of the domain can be devised. If this is done, it then also becomes possible, in principle, to interpret performance on the test with reference to how much of the domain in question has been mastered by individual learners. Thus, whereas norm-referenced tests provide interpretations of test scores relative to other learners, domain-referenced tests provide interpretations of test scores relative to an identified domain of knowledge or skill.

The important point here is that in order to be a frame of reference for test construction and interpretation, a domain must be finite and known. A well-described, finite domain is approximately equivalent to a large set of tasks. If one knows that the items that make up a test constitute an unbiased sample of tasks from the entire domain, then an interpretation with reference to the domain is possible. In order for a test to be amenable to domain-referenced interpretation, certain test development procedures must be followed – the most important one is the selection of an unbiased sample of tasks from the domain.

In contrast, without a well-defined domain, it is very difficult, if not impossible, to devise a test that lends itself to domain-referenced interpretation. Imagine being told to devise a test that would measure the ability to read all topics, in all possible academic disciplines, in all styles of written language, at any level of linguistic complexity, from any historical period, addressed to any group of readers, and presented in any manner. This example is certainly exaggerated, but it illustrates a major difficulty in satisfying the conditions for acceptable domain referencing. When a domain is broad and complex, like language, it is very difficult to attain consensus on what skills and, therefore, what tasks constitute the domain. This makes it difficult to select test items that reflect the domain adequately.

This is certainly an issue in language testing because of the open-ended nature of language proficiency. There has been much advocacy of domain-referenced testing in language education, but relatively little has been possible because of the lack of agreement on domain descriptions.

Objectives reference

Objectives referencing is similar to domain referencing in that it provides for the interpretation of test scores with respect to a defined area of knowledge or skills. The main difference is that it does not require consensus on the description of an *entire* domain, discipline, or field of study. Instead, it depends upon the description of the knowledge or skills that make up a particular lesson, unit, or course of instruction. In this form of testing, instructional objectives play an important role in defining the language domain of interest; for this reason, this kind of test is referred to as objectives referenced. Thus, what is important about objectives referencing is that the domain is conceptualized in local instructional terms. This means that the content of the test is derived from an understanding of the instructional objectives for a particular course, unit, or lesson. Instruction also figures in this method of testing insofar as instructional objectives and activities define how to instantiate the skills in test form. This means that, generally speaking, students should be tested in ways that resemble how they were taught. Of course, this makes sense only if the instructional methods are an appropriate reflection of the instructional objectives.

Interpretations of objectives-referenced test scores are made with reference to how many of or how well the instructional objectives have been attained. Interpretations of objectives-referenced test scores can be made only by people who are familiar with instruction. We discuss interpretation of objectives-referenced tests in more detail in Chapter 12. In addition, the people who can best develop objectives-referenced tests are those who are familiar with instruction – teachers. For these reasons, objectives-referenced testing is especially well suited for classroom-based evaluation.

Classification of second language tests

Second language tests have been classified in many ways. In this section, we review some of the classifications that have been used in scholarly and professional publications on educational and language testing. Alternative ways of classifying tests can be useful up to a point. Unfortunately, however, there has been a proliferation of classification types. All too often, this has tended to obscure rather than clarify second language testing. Part of the problem is that many of the terms that refer to different kinds of tests are not mutually exclusive; for example, the same test (e.g., an essay test) can be regarded as a proficiency test, a grammar test, an achievement test, a placement test, a diagnostic test, an integrative test, or a test of linguistic competence. Our purpose in reviewing these classifications is simply to alert you to these alternative terms for talking about tests so that you will recognize them in your independent reading. We do not promote or even refer to these classifications in the rest of the book because we do not find them to be particularly useful.

Second language tests have been classified according to whether they focus on:

1. Underlying linguistic competence
2. Specific aspects or subskills of language
3. A specific testing method
4. A particular kind of information, or
5. Certain kinds of decisions

Linguistic competence refers to the underlying linguistic abilities or knowledge of language that language learners have acquired. It is an abstraction that cannot be observed directly; we can observe only linguistic performance directly. Linguistic competence is inferred on the basis of linguistic performance, which is an individual's ability to use language appropriately or correctly in a variety of situations. Grammatical competence, pragmatic competence, sociolinguistic competence, strategic competence, and communicative competence are all examples of linguistic competence that second language theoreticians and testers have been interested in.

Some language tests refer to specific *linguistic subskills* that learners have acquired. These are often described in terms of the structural or grammatical features of language – spelling, vocabulary, grammar (or syntax), pronunciation, etc. These categories have been used traditionally to organize language instruction. These kinds of tests refer to the test content. There are as many descriptors for test content as there are ways of describing the content of language. Some such tests – called *discrete-point tests* – claim to focus on one specific aspect of language. Tests that call on a number of subskills operating in concert are sometimes referred to as *integrative tests.* In fact, tests are seldom truly discrete points in nature because no test or test item depends solely on one subskill to the exclusion of all others. Performance on a grammar test, for example, can also reflect the test taker's spelling, vocabulary, or even organizational skills with language. It follows, therefore, that the test could also be scored for either grammar, spelling, vocabulary, or discourse structure. Thus, it is important to recognize that tests that purport to assess a single language skill often also call on other skills at the same time. What a test is actually called depends on what the tester chooses to focus on, that is, what he chooses to score.

Other types of tests refer to a method of testing. A cloze test, for example, is a testing method in which words of a written text have been deleted and replaced by blanks. The test taker's task is to fill in the blanks with appropriate words. Other specialized methods of testing are dictation, interview, information gap, multiple choice, and essay. The number of different methods is unlimited if one takes cognizance of minor differences. When we discuss test tasks in Chapter 11, we subsume most of these diverse methods under three general types: open-ended, closed-ended, and limited-response formats. Test types that refer to testing methods tell you nothing about the general linguistic competence or specific skills that are being tested. For example, essays can be scored for spelling, grammar, organization, or some other feature, and so can other methods.

Achievement, proficiency, and performance tests refer to the types of information provided by the tests. Achievement tests provide information about student attainment in relation to instructional objectives or a defined domain of language. Proficiency tests yield information about student ability to use language in certain ways, for example, a store clerk's ability to use language to serve customers. Performance tests elicit information about students' ability to use the language to perform authentic tasks, for example, work as a telephone operator or in a bank. Diagnostic is a term used to describe tests that provide information about students' relative strengths and weaknesses.

Another category of test types describes the kinds of decisions that can be made using test results. Placement tests, for example, identify appropriate levels or types of instruction for individual students. Screening tests are used to admit or reject students for participation in particular courses or programs of instruction. Final examinations are used to promote students to the next level of instruction or to award a certificate of success or completion. A distinction is often made between summative and formative testing (this distinction is not specific to language tests but applies to any kind of testing). Summative testing comes at the end of a course or program of instruction and helps teachers make decisions about passing, failing, or promotion or about the overall effectiveness of the program or course. Formative testing is ongoing and takes place throughout a course or program of instruction. The results of formative testing can be used to modify instruction while the course is in progress. Once again, these test types do not specify the language competence or skills being assessed, nor do they identify the method of testing or the type of information revealed by test performance.

Task 4

Discuss how a test in which students were asked to
write a two-page essay on a topic of their choice
could be treated as an achievement test, a diagnostic
test, a placement test, or a grammar test.

Our primary focus in this book is on achievement testing because we are
concerned with classroom-based evaluation and, in particular, with the
importance of testing student attainment of instructional objectives in order
to determine the effectiveness of instruction. We do not promote or refer to
these other types of tests because we do not find them to be generally
useful. Classrooms differ in many ways. Each is unique. The particular
needs for test information in each classroom are also unique. Thus, it is
impossible to make generalizations about the use of the kinds of tests we
have reviewed here. Instead, we consider how the characteristics of classroom instruction define the characteristics of useful tests in those
classrooms.

Summary

In this chapter, we defined a language test as a set of tasks requiring
observable responses to language or in language that can be scored and
interpreted with reference to norms, domains, or instructional objectives.
We pointed out that language tests cannot be distinguished in any simple
and unique way from other methods of collecting assessment information.
In lieu of discussing the unique features of tests, we talked about tests from
the points of view of content, method, and measurement. We pointed out
that the construction of language tests requires knowledge about language
and an understanding of testing methods. Testing methods call on skills or
knowledge that can be independent of language itself but influence test
performance nevertheless. Therefore, it is important to select testing
methods (tasks) that, on the one hand, accurately reflect the kinds of language skills you want to test and, on the other hand, do not contaminate test
performance by calling on skills or knowledge that are irrelevant to your
interests.

In addition, the use of tests requires an understanding of some general
notions of measurement and, in particular, the notion of reference. Test
scores can derive meaning by reference to the performance of others (norm
referencing) or to a defined domain of skill or knowledge (domain and

objectives referencing). For classroom evaluation purposes, objectives-referenced testing is quite useful because the content and methods they employ are based on the instructional objectives and practices of specific classrooms.

Interpreting test performance calls for inferencing. There are two reasons for this: First, the content of language tests is only an indicator or sample of the language skills we want to know about. Thus, based on the learners' test performance, we infer their overall proficiency, competence, or ability with respect to the skill being examined. Second, there is no definitive method for testing language skills; hence, one must again infer language proficiency based on students' performance on one test task. In order to make sound educational decisions about students' language proficiency, the language skills included in your tests must be a representative sample of those skills described in your instructional objectives and plans, and you must base your judgment of students' abilities on multiple test tasks.

Finally, language tests have been discussed by others in terms of underlying linguistic competence, specific linguistic subskills, testing methods, the kinds of information emanating from tests, or the kinds of decisions that can be made. We do not promote any particular types of tests. Instead, we believe that tests need to be devised that permit individual teachers to collect the kinds of information they need for important decision making.

Discussion questions

1. What are some common criticisms of tests? Based on the material in this chapter, suggest ways to modify tests or how they are used to respond to these criticisms.
2. How are conferences different from and similar to tests?
3. List as many test methods or tasks that you can think of in three minutes. Examine each carefully from the point of view of (a) language performance demands and (b) extraneous task demands.
4. What are some skills, outside the language domain, that lend themselves to domain-referenced testing? Be sure to keep in mind the description of domain-referencing given in this chapter. Why is domain-referenced testing problematic for language assessment?
5. Select a norm-referenced (standardized) test that appears to be relevant to the kinds of students you work with. Carefully examine the test's technical manual for information describing the norming group. Then compare the norming/reference group for this test with the kinds of students you work with. Do you think this test is relevant for testing your students? If not, why not?

6. Are there any kinds of language skills you can think of that lend themselves to measurement of kind?
7. Devise a short answer test of the material contained in this chapter (one-hour duration); include a scoring scheme for the test. Compare your test and scoring scheme with those of other students in the class, if you are reading this book as part of a course. Critique one another's tests.
8. Use the conversion tables in Figure 2 to answer the following questions:
   a. Yuriko got a score of 63 on the comprehension subtest on page 148 and a score of 58 on the vocabulary subtest. What was her percentile ranking in each, and what does this tell us about her performance relative to each subtest and to other students?
   b. Juan got a raw score of 28 on the French comprehension test on page 149. How well did he do in comparison with the norming group?
   c. Which score on the hypothetical vocabulary test on page 148 is better: a stanine of 5 or a percentile of 62?
   d. What does a percentile score of 50 tell you about a test taker's level of performance on a test?

Readings

Bachman, L. F. (1990). *Fundamental considerations in language testing.* Oxford: Oxford University Press.
Barik, H. (1976). *French Comprehension Test,* Level 1. Toronto: OISE Press.
Carroll, B. J. (1980). *Testing communicative performance.* Oxford: Pergamon.
Cohen, A. (1980). *Testing language ability in the classroom.* Rowley, Mass.: Newbury House.
Finocchiaro, M., and S. Sako. (1983). *Foreign language testing: A practical approach.* New York: Regents.
Hambleton, R. K., and H. Swaminathan. (1978). Criterion-referenced testing and measurement: A review of technical issues and development. *Review of Educational Research, 48,* 1–47.
Harris, D. P. (1969). *Testing English as a second language.* New York: McGraw-Hill.
Henning, G. (1987). *A guide to language testing.* Cambridge, Mass.: Newbury House.
Hughes, A. (1989). *Testing for language teachers.* New York: Cambridge University Press.
Madsen, H. S. (1983). *Techniques in testing.* New York: Oxford University Press.
Rhea-Dickens, P., and K. Germaine. (1992). *Evaluation.* Oxford: Oxford University Press.
Stansfield, C. W. (Ed.). (1986). *Technology and language testing.* Washington, D.C.: TESOL.

Valette, R. M. (1977). *Modern language testing.* New York: Harcourt Brace Jovanovich.

Wesche, M. (1981). Communicative testing in a second language. *Canadian Modern Language Review, 37,* 551–571.

Weir, C. (1993). *Understanding and developing language tests.* New York: Prentice-Hall.

9 *Objectives-referenced testing*

- Introduction
- Describing instructional objectives
- Selecting objectives to test
- Test tasks
- Choosing test task types
- Summary

Preview questions

1. Have you ever taken a class test and were unhappy with it? What were you unhappy about, and how could this problem be solved? If you are teaching or have taught, what do your students complain about when you give them tests? Evaluate the validity of their criticisms and suggest solutions to the problems.
2. How do you currently decide what the content of a final examination or test will be? How do you ensure that it is an adequate sample of what you have taught?
3. What kinds of formats do you use in your tests (short answer, open-ended, multiple-choice, etc.)? Why do you use these?
4. In your opinion, what are the advantages and disadvantages of using multiple-choice tests?
5. Do you think objectives are an important part of teaching? Explain. What is your understanding of an objective?
6. Do you use objectives to plan instruction? Where do they come from? How do you use them when you devise tests? If you do not use objectives, how do you know what to teach?
7. If you use objectives, do you discuss them with your students? If so, why? If not, why not?

Introduction

In the preceding chapter, we pointed out that tests can be classified according to their *reference,* that is, according to something external that serves to give test scores meaning. A person's test score can have meaning in reference to the performance of other people who have taken the same test. We call tests that gain their meaning in this way *norm referenced.* In other

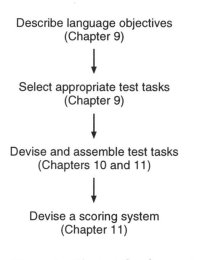

Describe language objectives
(Chapter 9)

Select appropriate test tasks
(Chapter 9)

Devise and assemble test tasks
(Chapters 10 and 11)

Devise a scoring system
(Chapter 11)

Figure 1   The test development process.

cases, a score on a test can have meaning in reference to a well-defined, general domain of skill or knowledge. Such tests are known as *domain-referenced*. In yet other instances, tests can derive significance through reference to more restricted domains of skill or knowledge such as those delineated in instructional purposes, plans, and practices. These are called *objectives-referenced* tests. The focus in this book is on objectives-referenced tests because of their particular relevance to evaluation in second language classrooms.

It is hard work to make good tests. This is true of all three test types mentioned in the preceding paragraph. Constructing classroom tests involves several stages; see Figure 1 for a schematic summary of these stages. To start, a careful description of instructional objectives is needed. Then appropriate test tasks must be selected. We discuss each of these aspects of test construction in this chapter.

Describing instructional objectives

In the discussion that follows, we sometimes distinguish between two sorts of objectives based on their generality. There are general instructional objectives, which include the skills, abilities, or knowledge students are expected to learn from extended instruction, such as an entire course. These may also be referred to as course or curriculum objectives, depending on the setting in which you are teaching. They are often expressed in teachers' manuals or textbooks as the overarching goals of the course, textbook, and so forth. In addition, there are specific instructional objectives that figure in day-to-day instruction of units and lessons. The specific objectives provide a definition (or a specification) of general instructional objectives. These more specific kinds of objectives are variously referred to as syllabus, unit, or lesson objectives, and they are associated with individual chapters in a textbook or with lessons and units of instruction. They are the objectives around which actual instruction is usually planned. (These were discussed in Chapter 2.)

The first step in devising an objectives-referenced test is to describe the general instructional objectives, or the objectives for that part of instruction – a lesson, unit, or series of units – you are planning to test. Although there are different kinds of objectives that teachers aim for in their classrooms, we focus here on language learning objectives. It is crucial that the description of your language objectives be complete and accurate and in a form that is useful for making tests. Not all ways of describing objectives are equally useful. We discuss two methods of describing language objectives for the purposes of devising objectives-referenced tests.

Method one: Objectives as tasks

The most direct way of stating language objectives is in terms of test tasks. Consider the following three examples for an imaginary university ESL course:

1. At the end of the course, students will be able to sustain a conversation in English with a native speaker for five minutes. They should be able to converse about everyday affairs and about their out-of-class work or field of study.
2. At the end of the course, the students should be able to answer correctly 80 percent of multiple-choice vocabulary items based upon words in the vocabulary lists in the textbook. The form of the test items is as follows:

   You should learn to ski or to skate or to do some other _____ sport.

   > autumn
   > spring
   > winter
   > summer

3. At the end of Unit Six, the students will be able to answer factual questions including in their answers at least three levels of probability. For example:

   > Q: Is it going to rain this afternoon?
   > A: It doesn't seem much like it, or
   >   Probably not, or
   >   It shouldn't, and so on.

Q: Can we make it to the theater by eight?
A: I'm sure we can, or
    Most likely, and so on.

These three examples do not exhaust all possible objectives one might expect to find for an entire course. In addition, the first example has a skill focus; the second, a structure focus; and the third, a communicative (or notional) focus. It is more common for the general objectives of a course to have the same focus.

According to this method, objectives are described in terms of test tasks. The advantages of doing so are easy to appreciate. There is, first of all, a practical advantage. Objectives described in this way provide a virtual blueprint of the kind of test tasks to use to evaluate learning. You know not only the form of the tasks (conversation, multiple-choice, answering questions), but also the standard of performance expected (five minutes, 80 percent, three distinguishable degrees). The second advantage is a technical one having to do with the validity of tests. You will recall from Chapter 4 that one type of validity (content validity) can be assessed logically as the degree to which test tasks represent the skills you want to measure. Because you want to measure attainment of instructional objectives, stating objectives in terms of test tasks allows you to make a test that is a highly representative sample of the objectives. The links between teaching and testing are direct and obvious. Yet another advantage to this method is that such clear and precise statements of objectives allow teachers and students to focus their efforts. This can lead to greater efficiency in reaching objectives.

However, there are some drawbacks to this method of stating objectives. When defining objectives in terms of test tasks, there can be a tendency to concentrate on skills that are easy to test at the expense of skills that are not so easy to test. Language skills that may be important for the students to learn may be left out of instructional objectives simply because the person describing them cannot identify easy ways to test them. In other words, objectives may be chosen more because of their amenability to testing than because of their value to the language learners. This problem can be overcome if objectives are described independently of their use for testing alone. This brings us to Method Two.

Method two: Objectives for learning

When describing language objectives in the second way, one should consider the linguistic content focus and content range of the objective as well as the standard of performance expected of the students. Examples of objectives defined according to Method Two are given in Table 1.

Table 1. Example objectives for learning

A general course objective:

In this course students will learn to read and understand simple texts about familiar topics. Topics are those that have been themes of lessons in their textbook. Texts are 50 to 120 words in length and are illustrated. The style is informal. Texts are narrative and descriptive; information is concrete and not dense. Language is restricted to simple and compound sentences. No syntactic forms are used that have not been found in the textbook. No more than one new content word will be used per 50 words of text. Students should read at a rate of 20 words per minute. They should understand most of the major points in the text and some of the detail. They should comprehend sequence and the relations between ideas of (a) cause or reason, and (b) illustration or exemplification.

A unit objective:

In this unit, students will learn to write mini-biographies. These are six to ten sentences long and include two parts: an identification (name, nationality or residence, occupation, time of life, etc.), and note of some exceptional quality or accomplishment. Only simple sentences are required. No particular syntactic structures or lexicon needs to be employed. Any person that students know may be the subject. Drafts may be edited by the writer. Time is unlimited. The quality of writing must be sufficiently high that all propositions must be understandable – albeit with some effort by the reader. First language words or phrases will not be included.

A lesson objective:

In this lesson students will learn to offer oral apologies when required in brief conversations with another student or the teacher.

1. They will learn to recognize a request for an apology implied by questions of the form, "Why did you . . .?" or "Why didn't you . . .?"
2. They will state regret and then offer a reason, explanation, or excuse of the type (Oh,) I'm (very) sorry; I forgot . . .; I was busy . . .
3. Wait for the interlocutor to accept the apology.

Requests for apology will almost always be recognized. Apologies will invariably include both subfunctions. The basic grammar will be correct, but there may be errors in other parts, for example, in the phrase following *I had to*. Apologies will be highly fluent. Pronunciation will not be a hindrance for a listener.

CONTENT FOCUS

Instructional objectives can be described in terms of performance skills such as reading or speaking; they can be described in terms of communicative language use, including reference to the specific functions and notions that learners will be able to express in the second language; they can be described in terms of specific linguistic subskills or structures, such as intonation, word order, or pronoun reference; or they can include a combination of these. General instructional objectives often focus on performance skills, whereas specific unit objectives often have different foci.

In any case, for test construction purposes, the linguistic content that is the focus of instruction should be clearly identified in the objective. This is necessary if tasks appropriate for the measurement of these skills are to be selected for use in tests. In other words, the linguistic content described in the language objectives determines the linguistic focus of the test tasks. If the objectives specify multiple types of linguistic content, then test tasks that reflect these different foci must be devised if the test is to be a valid indicator of attainment of the objectives.

CONTENT RANGE

It is necessary to specify not only the nature of the linguistic skills or content to be learned but also the conditions in which learners are expected to demonstrate those skills – we refer to this as the range of the objective. The range fleshes out the language objective beyond what is specified by the content focus. The range can be specified in several ways. One is by identifying the issues, topics, or themes that the learners will be able to handle using their new language skills. For example, if the language focus identified in the objective is reading, one aspect of the range might be the topics that learners are expected to be able to read with comprehension – such as current events but not thermodynamics. This might be referred to as the *thematic* range of the objective.

Another aspect of range that can be specified in a language objective is the style or genre of language that learners are expected to handle, for example, everyday conversational language versus formal language of the type used to give public lectures or political speeches. This might be referred to as the *stylistic* range of the objective.

A third aspect of range concerns the *functional* range of the skills to be learned. Instructional objectives often specify only one aspect of language content to be learned and leave other features of the content focus unspecified. As a result, such objectives can be overly general. Specification of other aspects of the linguistic content is called for in order to make the statement of the objective useful for constructing valid tests. For example, imagine an objective that has as its focus a communicative function, such as requesting clarification. It is necessary to specify further whether the learner is expected to understand spoken requests or to utter them; to comprehend them in written form or to write them. In addition, if the student is supposed to learn to understand such requests, which particular grammatical forms should be understood? And if students should learn to produce clarification requests, are there particular grammatical forms for such requests that they should learn? In the absence of such specificity, the original objective is overly broad and, therefore, subject to a variety of methods of assessment.

Consider this example: If the objective is expressed in terms of linguistic structures, then the range must be specified in terms of performance skills and possibly even communication skills. Imagine that use of conditional verb forms is identified as the instructional objective for a lesson; this is a structural skill. The objective must be expanded to identify whether it is use of conditionals in oral or written language and in production and/or comprehension. Furthermore, are the students expected to be able to use conditional verb forms to make requests, formulate hypotheses, or conjecture about future plans? These communicative aspects of the objective need to be specified in order to narrow down the original structural objective. Without this additional specification, the initial objective is not clear because there are many different ways to use conditionals.

To summarize, in order for language objectives to be useful in test development, it is important to specify the range of language learning that is expected. We have identified three aspects of range that can be useful here – thematic, stylistic, and functional.

STANDARDS OF PERFORMANCE

Standards tell you what to look for in order to determine whether the objective has been attained. They specify both the quality and the level of performance that students are expected to attain if learning is successful. For example, reading proficiency might be assessed on the basis of comprehension accuracy; the desired level might be that of native speakers in grade six. We discuss each of these aspects of standards in more detail now.

• **Quality**   Two of the most common bases for assessing language proficiency are accuracy and effectiveness. We are all quite familiar with how both of these can be used to assess speaking and writing skills: Accuracy can be used as the basis for assessing spelling and grammar in written language, for example, and effectiveness is often used when assessing communication skills – Can learners attain their communicative purposes (e.g., Can they convince others of the validity of their point of view on a controversial matter?)? These two qualities are not necessarily useful for assessing all language skills – effectiveness does not generally apply to comprehension skills, for example.

Another frequently assessed quality is appropriateness, which can be relevant when assessing the use of forms of address in spoken language (i.e., familiar or formal forms of pronouns and verbs). Other qualities used in assessment are authenticity and quantity. Authenticity, or similarity to what a native speaker might do, is used mostly when evaluating speaking and writing skills. Quantity, or amount, can be used as a basis for assessing speaking and writing: How long can students speak on a topic? or How much can they write? Speed is yet another quality that is sometimes assessed, most often with respect to reading and sometimes speaking skills.

There is no single quality that can serve as a basis for all assessment. There is no one correct quality for the assessment of every type of language skill. Moreover, the assessment of a given objective need not be carried out with respect to only one quality. In fact, it is quite common for teachers to want students to read accurately and quickly, and to speak accurately, effectively, appropriately, and even authentically. At the same time, since a given language objective can be assessed in different ways, the particular quality to be learned and ultimately assessed should be specified at the outset of instruction because this identifies to both teachers and students an important additional aspect of what students are expected to derive from instruction.

• **Level**   Quality tells the teacher what aspect of linguistic performance to consider when assessing proficiency. Level is a matter of how good student performance must be with respect to a particular quality for the teacher to conclude that the objective has been attained. When objectives are stated in terms of test tasks, it is possible to be quite precise about the level of performance expected of learners. However, this way of describing language objectives is somewhat arbitrary and potentially limiting because language skills that cannot be tested easily, but are nonetheless important, may be excluded.

When language learning objectives are stated in terms that are independent of the tasks used to test them, it is often very difficult to describe in words the level of performance we are looking for if learning is successful. This is true when it comes to describing the level of attainment of any complex skill. In comparison, it is relatively easy to recognize levels of performance when provided with a sample or model. Thus, a useful way of defining levels of performance for assessment purposes is to provide models or samples of performance that reflect the level of performance you expect of successful students. For example, a set of model compositions or

Table 2.   Important aspects of objectives to consider in language test development

---

Content focus:

- Structural
- Notional
- Functional
- Other

Content Range:

- Thematic
- Stylistic
- Functional

Standards of Performance:

- Quality
- Level

---

recordings of speaking skills is an efficient and effective way of illustrating a desired level of particular qualities in writing or speaking performance. These models can then be used to judge the level of an individual student's performance on similar tasks. People generally find it reasonably easy to judge whether a sample of a student's writing or speaking is as good as a model; it is much harder to judge whether samples of their writing or speaking skills match a verbal description. Even if verbal descriptions of the level of performance expected of students are possible, it is a good idea to have models as well.

Task 1

Examine the sample objectives from Table 1 using the criteria proposed in Table 2.

Selecting objectives to test

Once language learning objectives have been defined, the next task is to select those you wish to test. In some cases, only one objective may have been the focus of instruction, and, therefore, there is only one objective to be tested. This is likely to occur after a lesson because single lessons often focus on a single objective. More often, however, you must choose among a number of different objectives. This situation arises when testing is done after several lessons or a unit or at the end of a semester or an entire year of instruction. In these cases, a variety of interrelated objectives have usually figured in your teaching and, therefore, need to be tested. Selecting from among alternative objectives is required when it is not feasible to test all the objectives you have been aiming for.

It is preferable to select a sample of objectives to test before beginning test construction in order to avoid biases that can arise otherwise. The most common biases arise from natural tendencies to assess what is easiest to test as well as those things that stood out in class because they were recently taught or students had difficulty with them, enjoyed them, and so on. Two commonly used procedures for selecting objectives to test are random sampling procedures and stratified sampling.

RANDOM SAMPLING

Random sampling is easy to understand. What one does is essentially this: Write out all of the objectives to be covered by the test on separate slips of paper and put them in a hat. Then, without looking, take out as many slips as you plan to test given time constraints, and so forth. You will then test for each of these objectives. Random sampling of objectives is recommended only if all objectives are equally important. Random sampling of objectives of unequal importance runs the risk that some important objectives will not be selected and, therefore, not tested. This may be viewed as unfair by the test takers, and, furthermore, it may yield test results that omit important information about student achievement.

STRATIFIED SAMPLING

As just noted, there are times when random selection of objectives to include in a test is not the best procedure. Nonrandom selection is desirable when the objectives are not equally important. In this case, the test objectives are best represented according to their relative importance, with more important objectives represented in greater number than less important objectives; alternatively, more important objectives would receive more value than less important objectives, regardless of the number of items. When there are too many objectives to include in the test, the least important may in fact be omitted altogether.

Stratified (or nonrandom) sampling of objectives requires that all possible objectives be identified and then organized according to some criterion of importance, for example, according to their communicative importance, the amount of time spent on each in class, or their frequency of use. Alternatively, objectives can be organized and sampled according to unit or lesson, by linguistic structures, by language purpose (e.g., exchanging information, establishing and maintaining social relationships), by time segments of a course (e.g., first month, second month), and so on. The choice of appropriate categories for grouping objectives depends on the nature of the course.

Once you have identified the objectives to be represented in the test, test tasks that tap those objectives must be selected.

Test tasks

Constructing language tests means selecting a task or tasks that will elicit the kind(s) of language skills you are interested in assessing. When selecting these tasks, be sure to consider the response characteristics or demands of the task. In other words, what kinds of responses are possible or required by the test task presented to the students? This is important because certain kinds of tests elicit or call for certain kinds of skills that may be irrelevant to the actual language skills you are interested in. For example, multiple-choice listening comprehension tests put heavy demands on the test taker's memory and require reading skills if the response alternatives are written. You should avoid items in which the task demands exceed or interfere with the language skills of interest. Identifying task demands calls for analysis and intuition.

Generally speaking, the response characteristics of test tasks can be described as:

1. Closed ended
2. Limited
3. Open ended

Closed-ended test tasks call for the most limited and most predictable responses, and open-ended tasks call for the least limited and least predictable responses; limited response tasks fall in between these two.

CLOSED-ENDED RESPONSE TASKS

Closed-ended tasks include a prompt, stem, or elicitation followed by alternative responses or answers. Students select their answers from the alternatives that are given. These are what are commonly known as multiple-choice questions. The task is basically one of recognition of the correct or appropriate answer. Closed-ended test tasks are suitable for assessing comprehension skills. They do not involve language production and, therefore, cannot be used to assess speaking and writing skills directly. Different kinds of prompts and response alternatives can be used. For example, the prompt might be a single word, a sentence, or a paragraph. It can even be nonlinguistic in nature, for example, a picture or a real object. The response alternatives might take the form of a judgment of correct or incorrect, appropriate or inappropriate, or true or false. Or they might take the form of an actual linguistic response, such as words, phrases, or sentences. Examples of closed-ended test tasks are:

1. *Cloze* tasks in which a word or words have been deleted from a sentence or paragraph of written text and students must fill in the missing words by choosing from a number of alternatives provided by the examiner. Here is an example:

   • The boy _____ sick yesterday, so he could not come to school.

      a. was
      b. were
      c. is
      d. had

2. *Picture or object elicitation* tasks with alternatives; for example, the student is shown an object or picture of an object and has to identify the name of the object from alternatives given by the examiner:

   • A picture of an apple is shown and the test taker must identify the name of the object from the following alternatives:

      a. apple
      b. orange
      c. pear
      d. tomato

3. *Judgment* tasks in which the student responds to an item with an answer of correct or incorrect, true or false, same or different, or appropriate or inappropriate. Here is an example:

   • A chicken is a type of clothing. True or false?

4. Picture and object elicitation tasks can be seen as special cases of judgment tasks in that a series of true or false, correct or incorrect, or appropriate or inappropriate judgments is called for when considering each alternative.

When scoring closed-ended tasks, one simply needs to see whether the student has selected the correct alternative. Closed-ended tasks are often referred to as objective test tasks since deciding whether the response is right or wrong does not depend on the examiner's subjective judgment or opinion.

LIMITED-RESPONSE TASKS

In limited-response tasks, the range of responses available to the student is not fixed by the examiner as it is in the case of closed-ended tasks. At the same time, the range of possible responses is limited. All of the task types described under closed-ended response tasks can be used as limited-response tasks if alternative answers are not provided by the examiner. There are also other kinds of limited-response tasks, for example:

1. *Elicitation* tasks in which a carefully selected stimulus or prompt is used to elicit specific responses from the student, but no response alternatives are actually given; the student must provide the response:

   - The student is shown a picture of an apple and is asked to name it.

   Limited-response elicitation tasks can contain more complex prompts. For example, the student is presented with a picture depicting an interaction between a student and her teacher and is told that the student does not agree with the way the teacher has graded her composition; the person taking the test is asked how the student would express her disagreement in an appropriate way. This type of format is considered a limited-response task because both the nonlinguistic content and the linguistic form of the response expected of the student are restrained in important ways by the prompt.

2. *Cloze* tests with no alternative responses provided; students must fill in the blanks with their own responses:

   - The boy _____ sick yesterday, so he could not come to school.

   In cloze tests, the response alternatives are limited by the grammatical and semantic context of the missing word. In our example, the answer is limited to a single word and, in particular, a verb.

3. *Dictation* and *imitation* tests in which the student is asked to reproduce orally or in writing what the examiner has said. The range of responses in these cases is obviously limited by the material to be imitated or reproduced. At the same time, there is some variation in possible response in the way the student spells or pronounces the target words.

4. *Transformation* tasks in which the student is asked to transform an item as directed by the examiner: for example, change present tense verbs to past tense; replace nouns with pronouns; change singular forms into plural forms, and so on.

5. *Rearrangement* and *matching* tasks in which the student is given a set of items and has to arrange them in a correct or meaningful order or so that they go together in some way (e.g., the student is given a set of sentence

fragments in random order and must arrange them into a correct sentence).

In contrast to closed-ended response formats, more than recognition is called for by limited-response formats. Students must actually produce a correct or appropriate response, and, therefore, they must be able to recall the correct grammar rule, word, expression, pronunciation, and so on. Scoring of limited-response items also differs from closed-ended items in that responses can be not only correct but also appropriate or acceptable. This follows from the fact that there is not necessarily a single, fixed, linguistically correct response to limited-response items; a range of responses is possible, and, therefore, judgment is called for on the part of the scorer.

OPEN-ENDED RESPONSE TASKS

In open-ended tasks, the response alternatives are not limited by the examiner or test item, and students are free to give a wide variety of possible responses. In other words, the examiner has relatively little knowledge beforehand of what students will say or write and how they will express it linguistically. Open-ended test tasks are suitable for assessing speaking, listening, and other language skills that call for the production or generation of language. Examples of open-ended tasks are:

- *Oral interviews* in which the content is not prespecified.
- *Role-plays* and *interviews* in which the content is specified.
- *Written compositions* or other writing tasks in which the student is free to choose the content, for the most part. This applies even to writing compositions, term papers, and so on where the general topic or topics might be provided. A great deal of choice with respect to the ideas, concepts, details, and linguistic forms used to express them is still possible within such general topics.
- *Information-gap tasks* in which students are asked to provide information that is not known to the examiner; these tasks may take the form of questions about aspects of the students' family life, opinions, values, beliefs, interests, or knowledge that are not known to the examiner (e.g., students might be asked a series of questions about family, summer holidays, goals for studying a second language, or opinions about a recent political event). There are also a number of games that can be used as information-gap test tasks. Typically, in these games, students are given information that they must describe to another student or the teacher. Conversely, students may have to question another student or the teacher for information they need to complete a task.

Table 3.   Examples of test task types

Closed-ended

- Cloze
- Elicitation
- Judgment (e.g., true or false)
- Multiple-choice

Limited-response

- Dictation
- Imitation
- Transformation
- Rearrangement
- Matching

Open-ended

- Interviews
- Essays
- Information gap
- Oral or written reports

Open-ended test tasks are by far the most complex tasks to score since students' responses are not predictable. A great deal of subjective judgment is called for, and, therefore, these tests are sometimes referred to as *subjective* tests. In order to ensure that scoring is reliable and fair, one must pay a great deal of attention to deciding how to score such tests before scoring begins. In general, it is advisable to develop a scoring protocol that specifies the rules for scoring the test. The examiner or scorer then uses this as a guide to assist her in awarding points to the student. (Scoring is discussed further in Chapter 11.)

The examples of test tasks mentioned here are general and not exhaustive. For more specific suggestions, you may want to refer to books by Cohen (1980), Finocchiaro and Sako (1983), Harris (1969), Madsen (1983), Omaggio (1983), Underhill (1987), Valette (1977), Weir (1993), for other examples of item format types.

Task 2

Identify open- and closed-ended test tasks in addition to those listed in Table 3.

Summary

In this chapter, we reviewed two ways of describing language learning objectives for use in making classroom tests; according to the first method, objectives can be described in terms of test tasks, and according to the second method, they can be described in terms of linguistic focus, range, and standards of performance. We favor the latter method because it is more likely to include the full range of language skills that are important for learners to acquire. In the former case, ease of testing may influence the objectives that are emphasized and evaluated.

We discussed those aspects of focus, range, and standards that are important to specify when describing objectives for testing purposes and pointed out that overly general objectives can be unclear. Explicit, detailed descriptions of language learning objectives are important not only for valid assessment of learning but also for effective teaching. If the desired linguistic focus, range, and standards of performance are not specified in the objectives, then instruction may lack focus and, as a result, be less effective.

We also discussed the general characteristics and uses of three types of test tasks: open-ended, closed-ended, and limited-response. In the next chapter, we present specific guidelines for choosing from among these alternatives and for constructing open- and closed-ended test tasks. We do not discuss limited-response tasks since the guidelines for the other two types can be adapted for constructing limited-response items.

Discussion questions

1. How do you currently decide what the focus of a final examination will be? How would you change the way you select the focus based on what you have read in this chapter?
2. What criteria do you use, in general, to assign points to questions in your tests? Would you make changes to the way you decide on the value of test items based on the material in this chapter?
3. Select a general objective from the curriculum or textbook you are currently using or have used, and then examine the adequacy of this objective based on the suggestions in this chapter, that is, from the point of view of the focus, range, and standard of performance of the objective. How could this objective be improved?
4. Imagine that you want to devise a test to assess understanding of this chapter: (a) Describe the content of this chapter as a basis for devising a test of it, (b) prepare three objectives pertinent to the content that could be the basis for a test, and (c) select three different test task types to assess each of these objectives.

5. Select one or two instructional objectives that you are currently using or have used in the past and examine them critically using the guidelines in this chapter.
6. Are there standards of performance for assessing language proficiency in addition to those suggested in this chapter?
7. List as many test tasks as you can in three minutes, and then consider how these tasks could be used as open-ended or closed-ended formats.
8. Select a learning objective based on a lesson or unit of instruction. Then devise the following kinds of test tasks to assess attainment of the objective: (a) open-ended, (b) limited response, and (c) closed-ended. Compare and assess these different task types.
9. Select a chapter from a second language textbook and identify all the types of language content contained in the chapter. What is the most important? the least important? Then define the minimal range of performance expected of a student who successfully learns the content of the chapter. Next, expand the range expected of a successful student.

Readings

Berk, R. A. (Ed.). (1986). *Performance assessment: Methods and applications.* Baltimore, Md.: The Johns Hopkins University Press.

Canale, M., and M. Swain. (1980). Theoretical bases of communicative approaches to second language teaching and testing. *Applied Linguistics, 1,* 1–47.

Carroll, J. B. (1980). *Testing communicative performance.* Oxford: Pergamon Press.

Cohen, A. (1980). *Testing language ability in the classroom.* Rowley, Mass.: Newbury House.

Finocchiaro, M., and S. Sako. (1983). *Foreign language testing: A practical approach.* New York: Regents.

Harris, D. (1969). *Testing English as a second language.* New York: McGraw-Hill.

Hauptmann, P. C., R. Leblanc, and M. B. Wesche. (Eds.). (1985). *Second language performance testing.* Ottawa: University of Ottawa Press.

Madsen, H. (1983). *Techniques in testing.* New York: Oxford University Press.

Omaggio, A. (1983). *Proficiency-oriented classroom testing.* Washington, D.C.: Center for Applied Linguistics.

Seliger, H. W. (1982). Testing authentic language: The problem of meaning. *Language Testing, 2,* 60–73.

Shohamy, E., and R. Reves. (1982). Authentic language tests: Where from and where to? *Language Testing, 2,* 48–59.

Underhill, N. (1987). *Testing spoken language: A handbook of oral testing techniques.* London: Cambridge University Press.

Valette, R. (1977). *Modern language testing.* New York: Harcourt Brace Jovanovich.

Weir, C. (1993). *Understanding and developing language tests.* New York: Prentice-Hall.

10 *Choosing and devising test tasks*

- Introduction
- Choosing test tasks
- Guidelines for making open-ended test tasks
- Guidelines for making closed-ended test tasks
- Summary

Preview questions

1. What are the advantages of tests in comparison to the other methods of collecting information for evaluation that we have discussed in this book? What are their disadvantages?
2. Do you use (or have you used) multiple-choice questions to test your students' language skills? What did you find difficult about making up such tests? What did you find useful about them?
3. Do you use essay-type (or open-ended type) questions in your tests? When and why do you use this format? What are the easy and the difficult parts to making up and using such test formats?
4. If you have ever taken multiple-choice tests, what did you personally like and dislike about them? Did you feel that your performance was a fair reflection of what you knew? If not, why not?
5. When you have had to do essay-type tests, what did you personally find difficult about them? Did you have to study in any particular way for such a test in comparison with multiple-choice tests? Is one way of studying better than another?
6. What distinguishes authentic language use from nonauthentic language? Suggest some examples of authentic language use and some ways of testing proficiency in using language in these ways.
7. Are there some authentic language tasks that could be tested validly using multiple-choice task formats? Name them.

Introduction

In this chapter, we talk about how to choose among the three general test task types reviewed in Chapter 9. We also present guidelines for devising closed-ended and open-ended test tasks; we do not discuss limited-response formats because the guidelines presented for the open- and closed-ended formats can be adapted for this purpose. These guidelines are part of the larger process of devising valid tests that are compatible with instructional objectives and, specifically, with the focus, range, and standards of performance specified or included in your objectives.

Choosing test tasks

Choosing the type or types of tasks to include in a language test depends on a combination of factors:

1. Instructional objectives
2. The students' level of proficiency
3. Instructional activities
4. Available testing resources

What follows are general suggestions to assist you in the selection of test tasks.

Instructional objectives

Clearly, the most important factor to consider when choosing which type of test task to use is your objectives. Choose tasks that focus on the same kinds of language skills described in the objectives as well as the range and standards of performance expected of the students. Closed-ended tasks permit assessment of comprehension skills in both reading and listening, but they do not lend themselves to directly assessing production skills: speaking or writing. This is to say, one's ability to perform on a closed-ended test task does not necessarily mean that the individual would be able to produce the corresponding language in an open-ended task. Also related to language objectives, closed-ended tasks permit the examiner to assess specific language skills – this follows from the fact that the responses permitted by closed-ended tasks are controlled totally by the examiner. In comparison, limited-response and open-ended response tasks do not control the students' specific responses – students can often find ways of responding to test items that are different from what was intended by the examiner.

The range of language skills elicited by a closed-ended task is strictly under the control of test makers: they can include as broad or as narrow a range of language skills as desired. Moreover, closed-ended tasks force the test taker to respond to test items in specific ways so that the examiner can examine a specified range of skills. In comparison, test makers cannot control the range of language skills elicited by open-ended tasks. In principle, an open-ended task could elicit a very broad range of skills. In practice, however, learners may, and often do, limit their responses to those skills they have some confidence in. Thus, weaker students might produce a much more restricted range of language in response to a composition, for example, than more proficient students. Their performance may be nevertheless linguistically correct. If students do not use certain linguistic items or structures in an open-ended task, it is not possible to tell whether they do not know them or whether they simply chose not to use them. Thus, on the one hand, open-ended tasks can yield very rich samples of language and, on the other hand, may yield restricted samples because students choose not to use as broad a range of language as hoped for or because they avoid using language they do not have complete control over.

The same issue arises when considering the selection of open- versus closed-ended test tasks from the point of view of standards of performance. To the extent that open-ended tasks permit students to not use language that might be of interest to the examiner, then the examiner may not be able to assess the students' performance thoroughly with respect to certain standards of performance. Students can often find ingenious ways of avoiding language they do not know or know only poorly. In comparison, closed-ended tasks force students to respond to a limited range of alternatives that can be selected carefully to represent the standards of performance of interest to the examiner. At the same time, closed-ended tasks assess only recognition skills and, therefore, may not fully capture students' ability to actively use language according to these standards.

Level of proficiency

Closed-ended and limited-response tasks can be particularly suitable for assessing the language skills of beginning level second language learners. This does not mean that closed-ended and limited-response formats cannot be used for intermediate or advanced level students. Whether such tasks are suitable for more advanced students will depend upon the exact content of the item, not on the response characteristics per se. Open-ended tasks, in comparison, can be particularly suitable for assessing more advanced students. If different task types are used in a single test, it is generally desirable to start off with closed-ended tasks in order to put students at ease and to include limited- or open-ended response items later once the students have warmed up.

Instructional activities

Test tasks should be chosen by taking into account the kinds of instructional activities the learners have been exposed to. This ensures that students are familiar with and, therefore, understand the response demands of the task. It is unfair, for example, to use open-ended response tasks with learners who have been exposed to only closed-ended kinds of learning activities. Therefore, test tasks should always be chosen that are well understood by students, either by virtue of their classroom experiences with similar tasks during instruction or by virtue of clear instructions in the test.

Testing resources

Finally, test tasks should be practical given the resources available. An important resource to consider is time, both for administering the test and for scoring it. In general, open-ended test tasks take much longer to score than closed-ended or limited-response tasks. Either type of task can take a brief or a long time to administer, depending on the content of the test. The physical resources for testing are also important. Individual testing that requires private, quiet space (e.g., oral interviews) is impractical if the examiner does not have a separate area for conducting the interviews. Such a task might also be impractical if the examiner does not have the human resources to supervise other students who are not being tested.

Task 1

Identify a language skill to be tested (e.g., listening comprehension), and then brainstorm alternative open-ended and closed-ended tasks to test it. Discuss the merits of each alternative.

Guidelines for making open-ended test tasks

Introduction

As we just noted, in contrast to closed-ended test tasks, open-ended tasks do not control in a precise way the specific responses to be made by the test taker. Students are relatively free to respond in whatever way they choose. For example, in an oral interview, each test taker can respond to the interviewer's questions in a unique way, using different language structures, vocabulary, and so on. These kinds of tasks are particularly suitable for assessing language proficiency in many authentic situations that call for interactive, dynamic language use — such as a conversation between people or an encounter with a salesclerk in a store or a stranger on the street. Although many such situations are open-ended, they are always structured in particular ways. For example, a conversation has a certain structure or organization to it, although the topics of conversation may vary considerably; or a job interview also has a specific structure, and the interviewee can imagine beforehand the kinds of questions that may be asked. Assessing language proficiency in ways that resemble the actual situations and tasks for which language learning is taking place is sometimes called performance-based assessment.

At the same time, it is important to realize that not all authentic language tasks are open-ended; for example, filling out application forms and buying bus tickets, stamps, or gasoline are quite formulaic. Not all authentic language use involves oral communication; reading and writing are also characteristic of much authentic language use. Even taking multiple-choice tests can be an authentic language task for second language learners who are studying in schools in which the second language is the medium of instruction. Language performance in school often, although not always, calls for the ability to take tests, and preparing second language learners for such activities is common in many English language universities that enroll large numbers of nonnative speakers.

Because they are less structured than closed-ended tasks, open-ended tasks are often used to assess the skills of advanced level learners. In contrast, beginning level learners often need the structure imposed by closed-ended and limited-response tasks; oral tests for beginners, for example, often include such activities as picture naming and question answering. However, multiple-choice tasks, although well suited for testing beginning level learners, can nevertheless be demanding if care is not taken to avoid unnecessary complications.

Open-ended test tasks are suitable for testing speaking and writing skills because they require language production. They tend to be used to assess higher order skills, such as discourse and sociolinguistic skills in particular that cannot be elicited easily using closed-ended or limited-response test tasks. In fact, open-ended tasks call for a variety of language skills. For example, a written composition requires spelling, vocabulary, and grammar skills in addition to discourse and sociolinguistic skills. Thus, it is possible to score open-ended tasks for different language skills.

A great deal of judgment is called for when scoring open-ended tasks because each student's response can be different from other students' responses but no less correct. Consequently, scoring open-ended tasks is much more demanding and requires much more thought than scoring closed-ended tests. Moreover, if open-ended test tasks are used to assess language proficiency in authentic situations, then judgments of appropriateness, effectiveness, and correctness are often called for since these are important standards for assessing language use in situations in which language is normally used. Indeed, normally, correct use of language is not an end in itself but a means for negotiating social relations, transacting business, or achieving other goals. For instance, teaching assistants at the university level use language in order to help their students understand course material; computer salespersons use language to sell computers; and doctors use language to understand the source of their patients' medical problems. Language is vital for these people in the overall performance of their duties and jobs. Evidence of the success of their language skills lies in how well they perform these duties, not simply in how correctly they use language. Even when there is no face-to-face interaction, language use normally involves some form of interaction – someone who is listening or reading someone else's message. Even in these cases, appropriateness and effectiveness of communication can be important standards for assessment.

Because the specific responses to be made by test takers in open-ended tasks are not controlled in any precise way, devising such tasks does not require the same precision or technical care as closed-ended tasks, although they may require some ingenuity to ensure that the test task resembles the kinds of situations in which the learners will ultimately use their second language. Open-ended tests are different from closed-ended tests in that they usually consist of only one item (e.g., write a 250-word essay on a topic of your choice), although this is not always the case. In contrast, tests made up of closed-ended tasks generally include a number of items.

The guidelines in this section take the form of *general questions* you can ask about open-ended tasks rather than specific technical suggestions of the type provided for closed-ended test tasks.

General questions

When constructing open-ended test tasks, it is useful to ask the following general questions:

1. Is the task appropriate with respect to instructional objectives and in-structional activities?
2. Is the task understandable with respect to expected performance and assessment standards?
3. Is the task feasible with respect to topic, level of difficulty, and time?

Each of these general questions contains a number of specific questions. These are summarized in Table 1 and discussed next.

APPROPRIATE

When selecting an open-ended test task, follow the same general process used when choosing closed-ended test tasks; that is to say, it is important to select a task that is valid with respect to your instructional objectives. More

Table 1.   Guidelines for devising open-ended tests

Appropriateness

1. Can the task elicit the kinds of language skills identified in the instructional objectives?
2. Can the task elicit the range of language skills identified in the instructional objectives?
3. Do the language skills elicited by the task lend themselves to assessing the students' performance according to the standards expected of them?
4. Does the task reflect the actual performance demands of the situations in which the second language will ultimately be used?
5. Are the students prepared for the task?
6. Is this task workable with the students?

Understandability

1. Have the task demands of the test been made explicit and clear?
2. Have the standards of performance and evaluation been made explicit to the students?

Feasibility

1. Will the topic of the task elicit the kinds of language skills you want to examine?
2. Is the topic of interest to the students?
3. Is the topic biased?
4. Is the specific form of the task of appropriate difficulty?
5. Is there enough time for the students to complete the task? Conversely, has so much time been allotted that the test no longer reflects normal time constraints?

---

specifically, choose a task that reflects (1) the same linguistic focus, (2) the range of performance specified by the objectives, and (3) the standards of performance expected of the students. When using open-ended test tasks to assess language proficiency in authentic situations, try to select tasks that approximate the actual situations in which the students will use their second language skills as much as possible so that you elicit these skills and so that you can, in turn, make accurate predictions of your students' language performance. Most situations in which language is normally used are interactive, dynamic, and purposive in ways that extend beyond simply using language correctly. If your instructional objectives aim for proficient use of language in such situations, then an appropriate test task should also include these qualities. In addition, one should ensure that the full range of performance standards is part of the scoring system, including measures of how accurate, appropriate, and effective the students' performance is.

In some cases, special efforts need to be taken to simulate the performance demands of authentic situations in which the second language will ultimately be used because the target situations are different from those in the classroom. For example, in courses for people who are learning ESL for business purposes, the actual target situations are not likely to be part of the second language classroom. Teachers will need to exercise some ingenuity to simulate in their classroom the actual situations in which the language will be used if they want their assessment to reflect authentic language use. In contrast, when teaching ESL for academic purposes, the target situations in which English will ultimately be used can probably be found quite easily in the second language classroom itself. Much less effort is needed in these latter instances to create a testing situation that reflects the task demands of the target situation. The more closely your test task simulates the actual conditions in which the second language will be used, the greater the predictive validity of your test results.

When selecting appropriate test tasks, take into account the instructional activities that have been used in class. Students may not be able to demonstrate the full extent of their proficiency if a test task is selected that they have not seen before because the task demands may not be clear to them. For example, using role play for the first time as a test may not work with your students because they do not know what is called for, or they may simply be too self-conscious. Using the same kinds of tasks as have been used as instructional activities ensures that your students are familiar with the task demands.

At the same time, using exactly the same activities that were used in class will not tell you whether students can use their new language skills in new but related situations. Surely an indication of language proficiency is the ability to use language in different situations. This is particularly relevant when testing students at advanced levels of proficiency where generalizability would be expected. Judgment is called for when selecting test tasks that are different from but related to the activities you have used in class. You cannot know with any certainty whether your students can handle a new situation until you have tried it out.

Thus, when devising test tasks so that they are appropriate, there are a number of specific questions to ask:

1. Can the task elicit the kinds of language skills identified in the instructional objectives?
2. Can the task elicit the range of language skills identified in the instructional objectives?
3. Do the language skills elicited by the task lend themselves to assessing the students' performance according to the standards expected of them?

4. Does the task reflect the actual performance demands of the situations in which the second language will ultimately be used?
5. Are the students prepared for the task?
6. Is this task workable with the students?

UNDERSTANDABLE

Because open-ended test tasks allow wide variation in responding, test takers must understand what is expected of them. Test tasks that are not well understood become puzzles that require the student to guess what the examiner wants. Test takers who do not know what is expected of them might give wrong or inappropriate responses because of misunderstanding and not because of lack of language proficiency. Test instructions should be simple, straightforward, and unambiguous. Students should also have some specific indications of what counts in judging their performance. In a written composition, for example, does spelling count? Is originality important? In an oral interview, what exactly will be scored: pronunciation, grammar, the organization of their responses? What weight will different scoring components be given? Students need to be well informed in order to decide how to spend their time and energy during the test. The standards of performance that will be used to judge language performance should be made clear to the students prior to testing. Deciding on a scoring scheme after the test has been given or informing students of scoring criteria after the test is unfair.

Specific questions that can be asked about understandability are:

1. Have the task demands of the test been made explicit and clear to the students?
2. Have the standards of performance and evaluation been made explicit to the students?

FEASIBLE

Having chosen a certain open-ended test task, you must decide whether the task is feasible. There are at least three aspects of test tasks to examine from the point of view of feasibility: (1) task topic, (2) task difficulty, and (3) the time allotted to perform the task.

• **Topic**   Will or can the topic you have chosen elicit the kinds of language skills you are interested in? Sometimes topics that instructors think will work, do not. You may have to try them out beforehand with other students in order to determine this. Or even trying to do the task yourself can give you a general indication of the feasibility of the topic.

Is the topic realistic and authentic? Using topics that students do not regard as authentic will reduce the legitimacy of the test in your students' eyes and certainly will not elicit authentic language performance. Is the topic of interest to the test takers? If it is not, the test takers will not be motivated to respond seriously or enthusiastically. Interest and motivation are particularly important in open-ended tasks because the test takers are free to respond as much or as little as they want. Does the topic favor or disfavor individuals or subgroups of learners for reasons that have nothing to do with the course? That is to say, is there unfair bias in the topic? For example, is the topic culturally offensive to certain students? Do some of them have additional experience with the topic, such as a science topic that would allow students with a science background to perform better than students who do not have such a background?

From the examiner's point of view, will you be able to get the students to respond to the topic? Will the language samples produced in response to this task allow you to form a realistic picture of the student's ability with respect to the objectives you are testing? And can the language samples elicited by this topic be scored appropriately?

• Difficulty   Is the task of appropriate difficulty, or is it so difficult that students will be unable to demonstrate the language skills they have acquired? Conversely, is it so easy that all students will find it trivial or unchallenging?

From the examiner's point of view, is the exercise so easy that scores will fail to distinguish those students who have made more progress from those who have not progressed as much? Is the task so difficult or complex that the examiner will find it difficult to determine what anyone has learned?

• Time   Is there enough time for students to perform the task? On the one hand, students who are not given enough time will not be able to demonstrate their full achievement. On the other hand, students who are given too much time to do a test can treat it like a puzzle rather than an actual language task. So-called speeded or time-constrained tests are appropriate sometimes – namely, when the language skill they are testing is usually performed with time constraints; for example, an impromptu oral report or conversation should have time constraints but writing academic assignments probably should not. Speeded tests are usually used with material that is so easy that, given enough time, all test takers would be expected to respond correctly. Consequently, the test takers are being examined on their speed of performance rather than their skill or knowledge alone.

In contrast, a *power* test is one that allows enough time for nearly all test takers to complete it, but the material being examined is of sufficient difficulty that not all test takers are expected to get every item correct. Thus, power tests examine maximum level of skill or knowledge without time constraints. Test performance under speeded conditions is not usually the best indicator of maximum performance capabilities. Whether a speed or power test is appropriate will depend on your objectives. (We discuss time for testing further in Chapter 11.)

Specific questions to ask when considering the feasibility of test tasks include:

1. Will the topic of the task elicit the kinds of language skills you want to examine?
2. Is the topic of interest to the students?
3. Is the topic biased?
4. Is the specific form of the task of appropriate difficulty?
5. Is there enough time for the students to complete the task? Conversely, has so much time been allotted that the test no longer reflects normal time constraints for performance of such tasks?

Task 2

Compare the kind of information provided by a written test with that provided by students' journals or a writing conference. Discuss the uses and limitations of each method.

Guidelines for making closed-ended test tasks

Introduction

Closed-ended response tasks are suitable for testing skills involved in reading and listening because they involve comprehension skills. They do not require the test taker to produce or generate a response. Closed-ended response tasks can be particularly suitable for beginning level learners precisely because they do not require language production and because they are highly structured. Their use is not restricted to beginners, of course, and they can be made as complex as desired depending on the particular nature of the task and its content.

Most closed-ended test tasks are some form of what is commonly known as multiple-choice questions, although there are some variations that are not. Matching tasks in which the test taker must match one set of items, such as specific words, to another set, such as different "parts of speech" or grammatical terms, are an example. However, even this format can be conceived of as multiple-choice in that the grammatical items constitute a set of multiple-choice answers, only one of which is correct as a descriptor of each word. Multiple-choice question formats include a stem, or prompt, and alternative responses. The stem is, in effect, the question. The alternatives that are not correct are called *distractors.*

Closed-ended test tasks attempt to control in precise ways the particular response required to perform the task. Thus, they are especially useful for assessing particular aspects of language, such as certain grammar rules, functions, and vocabulary. A great deal of care is called for in making up these tasks in order to avoid ambiguous or misleading items that are confusing to the test taker and produce answers that are meaningless to the examiner. Thus, closed-ended tasks, and multiple-choice questions in particular, are difficult to construct. However, scoring is simply a matter of checking whether the correct alternative was chosen.

What follows are general guidelines for constructing multiple-choice types of closed-ended test tasks. These guidelines are summarized in Table 2. We present guidelines for preparing stems and response alternatives. Bear in mind that the guidelines presented for open-ended test tasks are also

Table 2.   Checklist for devising closed-ended tests

The stem

1. Is the stem simple and concise?
2. Are there unnecessary double negatives or other complex wordings in the stem?
3. Does the stem assess what it is supposed to?
4. Are there inadvertent cues to the right answer?
5. Is the stem a verbatim repetition of material taught in class? If so, is this desirable?

The response alternatives

1. Are the distractors of the same grammatical and semantic class as the correct response?
2. Are the response alternatives grammatically compatible with the stem?
3. Are all the alternatives equally attractive?
4. Are the distractors informative?
5. Are the alternatives equally difficult, complex, and long?
6. Is there more than one correct alternative?
7. Does the wording of the alternatives match the stem?
8. Can the correct response be derived from common knowledge?
9. Are the alternatives suitably simple?
10. Can the answer to any items be derived from other items?
11. Do any of the alternatives refer to other items?

---

relevant when devising closed-ended tasks. In other words, closed-ended tasks, like open-ended tasks, should be appropriate, understandable, and feasible.

The stem

The stem, or prompt, in a multiple-choice task can be linguistic or non-linguistic in nature. Nonlinguistic stems consist of pictures or realia (i.e., real objects). Linguistic stems can consist of single words, phrases, sentences, written text, oral passages, or discourse.

1. The stem should be presented in a simple, concise form so that the task or problem posed by the item is clear and unambiguous. In other words, it should be clear to the test taker what is called for after reading or hearing the stem. For example:

   The following item is ambiguous because it leads to more than one possible correct answer:

   - She watched her carefully _____ her coat on.
     a. put*
     b. puts
     c. to put
     d. while putting*

2. In most cases, it is advisable to avoid using negatively worded stems since they make extra and often unnecessary demands on the test taker. For example:

   - Which of the following is not true?

3. Make sure the stem is testing what it is supposed to be testing. In particular, make sure that the point that is being tested is the only source of difficulty in the stem. Otherwise, the task will demand more than you want to test. For example, if the item is testing vocabulary, make sure that any language used to provide context for the target item is familiar and comprehensible to the student; otherwise you might be testing knowledge of more than one vocabulary item. For example:

   - Jane *donated* a candelabrum to the charity bazaar.
     a. gave*
     b. sold
     c. sent
     d. wore

   In this stem, the target word is *donated,* but the use of the words *candelabrum* and *bazaar* may confuse and mislead students because they are not familiar with them.

Or if it is a sentence comprehension item, for example, make sure that obscure vocabulary that could impede comprehension is avoided, that is, unless you want to see whether the students can infer the meaning of unknown words from context. Obscure vocabulary in a sentence comprehension item turns the task from sentence comprehension to vocabulary knowledge.

4. Avoid stems that inadvertently give clues to the right answer for unimportant or uninteresting reasons. For example:

- Charlie is always late for school, so his mother is going to buy an _____ clock for him.

   a. ring
   b. alarm*
   c. morning
   d. bell

The correct answer in this case (alarm) is cued by the article *an* in addition to the meaning; *an* is always followed by a word that begins with a vowel, and *alarm* is the only alternative that begins with a vowel.

5. It is often advisable to avoid making the stem identical to material that has been taught or used in class in order to avoid correct responding on the basis of memory alone. There may be exceptions to this, such as testing for comprehension of idiomatic expressions.

The response alternatives

Like the stem, the alternative responses in a multiple-choice item can be linguistic or nonlinguistic in nature. The latter can consist of pictures of realia. For example, the examiner says a word, and the students must select from among four alternative pictures the one that corresponds to the word. More commonly, alternative responses are expressed in linguistic form. For example, the examiner says a word, and the students select from among four spoken alternative words the one that is a synonym of the target.

1. Distractors should belong to the same general grammatical or semantic category as the correct response. In other words, avoid distractors that are different from the correct alternative in structural or semantic terms. If the test taker has a general idea of the type of response called for, such differences might give inadvertent clues that certain responses are wrong.

    For example, if the stem consists of a sentence with a word missing (i.e., cloze format), then all alternative responses should belong to the grammatical category needed to fill in the blank. For example:

- She walked _____ up the steps to the library.
  - a. weak
  - b. slowly*
  - c. try
  - d. wisdom

In this case, the test taker might recognize that an adverb is called for. Since *slowly* is the only adverb among the alternatives, it would be selected regardless of its meaning. This would be an appropriate set of distractors if you want to test the test takers' understanding that an adverb, and not some other part of speech, is called for in this gap.

In reading comprehension tasks, the distractors should refer to the text in some way. Alternatives that are totally unrelated to the stem can be eliminated by the test taker simply on the basis of general understanding. For example:

- Japan has few natural resources. To prosper and survive, the country must import raw materials, maintain high standards of manufacturing, and sell finished goods in foreign markets.

Japanese prosperity depends *most* on:

  - a. discovering new raw materials
  - b. importing manufactured goods
  - c. her people's religion
  - d. high levels of international trade*

In this item, distractor c. could be eliminated easily because it has no relationship to the text.

2. When the stems are incomplete statements that call for completion, use distractors that are grammatically compatible with the stem. For example, in the item on Japanese prosperity, if alternative (d) had read *to sell finished goods internationally,* the item would have been much more difficult and confusing to the test taker because the grammatical form of the alternative does not fit with the stem.

3. In principle, all distractors should be equally attractive and plausible to the test taker; that is to say, each distractor will be chosen equally often by test takers who do not choose the right answer. Distractors that are never or seldom chosen instead of the right answer are not serving any useful function. In practice, it is difficult to create distractors that are equally attractive, but some effort should be put into achieving this.

When devising distractors, it might be helpful to (a) define the grammatical or semantic category to which the distractors should belong, and (b) think of alternatives that have some association with the stem or correct choice. In order to determine the attractiveness of distractors, it is necessary to keep a record of how often each distractor for a given question is chosen.

One method of identifying distractors is to choose them from the errors that students make in their spoken or written use of the language. Choosing distractors in this way means that you are likely to include plausible distractors that are attractive to the students who do not know the right answer.

4. Choose distractors that can tell you something about where the students are going wrong if they select them. A related point, avoid trick alternatives that distract the test taker for trivial or unimportant reasons. For example:

- Definition item: to cook by exposing to direct heat

  a. roost
  b. burn
  c. broil*
  d. fry

Roost is a trivial and tricky distractor because it confuses word meaning and pronunciation in a way that is not useful. It was chosen because of its resemblance to *roast.*

5. Choose distractors that have comparable difficulty, complexity, and length. Distractors that are obviously different from the alternatives might be especially salient to the test taker with the result that they are more likely to be eliminated or accepted. For example:

Choose the best definition of the underlined word:

- Mary is a very *bright* student; she got As in all of her courses.

  a. difficult
  b. erudite*
  c. shiny
  d. friendly

Erudite is a poor alternative since it is a much more sophisticated word than the others and might be chosen for that reason alone.

6. Avoid including more than one correct alternative. In this regard, avoid distractors that might be correct in another dialect, regional variation, or modality of the language. For example, if you are testing spoken language, avoid using language in the distractors that might be considered appropriate in the written form of the language. An exception to this is if you want to test sociolinguistic skills. The best way to avoid more than one correct alternative is to have someone else review your test items.

There should be no "missing link" between the stem and the alternative responses that would make more than one of them correct. This can happen when students assume some additional plausible context. For example:

- He left the office early _____ he could do some shopping.

  a. so*
  b. if*
  c. unless
  d. that

In this item, both *so* and *if* could be correct depending on the context you have in mind.

7. Avoid using alternative answers that contain words or phrases that match the stem if the other alternatives do not contain similar matching elements. An alternative that matches the stem while others do not might be chosen on the basis of the matching elements alone. In some cases this might lead to a correct choice, whereas in other cases it can lead to an incorrect choice. This is particularly important in comprehension tests.

8. It should not be possible to choose the correct response on the basis of general knowledge. In other words, choosing the correct response should depend on the content of the test. One way of examining this possibility is to have someone answer the questions without reading or hearing the text. For example:

- When tourists from Canada go to Florida on vacation, they travel

  _____.

  a. north
  b. west
  c. east
  d. south*

9. The alternative responses should be as simple as possible in keeping with the complexity of the test purposes. Avoid repetitious wording, redundancy, and unnecessary detail in the responses. For example:

- Robert went to the hospital

  a. because he wanted to visit his sick brother
  b. because he wanted to have his leg examined
  c. because he was a volunteer worker in the gift shop
  d. because his brother has asked him to

In this case, it would be better to include all of the repetitious elements in the stem: Robert went to the hospital because. . . .

10. In reading comprehension tasks, when several items are based on a single text, the answer to one question should not be given by the wording of another. For example:

1. What did Mary serve Sam?

   a. leftover casserole
   b. scrambled eggs
   c. hamburger and fries
   d. fresh salmon*

2. Where did Sam go for dinner?

   a. to Mary's*
   b. home
   c. to the school cafeteria
   d. to Joe's Restaurant

11. Avoid answers that refer to several other answer choices. For example:

- She didn't go to the party because she _____

  a. was sick.
  b. had nothing to wear.
  c. was expecting an important call.
  d. b and c but not a.

Task 3

Have each student in the class write a multiple-choice question to test knowledge of some point in this chapter. Present your question to other students for review and feedback.

Assembling multiple-choice questions

The following are a number of points to take into consideration when putting multiple-choice items together for a test or examination.

1. Make sure the stem is distinct from the alternative answers. In written tests this can be achieved by inserting extra spaces between the stem and the alternative responses and by listing and indenting the alternatives on separate lines, as in the examples used in this chapter. In oral tests, the stem can be distinguished from the alternative responses by presenting the stem in one voice, say a female voice, and the alternatives in another voice, a male voice.

Poor presentation

- The population of Denmark is: (a) 2 million, (b) 4 million, (c) 7 million, (d) 15 million

Good presentation

- The population of Denmark is:

    a. 2 million
    b. 4 million
    c. 7 million
    d. 15 million

2. Identify the stems and alternatives using different symbols: for example, numbers for the stems and letters for the alternatives. When using separate answer sheets, make sure that your method of identifying stems and alternatives on the test corresponds to that presented on the students' answer sheet.

3. The correct alternative should occur equally frequently in each option position. Avoid presenting the correct choice in a particular position.

4. Use as many alternatives as are both possible and reasonable. The chances of selecting the correct alternative by guessing alone diminishes with more alternatives. With three alternatives, students have a 33% chance of getting the correct answer by guessing; with five alternatives, the chances of a correct response due to guessing is reduced to 20 percent. However, increasing the number of alternatives makes it increasingly difficult to construct plausible, attractive, and appropriate distractors.

5. Allow plenty of space between questions so that the test does not appear to be compressed and jammed together.

Summary

In this chapter, we discussed some factors to consider when choosing tasks to use in devising tests. We also presented guidelines for preparing closed-ended and open-ended test tasks. In the case of open-ended tasks, they took the form of general and specific questions to be asked about the demands posed by different tasks. Open-ended tasks can be easy to devise but time consuming to score. They often have the advantage of reflecting the way authentic language is used. In the case of closed-ended tasks, the guidelines we presented took the form of specific technical suggestions. It is important to recognize that the guidelines we presented for open-ended test tasks also apply to the preparation of closed-ended test tasks. Good closed-ended test tasks require considerable time and thought to prepare. Whether it is worth investing the time and thought needed to devise these kinds of tests depends on how the test results will be used and the importance of the decisions based on those results. Clearly, the investment of a great deal of time and thought is warranted when there are a large number of students to be tested. Another consideration when deciding whether to use a closed-ended test format is authenticity: arguably, many closed-ended test formats often do not reflect the way authentic language is used. They may nevertheless be useful for evaluating specific aspects of language learning. In some cases, closed-ended test tasks do call on the kinds of language performance your students will be expected to demonstrate. As in other aspects of classroom-based evaluation, one form of testing is not necessarily desirable under all circumstances and for all purposes. Rather, judicious use of each form may be called for.

Discussion questions

1. List as many possible language skills you can think of that can be assessed adequately using closed-ended response tasks. Now do the same for open-ended test tasks. In each case, limit yourself to five minutes. Then compare the kinds of language skills you have included in each category.
2. What are the advantages and disadvantages of using closed-ended tasks? open-ended tasks?
3. Devise a set of open-ended items for the same purpose. In order to do this, you will need to devise learning objectives associated with the content of this chapter. Try doing this individually, and then compare the objectives prepared by different students.
4. Select a multiple-choice test that you or others have used (this could be a standardized test), and then carefully examine the following aspects of the test using the guidelines suggested in this chapter: (a) the stems, (b) the alternative responses, (d) the instructions and answer sheet, and (e) the layout.
5. Are there other suggestions you would make for devising open-ended tasks in addition to those suggested in this chapter?
6. Have you ever devised a multiple-choice test? For what purpose? What did you find difficult about making it? What did you find useful about it? What were its limitations, if any, with respect to informing you about student achievement?

7. Select (or imagine) an open-ended test task you have used recently. How did you decide on the content and format of the test? On what basis did you devise your scoring scheme?

Readings

Airasian, P. (1991). Performance assessment. In P. Airasian (Ed.), *Classroom assessment* (pp. 251–306). New York: McGraw-Hill.

Annual Review of Applied Linguistics. (1995). *15.*

Carlson, S. B. (1985). *Creative classroom testing.* Princeton, N.J:. Educational Testing Service.

Carroll, B. J. (1980). *Testing communicative performance.* Oxford: Pergamon.

Carroll, B. J., and P. J. Hall. (1985). *Making your own language tests.* Oxford: Pergamon.

deJong, J. H. A. L., and D. K. Stevenson. (1990). *Individualizing the assessment of language abilities.* Clevedon, England: Multilingual Matters.

Fradd, S. H., P. L. McGee, and D. K. Wilen. (1994). *Instructional assessment: An integrative approach to evaluating students.* Reading, Mass.: Addison-Wesley.

Hamp-Lyons, E. (1991). *Assessing second language writing in academic contexts.* Norwood, N.J.: Ablex.

Hauptmann, P. C., R. Leblanc, and M. B. Wesche. (Eds). (1985). *Second language performance testing.* Ottawa: University of Ottawa Press.

Heaton, J. B. (1975). *Writing English language tests.* London: Longman.

Hughes, A. (1989). *Testing for language teachers.* Cambridge: Cambridge University Press.

Jacobs, H. L., S. A. Zinkgraf, D. R. Wormuth, V. F. Hartfiel, and J. B. Hughey. (1981). *Testing ESL composition: A practical approach.* Rowley, Mass.: Newbury House.

Madsen, H. S. (1983). *Techniques in testing.* New York: Oxford University Press.

Omaggio, A. C. (1983). *Proficiency-oriented classroom testing.* Washington, D.C.: Center for Applied Linguistics.

Underhill, N. (1987). *Testing spoken language: A handbook for oral testing techniques.* Cambridge: Cambridge University Press.

Valette, R. M. (1977). *Modern language testing.* New York: Harcourt Brace Jovanovich.

Weir, C. (1993). *Understanding and developing language tests.* New York: Prentice-Hall.

11 *Assembling and scoring tests*

- Introduction
- Time
- Grading accuracy and time
- Test instructions
- Layout and format
- Tips on scoring
- Summary

Preview questions

1. Do you advise students before a test of the content of the test and your scoring scheme? If not, why not? If you do, what are the advantages and disadvantages of doing this?
2. Do you think it is a good idea to give students lots of time to complete tests? Do you think too much time could be a bad thing? Why? When might it be advisable to limit the time students have to do a test?
3. How do you decide how much to include in a test? What do you do if the test was too long for the time allotted?
4. On average, how often do you test your students? How do you know when to test them? Do your students think you test too much or too little?
5. Do you think it is advisable to base students' grades on one final examination? If so, explain. If not, why not?
6. Have you ever taken a test that confused you because the layout or instructions were unclear? What specifically was the problem?
7. Do you think your familiarity with some of your students has an influence on your assessment of their achievement? If so, what steps could be taken to reduce this?

Introduction

In Chapter 9, we identified and described language learning objectives for use in testing, and in Chapter 10 we discussed types of test tasks that can be used to assess language learning. In this chapter, we consider how to turn tasks into tests. We first consider some general issues related to time allocations for testing. In a related vein, we then examine the complex relationship between reliability of test results and the length and number of tests. At issue here is how much effort should be expended in order to obtain reliable test results. Finally, we discuss instructions, layout and format, and scoring – the practical requirements of putting tasks together into efficient tests.

Time

Students often complain that they have too little time to complete tests. This is a natural reaction from students who believe that a little more time will allow them to get a few more questions correct, to score a few more points. In many instances, however, second language tests allow too much time. When this happens, students are able to treat test items as puzzles rather than as examples of authentic language use, much of which occurs under time constraints (e.g., speaking, listening, and some kinds of reading and writing tasks, such as taking notes in class or taking examinations). Not all language use is constrained by time, however, for example, writing letters or reports, reading for pleasure, and conversing with others. Thus, when deciding how much time to allocate for a test, one needs to consider whether the language skills one is testing normally occur with or without real time constraints. If they do not usually occur with time constraints, then you can be generous in your time allocations. If they usually are time constrained, then it is important to build such constraints into the timing of your test; otherwise, the kind of performance elicited from students will not be a good indicator of their language proficiency in authentic situations.

An additional consideration is the level of proficiency of the learners. Speed of performance or the ability to use language according to normal time constraints is probably more important when testing the achievement of relatively advanced second language learners. In general, the standards of performance for advanced learners should approximate those of native speakers, including the ability to use language fluently in a variety of authentic situations. In comparison, speed of performance may be less important when assessing the skills of beginning level learners. In these cases, whether certain skills have been learned at all and to what extent is probably of greater concern than the speed with which the learners can demonstrate their accomplishments.

Task 1

Identify authentic language tasks that are time constrained and then some that are not.

Grading accuracy and time

As noted earlier, one should be careful not to give so much time for tests which are intended to assess language skills and are normally time-constrained that students treat the test as a puzzle rather than an instance of authentic language use. At the same time, as a general rule, the longer a test, the more reliable it will be. In addition, tests that have been carefully constructed, edited, tried out, and revised will be more reliable than tests that have been prepared in a hurry. Also, test items that can be objectively scored tend to yield more reliable scores than do items that require more subjective judgment in their scoring. Multiple-choice items, however, are usually somewhat less reliable than limited-response items, despite their objective scoring, because of the opportunity for guessing. Higher reliability means greater accuracy of measurement, no matter what you are measuring. Obviously, high levels of reliability are desirable.

Reliability and, in turn, accuracy in assigning grades can also be enhanced, in general, by increasing the sources of information one uses to formulate grades. Of specific relevance to our present discussion, accuracy in assigning grades can be enhanced by increasing the number of tests and/ or quizzes students take. But how many are necessary for grading to be accurate? The answer to this question is not simple; moreover, there is no single answer.

Table 1 illustrates the relationship between the accuracy with which grades can be assigned, the number of tests and/or quizzes required to attain specific levels of accuracy, and reliability. In preparing Table 1, we have assumed a grading scale of A, B, C, D, and F, in which relatively few As and Fs are given, and the most frequent grade is C. Accuracy is expressed in column 1 in terms of percentage grading errors. You can interpret these

Table 1.   Relation between grading accuracy, number of quizzes and tests, and reliability

1 *Percent grading error*	*2* *Number of quizzes*	*3* *Number of tests*	*4* *Reliability*
5	201	42	.99
9	99	31	.98
15	38	14	.95
23*	18	4	.90
33	8	2	.80
40	5	1	.70
50	2		.50

*Fewer than one double error per thousand.

entries as follows: The first entry represents a situation in which 5 percent of students would be assigned an erroneous score, whereas the remaining 95 percent would be assigned a score that is an accurate reflection of their achievement; the second entry in column 1 corresponds to a situation in which 9 percent of students would receive an erroneous score, and 91 percent, their true score; and so on. We have indicated in column 1 when double grading errors are likely to occur: when the grading error exceeds 23 percent. Double grading errors occur when students are assigned grades that are two grades lower than their true grades; for example, giving a C to a student whose real accomplishments rate an A. Column 4 indicates the statistical reliability associated with each error rate; reliability is simply another way of estimating error rate.

Columns 2 and 3 in Table 1 indicate how many ten-minute quizzes and one-hour-long tests would be required to attain certain error (or, conversely, accuracy) rates. To calculate these estimates, we have assumed that, on average, a ten-minute teacher-made test has a reliability of .33, and a one-hour teacher-made test, a reliability of .70. From column 2, it can be seen that to have a 95 percent accuracy rate and only a 5 percent error rate would require giving 201 quizzes or 42 tests; this is clearly unrealistic. To achieve a 77 percent accuracy rate and a 23 percent error rate would require 18 quizzes or 4 one-hour tests. Thus, if you want to avoid double grading errors, you must give at least 18 quizzes or 4 tests; otherwise, you run the risk of assigning some students grades that are two full grades lower (or higher) than they deserve. To ensure accuracy of 33 percent, you must give 8 quizzes or 2 tests. Although the amount of testing involved in the latter example is realistic, there is a cost in accuracy: a 33 percent error rate.

What generalizations can we reach from this discussion of accuracy, reliability, and number of tests? First, it is clear that perfect accuracy and reliability are virtually impossible in educational measurement. Even respectably high levels of accuracy require a considerable commitment in time and energy to devising and administering tests. Clearly, teachers must budget time for testing if they are to achieve even minimal levels of acceptable accuracy in grading. At the same time, they must budget time for testing in accordance with their needs for the kinds of information tests can provide. Teachers should not use time for testing when there is no need for the information tests provide. Since testing time reduces instruction time, these competing demands must be reconciled.

Second, important decisions about students should never be made on the basis of their performance on one test or quiz since a single test is likely to result in a number of students being assigned inappropriate grades. Important decisions about students, such as promotion, should always be based on multiple indicators of performance, including multiple tests. Teachers can gain a great deal of useful data for assigning grades during instruction using the assessment methods discussed in Chapters 5 to 7. Carefully maintained records of student performance during classroom activities can supplement information derived from tests and thereby improve the accuracy of grading.

Third, we must recognize the limitations of test-based measurement and be sympathetic to our students who often feel misjudged by the tests they take.

Test instructions

The primary job of test instructions is to let students know what they are supposed to do. We want to discover what students have learned, not how well they can understand test instructions or how well they can guess what they are supposed to do. They should be informed clearly what to do for each kind of task included in the test, and they should get enough information about the test as a whole to decide how best to expend their efforts in the time available. The instructions themselves should not be a test; in other words, instructions should be clear and meaningful to students. To achieve this, it might be useful, in some cases, to prepare the test instructions for students with a common first language in their native language. Clearly, this strategy is not feasible when a test is used for speakers of different languages. You will have to be doubly alert to potential problems with your instructions in such cases. Use the simplest and most straightforward language possible. It is always advisable to have someone else read or listen to your instructions before using them with your students in order to ensure that they are understandable.

General instructions for a test should provide students with general information that will orient them to the tasks ahead. Here is a brief list of some of the most important items to include in general instructions:

1. Purpose of the test: Is it for grades? for assessing program effectiveness only? for planning individual activities? or something else?
2. Weighting of test – this is especially important if it is to contribute to students' final grades
3. Time available or required for taking the test
4. Number of parts or blocks (sets of different task types) included in the test
5. Special test conditions, that is, things that are ordinarily allowed in your class but will not be allowed for the test. This includes activities such as talking with other students, referring to textbooks or notes, and so on.

It is also wise to include the following information where appropriate:

6. The kinds of input the student will have to work with (texts, written questions, an interlocutor, drawings, and so forth)
7. The kinds of responses expected (speech, writing, physical action, grading choices, and so on)
8. The extent of response expected: For example, in a role play of two students meeting in the school corridor, do you want (a) a strictly social exchange of a couple of turns by each speaker, or (b) a discussion of several minutes' duration, or (c) something else?
9. The procedures for recording their answers or responses: For example, a block of questions may require use of an answer sheet, whereas another block of items requires a tape recorder.
10. What the assessor will look for when scoring; this may be obvious for multiple-choice tasks, but in a composition, for example, will marks be awarded on the basis of spelling, grammatical accuracy, fluency, ideas, coherence, or authenticity?

The purpose of block instructions is to inform students of requirements of the task types that make up a block of the test. Block instructions should include the following information where applicable:

1. Time limits for the block and for subsections within a block
2. The number of marks allocated to the block
3. The number of marks allocated to items within the block
4. Special test conditions for the block

It makes sense to write out test instructions for older learners who are taking written tests. It can also be effective to give a set of written instructions to students who will be taking a test that is entirely oral. Written instructions seem to be especially calming for language learners beyond primary school. Regardless of whether instructions are given in writing, aloud, or both, all students must be given the opportunity to confirm their understanding of the instructions before they proceed. This is particularly important if the test is different from what students are accustomed to.

Two final suggestions to keep in mind: First, when students are already familiar with the task type – because it is used as a regular classroom activity – elaborate instructions may not be needed. Beware, however, of task types that are superficially identical to classroom activities. Elaborate instructions may be needed to point out the differences – and even then many students may revert to familiar methods before they have completed the block.

Second, one example can do the job of pages of instructions. Use examples whenever possible. If you are using a new test task but cannot think of an effective way to give an example, either prepare the students during class before giving the test or find an alternative task.

It can be difficult to identify all the information students might need to understand particular test tasks. Each test has its own requirements. Therefore, it is necessary for you to tailor instructions for the tests you use. Instructions are largely a matter of common sense – one tells the students what they need to know in order to do their best when taking a test. Nonetheless, teachers and even professional test publishers often produce tests with inadequate instructions. When students don't know what to do and must guess, they often make the wrong guesses. And when they guess wrong, tests will not tell you what you want to know about student achievement. If instructions are not good, the reliability and validity of student scores are invariably lowered.

Task 2

Are there circumstances in which it might not be advisable to inform students of the mark distribution for a test? Explain.

Layout and format

In this section, we talk about layout and format. As with instructions, our concern with layout and format is aimed at helping students demonstrate their attainment of instructional objectives. Like instructions, layout and format are also largely matters of common sense. But, whereas instructions – including the use of examples – are directed toward preventing wrong guesses about task requirements, layout and format are directed towards removing distractions. Even the best-informed student can be distracted.

Crowding

One of the most frequently encountered problems with teacher-made tests is a crowded page that is hard to read. Students can skip lines in reading, omit questions, write over things they haven't yet read, and so on – all because of crowded pages. White space between instructions and written test material and between the written questions themselves will make a real difference in the efficiency of test takers. One also needs to be careful about temporal crowding. For example, imagine the effect on two students in a crowded schedule of interviews with the teacher: The first student hasn't finished when the next student knocks at the door; the student at the door – who has come on time – is ready to go but has to stand in the hall and wait.

Ordering blocks of items

The same kinds of tasks or items should be kept together. For example, imagine that you are assessing pronunciation and comprehension skills. Your test includes two kinds of tasks for assessing each skill area (e.g., an imitation task and a naming task). It is preferable to group all items of the same type together – all imitation items together and all naming items together. It is best not to put the two pronunciation subtests together into a section and the comprehension subtests together in another even though this groups the skills together. This arrangement may be good for you for scoring pronunciation and listening skills. It is not good for the students, however, because it requires that they switch back and forth between the demands of each task type. Each change of mental gears that is entailed by a change in task type takes time and energy and introduces an occasion for students to go astray.

A more significant question concerns ordering of the blocks themselves. Which should come first? second? last? Here are some common ways of organizing blocks. Unfortunately, they do not always yield the same advice.

• Efficiency ordering   Order the blocks so that the one in which students can gain the greatest number of points in the least amount of time comes first. This would suggest that a block consisting of multiple-choice items would generally come first. (Of course, potential points per unit time depend upon both the marks allocated to the block *and* the time required to do the block.)

• Facility ordering   Order the blocks so that the one that you think will yield the best level of performance comes first. The other blocks follow until the one on which you believe performance will be poorest. This is to increase the likelihood that all students will get a chance to work at the blocks on which they will perform best.

• Difficulty ordering   This is just the opposite of facility ordering. The idea is to have students tackle the toughest tasks while they are freshest.

• Reactive ordering   If performance on block A is likely to have an adverse effect on students' performance on block B, then put block B before A. This seems an entirely reasonable principle but one we seldom pay attention to. For example, if a test requires students to answer a set of comprehension questions about a text and also to write a summary of the text, we might guess the following: The set of comprehension questions might make certain information in the text especially salient even though some of this information is not central. The students might then be likely to include the salient, but unimportant, information in their summaries. The summaries might not have included the extraneous matter had the comprehension questions been addressed afterward.

Reactive ordering seems the most difficult to figure out. It requires a critical and imaginative examination of test blocks. It is worth looking for, however, and it could be used to modify any of the other methods of ordering blocks we have described. Efficiency and facility ordering tend to yield somewhat similar arrangements of blocks. There are not many advocates of difficulty ordering, but that does not mean it is necessarily inappropriate in all situations. Consider each of these alternative ways of ordering and select the one that is most appropriate for your test and your students.

Ordering items

Item ordering refers to the way the items or tasks within a block are ordered. Two different procedures – with one thing in common – are suggested here. They both advocate starting the block with the easiest tasks or items. This makes sense for a number of reasons: it gives students confidence that they can perform tasks of this type; it gives them practice with some easy tasks; and it helps settle them down. We also encourage you to include one or two very easy, unscored items at the beginning of a block if the items take *very* little time. There is a difference of opinion about how to order the remaining items in the block.

• Facility ordering   Continue to order items according to your estimate of how well students will perform. The rationale for this procedure is that we want students to have maximum opportunity to try the items that they should do best on. This is an appealing rationale when test blocks are individually timed. The rationale suggests application of this procedure to the final block when there is a time limit for the entire test, but blocks do not have their own time limits.

• Random ordering   Following the initial easy items, put the remainder in random order. The rationale for this procedure is that students tend to become discouraged after encountering a series of items they cannot perform. Confidence, attention, and effort flag, and they fail items that they might otherwise have passed. If they see that relatively easy items can follow more difficult ones, they remain engaged and alert until the end.

There is no proof of the superiority of either of these methods. We find, however, the rationale for random ordering more persuasive when time limits or fatigue is not at issue.

Tips on scoring

Finally, some suggestions for scoring tests. Closed-ended test tasks can be scored easily and objectively because the range of possible responses is limited and the scoring criteria are straightforward. Limited-response tasks and especially open-ended test tasks, in comparison, are subjective and generally call for considerable judgment. It is necessary, when working with open-ended and limited-response tasks, to decide how to score students' work. There are two general types of scoring to choose from: *holistic* and *analytic*. In holistic scoring, a single score is assigned to a student's overall test performance. This is basically what teachers do when they assign number or letter grades to student tests, such as compositions. Holistic scores represent teachers' overall impressions and judgments. As such, they can serve as general incentives for learning, and they can distinguish students with respect to their general achievement in a particular skills area. However, because they provide no detailed information about specific aspects of performance, they are not very useful in guiding teaching and learning.

In analytic scoring, different components or features of the students' responses are given separate scores (on an essay, spelling, grammar, organization, and punctuation might be scored separately). An example of an analytic system for scoring ESL compositions is presented in Figure 1. The American Council on the Teaching of Foreign Languages has developed a comprehensive and detailed set of scoring criteria for the assessment of foreign language proficiency (see *ACTFL* in the list of additional readings). Individual analytic scores are sometimes added together to yield a total (holistic) score, but they are generally kept separate and form what is sometimes called a performance or test *profile*. The scoring categories included in an analytic system should reflect instructional objectives and plans. Determining levels of performance for each category generally reflects teachers' expectations, based on past experience, of previous students' performance. Analytic scoring provides useful feedback to students and diagnostic information to teachers about specific areas of performance that are satisfactory or unsatisfactory. This information can be useful for planning instruction and studying.

ESL COMPOSITION PROFILE

STUDENT   DATE   TOPIC

	SCORE	LEVEL	CRITERIA	COMMENTS
CONTENT		30–27	EXCELLENT TO VERY GOOD: knowledgeable • substantive • thorough development of thesis • relevant to assigned topic	
		26–22	GOOD TO AVERAGE: some knowledge of subject • adequate range • limited development of thesis • mostly relevant to topic, but lacks detail	
		21–17	FAIR TO POOR: limited knowledge of subject • little substance • inadequate development of topic	
		16–13	VERY POOR: does not show knowledge of subject • non-substantive • not pertinent • OR not enough to evaluate	
ORGANIZATION		20–18	EXCELLENT TO VERY GOOD: fluent expression • ideas clearly stated/supported • succinct • well-organized • logical sequencing • cohesive	
		17–14	GOOD TO AVERAGE: somewhat choppy • loosely organized but main ideas stand out • limited support • logical but incomplete sequencing	
		13–10	FAIR TO POOR: non-fluent • ideas confused or disconnected • lacks logical sequencing and development	
		9–7	VERY POOR: does not communicate • no organization • OR not enough to evaluate	
VOCABULARY		20–18	EXCELLENT TO VERY GOOD: sophisticated range • effective word/idiom choice and usage • word form mastery • appropriate register	
		17–14	GOOD TO AVERAGE: adequate range • occasional errors of word/idiom form, choice, usage *but meaning not obscured*	
		13–10	FAIR TO POOR: limited range • frequent errors of word/idiom form, choice, usage • *meaning confused or obscured*	
		9–7	VERY POOR: essentially translation • little knowledge of English vocabulary, idioms, word form • OR not enough to evaluate	
LANGUAGE USE		25–22	EXCELLENT TO VERY GOOD: effective complex constructions • few errors of agreement, tense, number, word order/function, articles, pronouns, prepositions	
		21–18	GOOD TO AVERAGE: effective but simple constructions • minor problems in complex constructions • several errors of agreement, tense, number, word order/function, articles, pronouns, prepositions *but meaning seldom obscured*	
		17–11	FAIR TO POOR: major problems in simple/complex constructions • frequent errors of negation, agreement, tense, number, word order/function, articles, pronouns, prepositions and/or fragments, run-ons, deletions • *meaning confused or obscured*	
		10–6	VERY POOR: virtually no mastery of sentence construction rules • dominated by errors • does not communicate • OR not enough to evaluate	
MECHANICS		5	EXCELLENT TO VERY GOOD: demonstrates mastery of conventions • few errors of spelling, punctuation, capitalization, paragraphing	
		4	GOOD TO AVERAGE: occasional errors of spelling, punctuation, capitalization, paragraphing *but meaning not obscured*	
		3	FAIR TO POOR: frequent errors of spelling, punctuation, capitalization, paragraphing • poor handwriting • *meaning confused or obscured*	
		2	VERY POOR: no mastery of conventions • dominated by errors of spelling, punctuation, capitalization, paragraphing • handwriting illegible • OR not enough to evaluate	

TOTAL SCORE   READER   COMMENTS

Figure 1   ESL composition profile. [From H. L. Jacobs et al., Testing ESL composition: A practical approach. *Rowley, Mass.: Newbury House.]*

Task 3

Identify a language skill, such as writing a science report, and then devise (a) a holistic scoring procedure including assessment criteria and (b) an analytic scoring procedure. Discuss the benefits and limitations of each.

A number of general scoring tips are suggested below:

1. Identify the features or qualities of good answers and communicate this information to the students before the test and again at the time of testing. The test instructions should contain a description of what criteria will be important when scoring the test. Examiners should do this ahead of time so that they can be sure the test lends itself to testing the features or qualities of interest. Students need to know what will be examined beforehand so they know what is important and where they should direct their study time. In the absence of such knowledge, students are left to guess what is important.

2. Establish the actual scoring scheme in advance and communicate this to the students. Decide whether to use analytic or holistic scoring. Other decisions involve how many points or what value each test item, section of the test, or aspect of performance contributes to the total score.

3. If there is more than one open-ended task on the test, score each student's answers to the first one before proceeding to the next one, and so on. This will make scoring more efficient and more objective since you need to work with only one set of standards or scoring criteria at a time. Scoring criteria can also be applied more consistently if this procedure is used. It also reduces the influence of positive or negative effects that result from scoring one answer before scoring another.

4. Whenever possible, reread open-ended test answers to check the reliability of your scoring, especially if important decisions are to be made based on the scores (e.g., decisions about promotion to the next grade or level based on end-of-year examinations). Ideally, this should be done by another teacher, although it is often impractical. At the very least, some sample of open-ended test answers should be reread to assess reliability.

5. Whenever possible, blind reading of answers to open-ended test tasks is recommended to avoid bias that is unrelated to the skills being assessed. This can be done by having students write their names on the backs of their answer books. However, even this method will not always work –

teachers become familiar with their students' handwriting as the course progresses, so the identity of the test taker may be evident even if names are not visible. And, of course, blind scoring of oral language tests is difficult unless samples of the students' oral language skills are tape-recorded, coded, and scored later. Once again, however, teachers can identify their students by voice alone once they have come to know them well.

Task 4

Devise holistic and analytic scoring procedures for the accompanying composition.[1] Discuss how you chose the qualities and levels of performance for scoring. Then compare the merits of each type of score from the points of view of (a) students and (b) teachers.

The role of agriculture in my country today

the role of agriculture in my country today is making a great development because is the principal industrial exportation. the first product that we produce is the coffee. this is an important product that we have because is ussualy consumed by the people. We are in the fourth position within the world of production of coffee.

Other product very important is "cotton" in the agriculture in my country. others are corn, sugar, bananas, etc.

My country is very small. It has an extension about eight thousand miles. Its name is El Salvador that is located in Central America.

The agriculture needs manteinance by many people. Our exportation is very little unless you think in coffee. In my country we have many volcanoes to cultive different products like coffee, bananas and many kind of fruit to bring them to the principal towns. Fishes and shrimps are getting in our coasts. Other principal thing is the cabbage that we have in our country the weather doesn't help the cultives in the coast just in tropical or cool parts of our territory.

to finish we, have many kinds of products in our country that help the founds to the state.

---

1 From H. L. Jacobs et al., *Testing ESL composition: A practical approach.* Rowley, Mass.: Newbury House.

Summary

In this chapter, we pointed out that authentic use of language is often time constrained and that, therefore, you should avoid giving students so much time to complete a test that they treat it like a puzzle to be solved. Clearly, this is more true for some kinds of language skills than for others – oral language use, for example, is often time constrained, whereas many forms of writing, such as writing business reports, are relatively unconstrained by time. Thus, judgment is called for when allocating time for different kinds of test tasks.

We also pointed out that the reliability and accuracy of test scores increases as the number of items in the test increases. Likewise, the accuracy of grade assignments increases as the number of tests that determine the grades increases. Thus, on the one hand, it is generally advisable to have more rather than fewer items in a test and to base your grades on several tests rather than on a single test. Whether it is worthwhile to increase the number of test items or to increase the number of tests depends on the significance of the decision to be made. Important decisions call for reliable tests and multiple sources of information. In this regard, the reliability and validity of such decisions can be enhanced by using information about student performance that is provided by the alternative methods of assessment discussed in Chapters 5 to 7, including observation, portfolios, conferences, and journals. Such data are useful for grading purposes to the extent that careful and systematic records have been kept.

We emphasized the importance of clear and well-considered instructions, layouts, and scoring procedures. These are largely a matter of common sense, and we encourage teachers to take the time when assembling tests to think about each carefully.

Discussion questions

1. If you assign final grades, how do you take into account the performance of students throughout the year or course? How could you do this better?
2. Based on the material in this chapter, do you think you test frequently enough to make reliable and valid grading decisions? Do you think you test too frequently?
3. Select a test you have recently used and examine it critically from the point of view of the instructions and the layout. Are there improvements that could be made?
4. How do you usually order items in your tests? Would you change the way you do this based on your reading of this chapter? Are there other

factors to consider when ordering test items in addition to those discussed in this chapter?
5. Do you check the reliability of your scoring of open-ended test questions? If so, how do you do it? When would it be most advisable to do this? Share your responses with other students in the course, if you are reading this book as part of a course on second language evaluation.
6. What kind of grading system do you use, if you use one? How do you assign students to each grade level (that is, what are the standards of performance you expect of a student at each level)? How do your tests and the scoring of your tests reflect these standards?
7. How do you assign scores (grades) to open-ended test tasks that you use? Do you use the results of these tests to modify your instruction or simply to assign grades?

Readings

Airasian, P. (1991). Paper-and-pencil test questions. In P. Airasian (Ed.), *Classroom assessment* (pp. 195–250). New York: McGraw-Hill.

American Council on the Teaching of Foreign Languages. (1986). *ACTFL proficiency guidelines*. New York: American Council on the Teaching of Foreign Languages.

Airasian, P. (1991). Grading pupil performance. In P. Airasian (Ed.), *Classroom assessment* (pp. 307–353). New York: McGraw-Hill.

Finocchiaro, M., and S. Sako. (1983). Grading systems for proficiency tests. In M. Finocchiaro & S. Sako (Eds.), *Foreign language testing: A practical approach*. New York: Regents.

Hopkins, C. D., and L. A. Richards. (1990). Marks and marking plans. In C. D. Hopkins and L. A. Richards (Eds.), *Classroom measurement and evaluation* (pp. 404–436). Itasca, Ill.: F. E. Peacock.

Jacobs, H. L., S. A. Zinkgraf, D. R. Wormuth, V. F. Hartfiel, and J. B. Hughey. (1981). *Testing ESL composition: A practical approach*. Rowley, Mass.: Newbury House.

Shohamy, E., and R. Reves. (1985). Authentic language tests: Where from and where to? *Language Testing, 2,* 48–59.

Underhill, N. (1987). Marking systems. In *Testing spoken language: A handbook for oral testing techniques*. Cambridge: Cambridge University Press.

12 *Interpreting test scores*

- Introduction
- Frames of reference for score interpretation
- Interpreting count and rating scores
- Developing meaningful interpretations of count scores
- Establishing other decision criteria
- Summary

Preview questions

1. Is it easier for students to argue about grades given on open-ended or closed-ended tests? Why? How can you minimize, or at least reduce, the likelihood that students will disagree with the grades you assign on open-ended tests?
2. How do you decide how difficult or easy to make a test? What do you do if the test appears to have been too easy or too hard?
3. Have you ever used a standardized test? Did you find the scores from these tests meaningful or useful? If yes, explain. If not, why not?
4. When a school or school district says that students must get a grade of 70 percent in order to pass, what does this mean? 70 percent of what?
5. Is it ever appropriate for all students in a class to get perfect or very high scores on a test? Explain.
6. If you are scoring students' essays, how would you assign grades? In other words, how do you know which essays should get high marks, which low marks, and which in-between?
7. What do you personally find to be the most difficult part of grading students?
8. Does your school or school district provide guidelines or requirements with respect to assigning grades? If so, what aspects of these guidelines do you agree with and disagree with, and why?

Introduction

In this chapter, we are concerned with interpreting test scores. We describe how they can and cannot be interpreted and explain two methods of providing interpretations for certain kinds of test scores that might otherwise be difficult to interpret meaningfully.

Test score interpretation generally depends on two factors: the frame of reference for the scores and the type of scores that are being interpreted. It also depends on how the test has been constructed.

Frames of reference for score interpretation

One way of interpreting test scores requires that we know the results of other learners who have taken the same test we are interested in. For example, if we know that the average score of tenth grade students on a reading test is 62, we can then interpret the scores of other students. Students who get a score of 62 on the test can be said to be reading at the level of the average tenth grade student, and those with scores higher or lower than 62 can be said to be reading above and below, respectively, the level of an average tenth grade student. Such norm-referenced interpretation of test scores requires that we know a great deal about how different students perform on a test, such as their grade level and even general language ability, if we are to be able to interpret the scores our students might obtain.

You are probably most familiar with norm-referenced score interpretation for standardized tests. In the case of standardized tests, there are formal statistical procedures for developing norm-referenced scores. Teachers often use a kind of informal norm referencing to interpret their students' scores on classroom tests. This happens when teachers interpret the test performance of their current students on the basis of their experiences with similar students in the past. In these cases, teachers have a kind of "mental norm" built up over the years that they use to interpret the performance of their current students. This sort of informal norm-referenced interpretation is useful for instructional planning to the extent that the mental norms include clear and specific indications of what constitutes good and poor performance. Interpretations based on unspecific mental impressions of normal student performance are not useful for instructional planning precisely because they are so general.

From an instructional point of view, it is important to understand that norm-referenced score interpretation permits you to assess the performance of students relative to some comparison group, but it does not usually permit you to identify specifically what students have or have not learned. Thus, it does not enable you to isolate aspects of instruction that need additional attention in order to enhance student achievement. Domain-referenced and objectives-referenced methods of score interpretation are useful for this purpose.

In principle, because domain-referenced tests reflect well-defined domains of skill or knowledge, they allow you to say that a given score represents achievement of some percentage of the domain. Similarly, since objectives-referenced tests represent certain instructional objectives, they permit you to interpret a score as acquisition of some percentage of what one is trying to teach. However, this is not always so straightforward. Objectives-referenced tests can be constructed to be more or less specific in focus and more or less difficult. The difficulty level of a test and the specificity of the content affect the kinds of interpretations of test results that are possible.

A classroom test that focuses on a specific and limited domain or set of objectives permits relatively specific interpretations of how much has been learned or how well it has been learned, assuming, of course, that the test is a fair and representative sample of the objectives and you have observed all the other features of good classroom test construction. In comparison, a generalized test is less amenable to such interpretations. However, even a test that focuses on a specific and limited objective or domain cannot be interpreted unambiguously with respect to level of mastery of the objective. The level of difficulty of the test also influences the sorts of interpretations that are possible.

There is no one way to assess a particular objective or set of objectives. A given objective can be tested using a relatively easy or difficult task. Of course, a difficult task will produce lower levels of student performance than an easy one. Student performance in this case would be influenced by both their level of mastery of the objective being tested and the difficulty of the task. Indeed, a very difficult test task could depress student performance so much that it might appear that no one has mastered the objective at all. In comparison, tests that focus on specific and limited content and are also sufficiently easy for all students – if they have attained the objective – are best for providing relatively unequivocal interpretations of mastery of objectives, provided they are an adequate sample of the objective being assessed. These are called *mastery tests.*

Mastery tests are constructed to determine if a minimum level of attainment of a particular objective or set of objectives has been reached. They are constructed so that most students are expected to perform at or near ceiling (maximum level). If, in fact, all or most students perform at ceiling on the test, then you know that your instructional objective has been reached by all or most students, and you can proceed with the next unit or lesson. However, if many students do not perform at ceiling, then you know that some modification of instruction is called for if students are to attain the objective. If only one or a few students fail to perform at ceiling, then you know that individualized instruction is advisable in order to bring these students up to mastery level. In this way, mastery tests can aid in formative instructional evaluation.

Mastery tests are most useful for the following:

1. Providing feedback for general instructional planning.
2. Assessing student achievement in an area in which all students are expected to perform at some minimum level (such as in a screening test).
3. Determining whether all students have acquired knowledge or skills that are prerequisites to undertaking new learning.
4. Individualizing instruction in which each student is assessed at the end of each unit of instruction.

Classroom tests need not always be easy. They can be designed to be of medium or high levels of difficulty with respect to a specific or general set of objectives. Such tests permit one to ascertain the students' complete range of attainment, including the top levels. Because they are relatively easy, mastery tests put a ceiling on the highest level of performance that can be demonstrated. Since tests of medium or high difficulty do not do this, they are sometimes referred to as *open-ended tests,* not to be confused with open-ended test tasks. In addition to assessing the complete range of achievement among students, open-ended tests permit one to differentiate among students in terms of their achievement. In comparison, mastery tests aim for uniformly good levels of performance.

Open-ended tests are useful for:

1. Summative evaluation of units of instruction for purposes of general instructional planning.
2. Summative evaluation of overall instruction at the end of a course with no intention that the feedback provided be used to modify instruction for the current students.
3. Summative student achievement of general instructional objectives at the end of the year or course for purposes of assigning grades.

The general point here is that the interpretations that can be made of classroom test scores depend on how the test is constructed – as a mastery test or as an open-ended test. Mastery tests lend themselves to interpretations in terms of mastery of instructional objectives and, therefore, the effectiveness of instruction. Open-ended tests lend themselves to interpretations in terms of the range of achievement among students and individual differences in achievement among students. Each kind of test, and its associated interpretations, is useful for most teachers at certain times. Which one you use and when you use it will depend on the interpretations you seek. To be of maximum benefit, the results of classroom tests should evaluate both student achievement and the effectiveness of instruction.

Interpreting count and rating scores

Test score interpretation is also affected by the nature of the scores. Generally speaking, the scores derived from objectives-referenced tests can be classified as either counts or ratings. Most scores based on ratings have built-in bases for interpretation, whereas some scores based on counts do not; therefore, bases for interpretation need to be provided. In this section, we discuss the characteristics of these types of scores and examine how to interpret them.

Words in a composition can be counted, and so can the number of correct items in a spelling test or the number of minutes a student speaks. Many other aspects of performance can be counted, but not all. The quality of an essay can be indicated by a number – a score – but that score is a rating, not a count. Most scores that indicate the quality of language performance are ratings. Ratings can be based on sophisticated guidelines, or they can be highly impressionistic. In either case, ratings are different from counts, and, in most cases, interpretation is built into the rating procedure, explicitly or implicitly. In contrast, counts derived from open-ended tests require interpretation; they cannot be interpreted in any simple fashion as a percentage of the objectives that have been mastered. Consequently, we need procedures for interpreting such count scores. We describe two such procedures shortly. But first, we discuss further the distinction between count and rating scores and why the latter but not the former usually includes built-in bases for interpretation.

Let us illustrate this difference using our earlier distinctions between closed-ended, limited-response, and open-ended test types. Scores from closed-ended tests are generally counts. The students' answers or choices are marked "right" or "wrong," and their scores on such a test are a count of the number of answers they got right. Sometimes, certain items in a closed-ended test may have different weights. In such cases, the score is the count of right choices multiplied by the weights for each of those items. Even when items are weighted, the final numbers are count scores.

Limited-response tests are also often scored as counts. Like closed-ended test items, limited-response items can be scored dichotomously as right or wrong. Some limited-response items may be scaled. That is, a score of 0, 1, or 2, for example, may be awarded to a single item. Usually no more than three or four scaled scores (including 0) are possible for a single limited-response item. Sometimes these scores represent counts (for example, if the item asks for two synonyms for "hurry"). Each synonym supplied would be credited one point. Or one point could be given for the discourse appropriateness of a response, another for grammatical accuracy.

Regardless of whether limited-response items are scored right or wrong or are scaled, the test scores are sums of the individual item scores. In this respect, scores from closed-ended tests and limited-response tests are derived in the same way. And the scores on both types of tests will be generally high or low depending on whether the test writer has produced items that are generally easy or hard. If the scores are derived from mastery tests, as discussed in the preceding section, then an interpretation with respect to achievement of a specified objective or content can be made easily. However, if the scores are derived from open-ended tests, there is no simple way to arrive at a content-referenced interpretation. We need a method of interpreting them that goes beyond the scores themselves. In the section that follows, we describe two procedures that provide meaningful interpretations of such scores.

In yet other instances, limited-response items might be rated to represent different degrees of quality of a response. For example, in a reading test question that asks for the major cause of some event reported in the text, one could award two points to students who give the major cause and one point to students who cite a secondary cause. Similarly, scores on open-ended tests are often based on ratings. Sometimes a number of different ratings are applied to the same task and then aggregated to form a single score. For example, an interview may be rated on the following qualities: fluency, grammatical accuracy, social appropriateness, pronunciation, and range of vocabulary. The scales used with open-ended tasks may have scores of 0–5, 0–10, 1–6, and so on. When several scales are used with a single task, the individual scale scores are sometimes added to yield an overall score for the task. In addition, ratings for several tasks may be added to yield a total test score.

Each level of a rating scale is often defined explicitly: For example, 5 on an oral proficiency scale ranging from 1 to 5 may equate to "expresses himself/herself like a native speaker with no discernible signs of accent or non-native usage." Each student's performance is compared to the definitions provided for each level. The performance is given the rating corresponding to the level whose definition best describes it. In effect, these explicit definitions are like standards of performance. Even when there are not explicit definitions of each level of rating, there is usually an implicit understanding of what each level means. The important point here is that interpretations are built into the rating procedure that results in assigning scores.

Another means of scoring open-ended tasks that includes interpretation as part of the scoring procedure deserves special attention and works as follows: Many school systems have conventional meanings for assigning marks. For example, 50 or 60 means that a student has attained a passing knowledge, and 90 means that the student has excelled. In such settings, a teacher can examine a student essay and decide on the quality of the work:

Does it look like a bare pass? Is the work clearly above the expected minimum? Is it a truly excellent essay? Once teachers have made a decision about quality, they can then express their assessment by means of the conventional numbers or grades. Note that these numbers do not represent counts of anything; they are merely synonyms for qualitative statements. In other words, these are not scores like the other scores we have considered; they do not have to be interpreted. Note also that a score of, say, 70 cannot be interpreted as knowledge of 70 percent of course objectives. Nothing has been counted to arrive at that number.

Teachers generally feel comfortable with this method of scoring. With experience, they develop a sense of what constitutes reasonable expectations of students in their classes; thus they can articulate the skills or knowledge students need in order to get specific scores. As we shall see, we can use this sense that teachers have acquired in order to develop interpretations of scores derived from counts on open-ended tests.

Generally speaking, scores can be classified as counts or ratings. Rating scores can usually be interpreted with reference to the descriptors that accompany each rating value. In this sense, they can be said to have built-in interpretations. Count scores based on mastery tests can also be interpreted in a relatively straightforward fashion – that is, with reference to mastery or nonmastery of the objective being tested. Count scores derived from open-ended tests, however, cannot be interpreted in either of these ways and require another means of interpretation.

Task 1

List some examples of count scores and rating scores you have used. What are the advantages and disadvantages of each?

Developing meaningful interpretations of count scores

In this section, we describe two procedures for giving meaningful interpretations to count scores based on open-ended tests. These procedures are not simple. They require, at a minimum, teachers who know their courses and what they are trying to accomplish and who know about the abilities of students who typically take the course. This means that these procedures are of limited use to inexperienced teachers or to those who are new to a course. For that reason, if they wish to use these procedures, new teachers should try to work together with experienced colleagues when developing interpretations of scores for important tests. In fact, we advocate that anyone using these procedures do so in groups whenever feasible.

The borderline student procedure

The essence of this procedure is to imagine a narrowly defined group of students and then to imagine how they would perform on each item of a test. It can be used for developing interpretations of scores for screening and placement tests or for tests of student achievement in a course. In each case, it is possible to develop interpretations that are appropriate to the kinds of decisions to be made. We begin with an example of a teacher deciding on a passing score for a classroom test, followed by a more formal screening example.

SETTING PASSING SCORES FOR CLASSROOM TESTS

We illustrate this procedure with an example of a teacher deciding informally on the passing score, a grade of C, for an examination she has just prepared. The teacher's exam has forty items in two sections of twenty items each. The first section, administered in the language lab, requires the students to tape brief answers to questions the teacher will pose about their homes and families, school life, interests, and leisure activities. Each response is scored from 0 to 3, with one point for understanding the question (that is, giving a factually appropriate answer), one point for a response that has no major formal error, and one point for an answer that is socially appropriate.

The second section requires students to read four short texts and then write short answers to five questions about each text. Responses are scored 0 to 2, with one point given for a right answer to the question and one point for writing a complete sentence with no major structural error or misuse of vocabulary. The maximum possible score on the test is, therefore, 80. The question the teacher has to answer is, What score should a student achieve in order to earn a grade of just C on the exam?

Because the teacher has taught this course before, she is able to remember a number of students who were true borderline learners; when they were in her class, she could never be sure whether their work would be good enough to pass. In fact, some of them had just made it, but not all of them did. For a while, the teacher reflects on those borderline students, remembering their strengths and weaknesses, their failures, and their successes. Then, with that group of students in mind, she scrutinizes the exam she has just prepared.

For each item in the exam, the teacher imagines how her borderline students would have done; she tries to figure how many of them would have earned each available point on the test. She looks at the first item, "What's your name?" (an easy question that all of the borderline students would probably understand and answer accurately). Everyone would earn the first point, so she writes down, next to item 1, the number 1 as the expected score (on average) for understanding. For the second available point, she decides that nine out of ten of her borderline students would make no major errors in their replies; perhaps one in ten would answer, "Your name is . . . " when referring to himself. She writes .9, also next to item 1, as the expected score, on average, for the second available point. Next she considers the point for social appropriateness and guesses that more than half of her borderline students would answer inappropriately, usually too formally, with, "My name is . . ," rather than "It's . . ," or with just their names. Together with her 1 and her .9, she writes down .4 as the expected value for the third available point on the first item. Adding these numbers (1 + .9 + .4 = 2.3), she sees that borderline students should average 2.3 points on the first item. Of course, no individual could get that fractional score. It would be the average for borderline students. Clearly failing students would average lower, and above average students would average higher.

The teacher goes through the entire exam in this fashion, trying to imagine what the borderline students would do for each item and recording the scores they would probably get, on average. Then all of the expected values are added up. The result is the teacher's best estimate of the total test score that would be achieved by a student who is right on the line between passing and failing. That is the score one of her current students must achieve in order to earn a C.

The teacher could repeat the procedure for borderline A and borderline B students in order to set realistic score standards for those grades. In practice, however, the passing grade is usually the most crucial one. Often a teacher will use the procedure for the passing grade and the highest grade and then extrapolate for the other grades.

A SCREENING EXAMPLE

The borderline student procedure can also be used in more formal testing contexts. Now we present an example to screen applicants for a well-defined second language course for high-intermediate students. Some of the steps and requirements of the procedure that were taken for granted in the previous illustration will now be made explicit. In screening tests, we want to be able to use test scores to answer questions of the following sort: Which applicants are good enough to enter a second language course? In our example, we assume that a test has been selected and that there are a number of teachers available (say six) to develop score interpretations. We also assume that the admissions officer knows the procedure and will take responsibility for implementing it. The five steps in the procedure are:

1. Selecting judges who know the course and its requirements
2. Defining the minimum qualifications for the course
3. Training the judges in the use of the test judgment procedure
4. Judging the test
5. Combining the judgments to set score interpretations

We briefly describe each of these steps as they might actually be applied.

1. *Selecting judges.* The judges selected to do this must be people who are qualified to know what knowledge and skill are necessary for applicants to succeed in the course. Ordinarily they will be teachers with experience in the course. Sometimes counsellors or others who have dealt extensively with marginal students, for example, and are familiar with the program may be good judges. Students who have already been through the first term of the course can also be good judges if they are sufficiently mature. In the present scenario, the admissions officer has assumed responsibility for the screening test program and selects the teachers who have taught in the course as judges.
2. *Defining qualifications.* The teachers are brought together for a meeting several months before the new screening test is to be used for the first time. First, the test is shown to the teachers so that they understand what it measures and what it is to be used for – deciding whether applicants satisfy prerequisites for the course. Their main task at this meeting is to define and describe those prerequisites. They begin the task by describing individually, in their own words, a person whose abilities are borderline for the program. They might describe borderline students based on students from their classes in the recent past. The admissions officer, who has had experience with this kind of procedure, might help the process along by asking appropriate questions. She might ask, for example, whether the borderline student should be able to converse in the language if the teachers' descriptions have mentioned only reading and writing.

   The teachers should be allowed plenty of time to agree on their definition and description. A second meeting may be necessary to provide time for reflection. They finally produce a written description of the borderline abilities required by the course together with a number of examples. This is the statement of the standard that the admission score will represent. Although agreement is desirable, it is not essential. Even when compromise is not possible, one can continue the procedure without serious problems.

3. *Training the judges.* Before the teachers can make their judgments about the test, they must know how it is scored and how to use the procedure for judging the test items. For multiple-choice items, scoring presents no problem; the student who gets the item right is given the number of points assigned to that question, ordinarily one. For questions that are not scored objectively, it is necessary to inform the judges clearly what students will have to do to be credited with a correct answer. For scaled questions (those for which a range of points may be awarded), the basis for scoring must be clearly and thoroughly explained. It is helpful to provide example answers and their scoring for nonobjective questions. When the teachers are satisfied that they understand the scoring system, they go on to the judging phase of the procedure.

For right-wrong questions, the teacher-judges imagine a group of 100 borderline applicants. (They have already defined and described this borderline.) Then they estimate the number of these 100 applicants who will get each of the questions correct. This number is then expressed as a proportion (from .00 to 1.00). This proportion correct is the same as the average score on the item. For multiple-choice questions, one would generally expect this proportion (or average score) to be higher than the probability of guessing the correct answer by chance.

For scaled-response questions, the task is slightly different. The teachers still imagine 100 borderline applicants, but then estimate the average score they will achieve on each of the scaled-response questions. This would be a number somewhere between 0 and the total number of points assigned to the question. The procedure for judging scaled-response questions is often less clear than the procedure for judging right-wrong questions. It is important, therefore, to be certain that all judges understand clearly what they are to do.

For practice, the six teachers make independent preliminary judgments for two right-wrong questions. Then they each announce the probabilities they have given for the two questions. For the first question, the probability estimates from each teacher are written on the blackboard. Then the teacher with the highest proportion and the teacher with the lowest proportion are asked to explain the basis for their decisions. The other four teachers are given an opportunity to comment. No attempt is made to sway a judge from an initial estimate. The same procedure is followed for the second right-wrong question. The judges are then told that they are free to change either of their probability estimates if they wish to do so. They are requested, however, not to announce any changes they make.

The same procedure is then followed for one, and then a second, scaled-response item. This time, of course, the numbers on the board are

Table 1. Example of one teacher's estimation sheet for a hypothetical ESL screening test

Question	Points	Probability average
1	1	.80
2	1	.55
3	1	.75
4	1	.4
5	1	.95
6	1	.65
7	4	2.5
8	4	3.0
9	4	1.0
10	4	1.5
Maximum score = 22		Expected score = 12.1

estimated average scores rather than probability estimates. Again, the judges are allowed to change their initial estimates.

4. *Judging the test.* The teacher-judges then independently estimate probabilities and average scores for the rest of the items in the test. When they have all finished their estimations, they go through the test together question by question. Any judge giving an unusually high or low estimate explains the reasoning behind the estimate. Other teachers are free to comment. All teachers are free to change their estimates, but none are pressured to do so. They do not announce any changes to the other judges. Finally, the teachers give their estimates to the admissions officer.

Table 1 illustrates one teacher's estimates. Note that the first six questions are right-wrong questions and the next four are four-point scaled-response questions. According to this teacher's estimate, an applicant who has the minimum qualifications for the course should score 12.1 points on the test out of a possible 22.

5. *Combining judgments.* The estimates of the six teachers are averaged for each of the ten questions. These averages are then added up. This is illustrated in Table 2. Note that the summary form is identical to the individual teacher's estimation form except for the last column. The sum of the last column is the expected test score for an individual who, in the view of the teacher-judges, has only the minimal qualifications for the program.

A score of 12 (approximately equal to the computed score of 11.96) was judged by these teachers to be the minimum score for admission.

Table 2. Example summary sheet of all six teachers for a hypothetical ESL screening test

Question	Points	Probability average
1	1	.72
2	1	.63
3	1	.77
4	1	.48
5	1	.89
6	1	.57
7	4	2.7
8	4	3.1
9	4	0.8
10	4	1.3
Maximum score = 22		Expected score = 11.96

Thus, the interpretation for 12 is: minimally qualified. The interpretation for scores less than 12 is: less than minimally qualified. And, of course, the interpretation for scores greater than 12 is: more than minimally qualified. All of these interpretations are consistent with admissions (screening) decisions. Ordinarily, the admission decision rule would be: Accept scores of 12 or above; reject scores below 12. But the admissions officer does not have to follow such a rule rigidly with every applicant. She may consider other information besides screening test scores before making a decision. Or the admissions officer may adopt a different decision rule. For example, she might set a cutoff score of 10 in order to have leeway for changing the interpretation of scores after applying another procedure for developing interpretations.

The contrasting-groups procedure

In the preceding section, we saw how an initial cutoff score was established for a screening test. In this section, we describe how this initial score can be monitored and adjusted during the first cycle of its use. The procedure for adjusting the cutoff score is similar to that for first setting the score, but there are important differences. In the first procedure, judges estimated the performance of an imaginary group of students who were all at the same level: borderline. In the present procedure, judges assess the actual performance of a real group of students who are not all at the same level.

The procedure for refining the cutoff score is called the contrasting-groups method. The steps in this method are:

1. Select judges to assess students
2. Define and describe acceptable and unacceptable levels of performance in the course
3. Select students to be the subjects for study
4. Obtain judgments and screening test scores
5. Curve the judgment data
6. Establish a criterion score

1. *Selecting judges.* Judges for this procedure should have the same qualifications as those for the preceding method. In addition, they should have had an opportunity to observe the newly admitted students during their first classes of the course. Imagine that the six teachers who set the initial cutoff score are selected as judges.
2. *Defining the qualified student.* In a procedure very similar to the one used for defining and describing qualifications for applicants, the judges define and describe the qualities of students who can do acceptable work in the course as evidenced by their performance during the first week or two. Once again, the descriptions of these qualifications should be written out; agreement and compromise are desirable but not essential.
3. *Selecting students.* In the present example, all of the students took the screening test, and all of the judges are teachers in the course. The admissions officer can easily have both a screening test score and a qualification judgment for all of the students. All students can be used in the procedure; no selection is necessary. In other cases, however, conditions may preclude using all of the students – there may be very large numbers of students involved, judging may be much more difficult, and so on. In those cases, it is important to plan who gets tested and judged in order to eliminate bias in the selection of students.
4. *Obtaining screening scores and judgments.* In our example, the admissions officer already has scores for all admitted students on the screening test. The minimum score for these students is 10 (the initial adjusted cutoff score), and the maximum possible score is 22. In fact, the highest score that any applicant attained was 19.

   In our hypothetical course, there are eight classes of students with 15 students in each class: 120 students in total. A class meets for three hours per day, each hour with a different teacher. All six teachers judge the performance of all of their students during the last day of the second week of the course, without knowing their screening test results. They judge whether each student is qualified to be taking the course using the qualifications they have agreed upon in Step 2 (Defining the Qualified Student). In contrast to the first procedure (when the teachers were judging whether prospective students might be qualified to take a course

Table 3.   Screening test scores and judgments

Screening score	Number	Number of students judged qualified	Cumulative percent
10	13	4	31
11	15	6	40
12	17	10	59
13	13	9	69
14	15	12	80
15	12	9	75
16	10	9	90
etc.	etc.	etc.	etc.

before they actually take it), now they are asked to judge whether the students are qualified for the course on the basis of their actual performance during the first two weeks of the course.

The admissions officer then collects all of these judgments and uses them to classify each of the 120 students in the course as either qualified or unqualified. If two or three of a student's three teachers judge the student to be qualified, that is the classification given. If only one or none of the teachers thinks a student is qualified, that student is classified as unqualified.

In actual practice, it is often possible to get only one judgment for each student – that is, the judgment from the student's class teacher. In these cases, the definition and description of what makes a student qualified are especially important. When only single judgments are possible, and especially when there is also a small number of students being judged, cutoff scores should be applied with great reservation.

5. *Curving the data.* The admissions officer first makes a table showing the number of students attaining each score on the screening test and the number of them who are judged to be qualified on the basis of the teachers' assessments during the first week of the course. Then she computes the percentage of qualified students at each score level of the screening test. (See Table 3.)

There is a clear relation between scores on the screening test and the teachers' judgments about the qualifications of students in the course. There is one aberration, however. A higher percentage of students scoring 14 were judged qualified than those scoring 15. You can always expect such aberrations because, even when appropriate tests are used, both tests and judgments are imperfect measures.

In order to get a clearer picture of the relation between screening test scores and teacher judgments, the admissions officer smooths the per-

Table 4. Screening test scores and smoothed judgments

Score	Number	Qualified	Smoothed percent
10	13	4	*
11	15	6	43
12	17	10	56
13	13	9	69
14	15	12	75
15	12	9	82
16	10	9	88†
etc.	etc.	etc.	etc.

*The lowest and highest values in a series cannot be smoothed.
†Assuming that the percentage reported for a score of 17 was 100.

centages by means of a sliding average. That is, the percentage of qualified students at any test score is the average of three percentages: the percentage for that score, the one for the score below it, and the one for the score above it. In the example above, the moving average percentage for a score of 11 is 43. That is: $(31 + 40 + 59)/3 = 43$. The smoothed percentages are shown in Table 4. The revised decision rule for admission to the program will be based upon these smoothed percentages.

6. *Establishing a criterion score.* The borderline student procedure yielded a single score that could be used as a screening score for decisions about admission to the course. The results of the contrasting-groups procedure is somewhat different. It does not yield a single cutoff score. Instead, it yields a smoothed curve that describes the relation between screening test scores and actual judged qualifications for the course. In other words, it gives an indication of the percentage of students at each score level of the screening test who are likely to be qualified for a particular course if admitted to it. This relation is shown in Figure 1.

It is possible to use the information provided by this procedure to set the cutoff score so that any desired quality of students is admitted. It becomes possible for the admissions department to establish its own admissions standards. On the one hand, if it is a relatively serious problem for unqualified students to be admitted, but a minor problem for applicants if they are refused admission, then one might want to set a high cutoff score. A cutoff score of 15 would ensure that more than three out of four students who are admitted to the course would be qualified. On the other hand, rejecting an applicant for a course could have very serious career consequences for the individual, although there would be no serious consequences if some unqualified students are admitted.

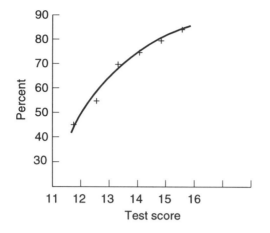

Figure 1   Smoothed relation between screening test scores and judgments of student qualifications for an ESL course.

This could be true of a course with a great deal of individualized instruction. In such a case, one might choose a cutoff score of, say, 11.5, a score at which the chances of an applicant being qualified are about 50 percent. In this way, the contrasting-group procedure allows one to establish a decision rule in accordance with one's own assessment of the two possible decision errors: admitting the unqualified and rejecting the qualified.

Establishing other decision criteria

In the preceding sections, we illustrated two methods for establishing interpretations for test scores. They were illustrated in the contexts of passing and screening scores. They are just as applicable, however, for setting criteria for other kinds of decisions. For example, screening out applicants who are already too capable for a course can be accomplished by the borderline method. Judges would estimate what the borderline passing student in a program would be able to do on each question of the test. Then applicants above the derived cutoff score would be refused admission.

It is also a simple matter to extend these methods to making rules for multiple category decisions. Grading is often a multiple category decision. One must decide whether to give an A, a B, a C, and so on. Placement is also a multiple category decision when more than two levels exist in a program. The difference in the borderline procedure is that judges must make estimates of performance of borderline students in each category. In the contrasting-groups method, students are classified into all decision categories (A students, B students, or F students, e.g.), not just into the categories qualified and unqualified.

The procedures illustrated here lead to defensible and meaningful interpretations of count scores. They establish scoring and decision criteria that take test difficulty into account. In contrast, arbitrary score interpretations that do not account for the difficulty of test tasks (e.g., 60 = D, 70 = C, 80 = B, 90 = A) can lead to unfair and irrational decision making.

Summary

In this chapter, we discussed different kinds of test scores and their interpretation. We pointed out that there are two basic ways to interpret test scores: (1) with reference to the performance of other students (norm-referencing) and (2) with reference to defined domains of knowledge or skill, such as might be described in instructional objectives. Norm-referenced score interpretation is not particularly useful for instructional planning. It is often used informally by teachers to score the test performance of their current students based on their accumulated experiences of student performance in the past. It is also often used by specialists to diagnose specific language problems that individual students might be experiencing, although there are relatively few standardized, norm-referenced second language tests. When it comes to providing feedback to students and teachers about learning and teaching, objectives-referenced test score interpretation is the most useful.

We pointed out that, although, in principle, objectives-referenced tests permit interpretations about mastery (or lack of mastery) of instructional objectives or content, this is not always the case. Mastery tests reflect a limited domain or set of objectives and are constructed so that most students are expected to perform well. Mastery tests provide useful feedback about the effectiveness of instruction. In comparison, open-ended tests are of greater difficulty and reveal the full range of student attainment as well as students' top levels of performance. Such tests are somewhat less informative about mastery of instructional objectives and the effectiveness of instruction. Both kinds of interpretations can be useful.

We also distinguished between count and rating scores. Most rating scales have the advantage of building interpretation into the scoring procedure. Count scores derived from mastery-type tests also provide a useful basis for score interpretation – that is, with respect to some minimal level of learning. Count scores derived from open-ended tests, however, lack a built-in basis for interpretation. We described two procedures for developing meaningful interpretations of such count scores. These procedures are most useful for making important decisions when large numbers of students are involved and a team of teachers is available. They are less practical for individual teachers working with small groups of students because they require considerable time and judgment.

Discussion questions

1. How do you interpret scores from class tests you currently use? Do you use predesignated categories? Do you interpret them relative to instructional objectives? If not, why not?
2. Do you use mental norms based on the performance of previous students? Do you make these norms explicit to your students? What if they do not attain these norms? Do you modify your objectives or your norms, or both?
3. How carefully do you take your instructional objectives into account when devising tests? When scoring tests? Based on the material presented in this chapter, would you modify the way you take objectives into account? If not, why not?
4. Do you currently use or have you ever used mastery tests? How were they helpful? If they are new to you, how could they be useful in your classroom? How could open-ended tests be helpful?
5. If you are reading this book as part of a course on second language evaluation, devise a screening test to select students for inclusion in this course; alternatively, select a second language textbook, and use this as a basis for devising a screening test. Using the borderline student method, establish cut-off scores for the selection of students who are minimally qualified to take this course.
6. Suggest ways that you can ensure reliability of scoring open-ended tests.

Readings

Airasian, P. W. (1991). *Classroom assessment.* New York: McGraw-Hill.
American Council on the Teaching of Foreign Languages, *ACTFL Proficiency Guidelines.* New York: American Council on the Teaching of Foreign Languages.
Harris, D. P. (1969). Interpreting and using test results. In D. P. Harris (Ed.), *Testing English as a second language* (pp. 121–134). New York: McGraw-Hill.
Heaton, J. B. (1975). Interpreting test scores. In *Writing English language tests* (pp. 167–184). Essex, England: Longman.
Hopkins, C. D., and L. A. Richards. (1990). Interpreting test scores. In C. D.

Hopkins and L. A. Richards (Eds.), *Classroom measurement and evaluation* (pp. 346–403). Itasca, Ill.: F. E. Peacock.

Jacobs, H. L., S. A. Zinkgraf, D. P. Wormuth, V. F. Hartfiel, and J. B. Hughey. (1981). Interpreting the test scores: Some general guidelines. In H. L. Jacobs et al. (Eds.), *Testing ESL composition: A practical approach* (pp. 56–68). Rowley, Mass.: Newbury House.

Livingston, S. A., and M. J. Zieky. (1982). *Passing scores: A manual for setting standards of performance on educational and occupational tests.* Princeton, N.J.: Educational Testing Service.

13 *Standardized tests*

- Introduction
- Why use a standardized language test
- Standardized test development
- Interpreting standardized test scores
- Evaluating standardized tests
- Summary

Preview questions

1. Have you ever used a standardized test? With whom and for what purpose? Did you find it useful? If yes, in what ways? If not, why not?
2. Are standardized tests better than teacher-made tests? Explain.
3. When is it useful to use standardized tests? When is it not useful?
4. Many people have made the claim that standardized tests are discriminatory. What are the bases for these claims? Do you agree or disagree with them?
5. What are the differences between a standardized test and teacher-made tests?
6. Have you ever taken a standardized test? What were your feelings before, during, and after taking it? What does this tell you about your students' taking standardized language tests, and how could you respond to these issues?

Introduction

In this chapter, we discuss standardized tests – why they are used, how they are constructed, and how to assess them. A great deal of thought and effort goes into the development of standardized tests to ensure that they are psychometrically sound. This entails compiling a large set of test items, administering these items to a tryout group in order to see how they work, selecting the items that work best, and in some cases developing norms for interpreting scores on the test. We talk about these various steps shortly so that you understand better what standardized tests are all about. Suffice it to say at this time that different procedures are used to make up standardized tests than classroom tests of the sort we have been talking about so far. It is not possible for most individual teachers to make standardized tests.

They involve too much work and very specialized training. Nor is this desirable because, as we shall see shortly, although standardized tests may be helpful for some purposes, they have limited useful application in the classroom.

Standardized tests usually consist of a set of materials including (1) a test booklet with the test items and instructions to the test taker, (2) an answer sheet, (3) an adminstration manual containing instructions on how to administer the test, and (4) a technical manual with information on uses of the test, how it was developed, how it is to be scored, and how the scores can be interpreted. Not all standardized tests include all these parts although they should, since all these components are necessary for effective use. If one or some of these parts are not included in the package, you will probably be lacking important information about the test.

Standardized language tests are used widely in some educational settings for both first and second language assessment. For example, bilingual education programs in the United States routinely require that limited-English-proficient students take standardized tests in English in order to determine their participation in bilingual versus mainstream English classes. Most foreign students applying to universities in the United States and Canada are required to take the TOEFL (Test of English as a Foreign Language) in order to qualify for admission. Many adult ESL programs screen and place students into their programs on the basis of the students' performance on a standardized ESL test, such as the Michigan Test of English Language Proficiency or the Comprehensive English Language Test.

You may be called upon to select and administer a standardized test, or you may simply be called upon to interpret students' scores on a standardized test. In either case, it is important to understand these tests: Why they are used, how they are constructed, how scores on them can be interpreted, and how to assess them. We address each of these questions in the following sections. First of all, we consider why one might use a standardized language test rather than making up one's own test.

Why use a standardized language test?

There are a number of reasons why standardized tests are used instead of nonstandardized or teacher-made tests. Standardized tests are often used because of their practicality – it is sometimes easier to use a test that is already available than to make up one's own. Moreover, the procedures for administering, scoring, and interpreting the test have already been worked out. Practicality alone is not a sufficient reason for using standardized tests, however.

Standardized tests are also used by school districts or educational authorities and professionals who want a common basis for making decisions about students. These decisions often pertain to which students should be admitted into a particular program or course (e.g., an English language university, a mainstream English elementary school class) and how students should be placed in special programs or streams (e.g., bilingual education, catch-up ESL classes). Indeed, one of the most common uses of standardized tests is to make screening and placement decisions.

The TOEFL is a good example of a standardized test that is used to decide who will be admitted into a course or program. Students who do not attain the requisite score on the TOEFL are not permitted to take regular university courses and are required to take additional ESL training as preparation for retaking the TOEFL, that is, if they would like to try again. For those students referred to ESL instruction, a standardized placement test might be used to identify their particular language strengths and weaknesses in order to place them in the most appropriate language courses.

Standardized tests are also often used to determine whether individuals have achieved certain levels of language proficiency and therefore qualify for language accreditation. For example, in Quebec, Canada, it is necessary for individuals who do not speak French as a first language to pass a language test in French in order to practice certain professions. In this case, the same language test is given to all professionals in a particular field (e.g., doctors) who are not native speakers of French.

Standardized language tests may be used as diagnostic instruments to detect problems that individual students might have. Standardized tests are useful in this case because they provide norms that can show who is having problems and who is performing within the normal range.

Standardized tests may be used as part of formal program evaluation at the district, regional, or national level. In this case, the interest is not in making decisions about students, but in deciding whether language programs in the school system are working. For example, schools in the United States routinely administer standardized achievement tests in a variety of subject areas, including language, as part of a strategy of general accountability. Standardized tests aid in this process precisely because they are standardized in content and in administration and scoring procedures. This type of program evaluation differs from the type of informal evaluation discussed in this book in that the focus in informal evaluation is on tailoring the evaluation procedures to specific classrooms so as to maximize learning. In contrast, in formal program evaluation, standard evaluation procedures are used despite what might be considerable differences in the actual programs or classes being assessed.

Use of standardized tests during instruction or for instructional planning is rare and not usually advisable, because these tests are not tailored to the instructional objectives and plans of particular programs, courses, or classes. This point will become clearer in the next section when we discuss how standardized tests are constructed. Standardized tests might be employed during a program or course as part of continuous program evaluation, in which case the test results will probably not be used to make decisions about individual students or to make adjustments to teaching plans and practices.

Task 1

Identify the uses of standardized tests and discuss how they are better suited for these purposes than classroom tests.

Standardized test development

In the introduction to this chapter we pointed out that standardized tests are constructed using procedures that are different from those used with classroom or teacher-made tests. We then observed that standardized tests are not based on the content of particular programs or courses. The question arises, How are standardized tests made? In this section, we describe in general terms how standardized tests are developed so that you will have a better understanding of them. We focus on a particular type of standardized test, namely, norm-referenced tests, which are special in that score interpretation is done by comparing an individual test taker's score to the scores attained by a norming group.

In general, these steps are followed in the development of standardized tests:

1. Definition of the test purpose(s)
2. Preparation of test specifications and creation of a pool of test items
3. Administration of test items to a tryout sample
4. Analyses of initial items and selection of final items
5. Determination of test norms

This is an oversimplification, but it serves to illustrate a number of important procedures in the development of standardized tests.

As in the development of any test, standardized test development begins by defining the purpose of the test. Teacher-made tests are devised to assess achievement as a result of exposure to specific instructional activities; therefore, the content of such tests is determined largely by specific instructional objectives, plans, and practices, as we pointed out earlier. In contrast, standardized tests are not made to assess achievement in a particular program or course of instruction. They are intended to measure more general language skills or knowledge. Therefore, the statement of purpose is usually quite general, more so than that of a classroom test. For example:

The purpose of the test is to assess the child's ability to produce standard grammatical and phonological features when he speaks. (Michigan Oral Language Productive Tests 1970)

The primary purpose of the Test of Spoken English (TSE) is to evaluate the English speaking proficiency of persons whose native language is not English. (Test of Spoken English 1982)

Since standardized tests are not objectives-referenced, it also follows that there is no predetermined language content or set of instructional activities to draw on when deciding what language skills should be included in the test and what form the test tasks should take. In order to do this, the test developer calls on a group of experts to develop specifications for creating test items that will correspond to the general purpose for which the test is being developed. The test specifications serve two main functions. First, they communicate to users what it is that the test measures. Second, they lay out the details of the language domain being assessed so that item writers can generate pools of similar items. An example of a general test specification of the type that might be appropriate for a language test is given by Popham (p. 128):

When given brief, previously unseen fictitious accounts of the research activities of natural and physical scientists, students will answer questions . . . calling for the identification of particular phases of the scientific method being illustrated.

A group of item writers then prepares a pool of test items that satisfy the requirements of the test specifications. The item pool is deliberately much larger than will be used in the final version of the test. It is assumed that not all of the items will work, so more are created than are required.

This pool of test items is then administered to a tryout sample under conditions that closely match those that will be used with the final version. The tryout sample is selected to be as representative or typical as possible of the people who are likely to be given the final version. The responses of the tryout sample to the individual test items are then analyzed, primarily with respect to two characteristics: (1) how hard each item is (its difficulty) and (2) how well each item distinguishes among test takers with different levels of ability (its discriminability). One of the simplest measures of difficulty (in practice, more sophisticated measures are used) is simply the proportion of the tryout sample who fail or respond incorrectly to each item. Discriminability is determined in a number of different ways, all of which compare item performance by more able and less able examinees.

For example, if an item is of middling difficulty, most examinees with little ability should fail the item, about half of the examinees with middling ability should pass the item, and most examinees with high ability should pass the item. Looked at another way, the likelihood that an examinee will pass an item should depend upon his ability as compared to the difficulty of the item. When this is true, the item is said to have high discriminability. It does not always work with every item, however. An item might contain a red herring that only the more able will fall for. Or the item may call for some bit of factual information that some low-ability examinees are likely to possess. There are mathematical formulas for calculating discriminability.

After the item analyses are completed, the test developers choose which items to include in the final version of the test and which to reject. The general rule of thumb is to keep those items that were neither very easy nor very difficult in the tryout. Items included in the final version of the test are also selected to have good discriminability. In general, the higher the discriminability, the better.

The final task in developing norm-referenced standardized tests is to develop norms. The developer administers the final version of the test to another group or groups of individuals; these groups are called "norming groups." The norming groups are selected to be the same as or similar to the individuals for whom the test is intended. Their scores on the test are analyzed in order to describe their average and range of performance on the test. These results are then used to interpret individual test scores once the test becomes operational.

Interpreting standardized test scores

There are a number of important consequences of this test development procedure for interpreting standardized test scores. One is that items that most test takers would get correct and those that most would get wrong are not included in standardized tests. Therefore, skills that most learners would have acquired or would not have acquired are not tested. As a result, it is virtually impossible when using standardized tests to ascertain skills everyone in a particular group might have acquired or failed to acquire. This contrasts markedly with teacher-made tests, especially of the mastery variety, where it is possible and very useful to know what all or none of your students have learned.

Another consequence of this procedure is that students taking the final version of the test are likely to obtain a wide range of scores. In fact, standardized tests are developed deliberately to yield a range of scores among test takers. Viewed differently, standardized tests are useful for identifying individual differences among test takers. This is done for mathematical reasons that may have very little to do with second language learning in a particular program. In this respect, standardized tests resemble open-ended tests, which we discussed in the preceding chapter.

A third and very important consequence of this procedure is that the final selection of test items is not necessarily a good reflection of the language skills or knowledge of interest to a particular teacher or school setting. It most certainly is not likely to be a good representation of the language content identified as important in your instructional objectives. The final selection of items in a standardized test is guided largely by statistical considerations. The consequence of this is that standardized test scores by themselves may tell you very little about what the test takers do or do not know relative to the objectives that guide instruction.

To illustrate this point simply, recall that test items that were answered correctly or incorrectly by most of the test takers in the tryout sample were eliminated from the final version of the test. This means that you cannot tell from a standardized test what language skills are known by all of your students. Similarly, you can never know what language skills none of them know. What standardized tests do tell you is that some students have scored higher in a particular language domain than others, but you do not know what skills their higher scores actually comprise. Consequently, standardized tests are of limited value for planning and assessing classroom instruction.

Now that you understand some of the severe limitations of standardized test interpretation, we address ways to make sense of standardized test scores.

Scaled scores and norms

Making sense of a standardized test score depends upon two operations conducted by the test developers: scaling and norming. Scaling allows us to interpret scores from any form of a standardized test in the same way that we would interpret a score from any other form of that test. The Test of English as a Foreign Language, for example, produces a dozen forms per year, year after year. Scaling is the procedure that adjusts for the inevitable differences in test and item difficulty from form to form so that a given score on any form has the same meaning. The standardized test manual provides tables that show how to transform a score on any test form to a scaled score. We give meaning to individual scores on standardized tests by reference to norms. These are descriptions of the performance of clearly identified groups of individuals on the test. Norms are essential for norm-referenced, standardized test interpretation and are included in the test manual. There are five common ways of presenting norms:

- Age-equivalent scores
- Grade-equivalent scores
- Percentile ranks
- Standard scores
- Stanines

These will be briefly described here, but you will probably want to read more about the kinds of norms reported for tests that you may use. Consult the references in the reading list at the end of this chapter.

Age-equivalent score norms represent the typical score achieved by learners of different ages. Figure 1 shows an example of age-equivalent norms for a second language reading test designed for immigrant children. If a learner takes the test and attains a scaled score of 41, for example, you see that she is reading slightly better than the typical ten-year-old immigrant child. Grade-equivalent scores work in the same way, only the typical scores are given for learners at different grade levels.

Age and grade equivalents give one typical score for each of a number of groups. Another kind of norm gives information about the range of scores achieved by a single group. Percentile ranks are probably the easiest to understand. Figure 2 illustrates percentile ranks for nine-year-olds on the same test illustrated in Figure 1.

Age equivalent	Median scaled score
8;0	18
8;6	22
9;0	26
9;6	31
10;0	39
10;6	45
11;0	52
11;6	58

Figure 1   Sample conversion table for age-equivalent scores.

Percentile rank	Scaled score
90	49
75	33
50	26
25	19
10	12

Figure 2   Sample conversion table for percentile scores.

Figure 2 is used as follows: A child between 9 years and 9 years and 6 months of age could have his score interpreted with this table. If he attains a score of 26, he is as good as or better than half of the children in his age group. If his score is 19, that score equals or exceeds only 25 percent of scores achieved by others in his age group. If he scores 30, he equals or surpasses (by extrapolation) approximately 65 percent of the norm group. Stated another way, he is in the top 35 percent of nine-year-olds. (Additional examples of standardized test score norms are presented in Chapter 8, Table 2.)

Standard and stanine scores indicate how high or low a given score is in comparison to the range of scores attained by a norm group. They are not so transparent as percentile ranks, however. Fortunately, manuals that present norms as some version of standard score or stanine should provide you with the information necessary to translate them into percentile ranks. You should, nonetheless, read more about standard scores if you are called on to interpret them.

The use of norms for interpreting scores is relatively simple and straightforward. There are a few cautions that should be considered, however. These concern the quality of norms, the appropriacy of norms, and the interpretation of group averages. First of all, good norms require (1) large numbers of test takers who are (2) representative of the group described and who (3) take the test under the same conditions as the learners you will test. The manual should provide the information you need to judge the quality of the reported norms.

In order to interpret a score with reference to published norms, it is essential that those norms be appropriate. Otherwise, decisions based upon those interpretations will not have the same validity as that claimed in the manual. In order for norms to be appropriate, the students whose scores you want to interpret must be similar to the norm group. When you read the description of the norm group, you should be able to imagine your students as having been included. An appropriate norm group should include people of the same age, cultural and ethnic background, educational level and type, gender, and linguistic background. The most appropriate norm group is one that is quite homogeneous and also quite similar to your own test takers.

A common mistake in using norms occurs when the average score attained by several test takers is interpreted with respect to norms developed for individual test takers, for example, when the average score of an entire class or school is compared with published norms. Most norms represent the scores attained by a large number of individuals, and, therefore, only individual scores can be interpreted in reference to these norms. When compared to a set of norms for individuals, the average score for a very good class would most likely seem quite mediocre; it might even be below average. If you want to interpret class averages, you must refer to norms that are made from a large number of class averages. Unfortunately, such norms are almost never available.

In summary, test developers provide norms in order to make standardized test scores meaningful. Norms are statistical descriptions of how the norming group scored; they help you to interpret standardized test scores by indicating how individual test takers scored in comparison with the norming group. Norms do not generally work for interpreting average scores of groups. Valid decision making requires norms of high quality that are appropriate to the people whose scores you are interpreting.

Task 2

What do age-equivalent, grade-equivalent, and percentile scores tell you about students' language abilities? How is this information different from the information provided by scores on classroom tests?

Evaluating standardized tests

Teachers are often called on to use or interpret standardized tests; therefore, it is important that they be able to assess them. We discuss six criteria here that can be used for judging the quality of standardized tests:

1. Test content and purpose
2. Appropriateness
3. Practicality
4. User qualities
5. Reliability
6. Validity

1. Test content and purpose

When assessing standardized tests, look at (1) the language skills or subskills you are interested in testing and (2) the kinds of decisions you want to make. Naturally, you will want to consider seriously only those standardized tests that examine the same kinds of language skills or knowledge that you wish to assess. It is important to examine in detail specific skills included in the test to ensure they correspond to the skills you are interested in. Do this by examining the description of the test content contained in the test manual and, more importantly, by examining the actual content of the test. It is very important to scrutinize the test content itself because the test title or manual may give an incomplete, inadequate, and, in some cases, inaccurate description of what is actually included.

You will also want to start by selecting only those tests that allow you to make the kinds of decisions you want to make. For example, if you want a standardized test that will allow you to decide which students are able to write in English at the level required in university courses, then you would exclude from further consideration tests that do not pertain to such a decision. The test manual should contain a description of the kinds of decisions that can be made on the basis of scores obtained using that test. As in the case of test content, it is important to examine what the manual says about decision making and what appears to you to be the actual case. You should be critical of the claims of test developers; you may not agree with what they say.

2. Appropriateness

Appropriateness includes comparisons between the students to be tested and students for whom the test was designed. It includes the following:

a. *Age or grade level.* Is the test appropriate for the age or grade level of the students you want to test?
b. *Educational background.* Is the test appropriate for use with students with the kind of educational background you want to test? For example, if you plan to test students with little formal education, you should select a test that does not involve language tasks (such as multiple-choice questions) that might be unfamiliar to your students.
c. *Proficiency level.* Is the general level of proficiency required by the test appropriate for the students to be tested?

Appropriateness also includes the question of whether the test is acceptable to the students, teachers, school administrators, and possibly parents or other members of the community implicated by use of the test. In recent years, standardized tests have come under close public scrutiny. It may not be advisable to consider using standardized language tests because one or a number of these groups considers the test to be unfair, biased, or invalid. As a result, they may be antagonistic to the use of the test results or decisions based on them.

3. Practicality

Is the test practical with respect to financial considerations, time, space, administration, scoring, and special materials or equipment? Here are some questions about practicality to ask:

- Is the test affordable?
- Is there sufficient time available to give the test according to the developers'guidelines?
- Is the space required to give the test available (e.g., a classroom that will seat twenty-five students at separate desks at one time; a soundproof room)?
- Does administration of the test require specialized training of the examiner? For example, some oral interview procedures cannot be done by untrained people; they require intensive, specialized training. Is it practical to obtain such training?
- Does the test require special scoring procedures? For example, some standardized tests cannot be scored by the teacher or person administering the test. They must be sent away to be scored by specialists, sometimes for an additional fee. Is this practical? If the results are needed immediately or if there are no additional funds for such scoring services, then this would not be a practical test.
- Are specialized materials or equipment needed to administer the test (e.g., tape recorders, videorecorders, slide projectors)? Is such equipment available?

Task 3

Select a standardized second language test and consider its appropriateness for your students.

---

4. User qualities

It is important to examine standardized tests from the point of view of both teachers and students as users.

The following questions pertain to student-users:

a. Does the test explain to students its purpose, intent, or recommended use in an honest and straightforward way?
b. Are test instructions thorough, clear, and specific?
c. Are there example test items? Are they adequate?
d. Do the test booklet and answer sheet have layouts that facilitate comprehension and responding? Consider the following:

- Is the typeface clear and legible?
- Is it easy to differentiate questions from answers in the case of multiple-choice items?
- Are the numbering and lettering of different items clear?

- Are pictures and other graphic designs clear and easy to interpret?

e. Are the test items unbiased, personally inoffensive, culturally appropriate, and interesting to the students?

The following questions pertain to teacher-users:

a. Are administrative procedures described clearly and simply in the manual? Who is to administer the test? How much time is to be allotted? Do students answer all items, and, if not, what items do what students answer?
b. Does the test manual indicate clearly and precisely what instructions are to be given to students?
c. Are scoring procedures described clearly and simply?
d. Are norms provided? Are they provided for different subgroups of test takers? Are normed or transformed scores explained simply and clearly?
e. Are instructions given for converting raw scores into scaled scores?
f. Are instructions provided on how to interpret test scores?
g. Does the manual provide guidelines about the kinds of decisions that can be made and how they can be made using test scores?
h. Is there a technical manual? If so, does it provide complete and clear descriptions of the standardization sample(s), item selection procedures, reliability, and validity?

Task 4

Assess the practicality and user qualities of the test selected for Task 3.

---

5. Reliability

Information pertaining to test reliability should be included in the technical manual or general description of a standardized test. This information should include reliability estimates and the means used for calculating them. Without this information, it is impossible to know how reliable a test is and, therefore, how much confidence you can have in the scores. Standardized tests that do not include this information should be used only with great caution.

As discussed in Chapter 4, reliability refers to the consistency of test scores for the same individuals. For example, a test that yields the same score for a given individual on two separate occasions would be considered reliable. A test that yields different scores for the same individual on separate occasions would be considered relatively unreliable and should be avoided. A test that is not reliable cannot be valid. A valid test is one that measures what it is supposed to measure – no more, no less. An unreliable test is invalid because a large part of the score is due to error and not to the presence of the quality being measured. We discuss validity in greater detail in the next section.

Sources of unreliability

As discussed in Chapter 4, different sources of error can lower the reliability of test scores. There are error sources related to (1) the test itself; (2) the testing conditions, including the testers; and (3) the persons being assessed. Briefly, characteristics of the test itself can lower reliability. For example, if the instructions are not clear or if they vary from one occasion to the next, then performance on the test might vary because of confusion on the part of the test taker or because of inconsistency in instructions. The conditions in which a test is given can affect results – for example, the time of day, temperature of the testing room, lighting conditions, noise level, and so on. Test scores can also be affected by how the test taker feels at the time of the test – for example, tired, hungry, angry, and so forth.

It is important to understand that these sources of error can influence test scores but are not part of the skill you really want to measure. A test might be susceptible to any or all of these sources of error. A good test is not highly susceptible to error. That is, it is very reliable. When assessing standardized tests, it is important to ascertain its reliability and to decide whether it is sufficiently reliable for you to have confidence in it.

Types of reliability

There are a number of different kinds of reliability that pertain to different sources of error. Of particular relevance are (1) test-retest reliability, (2) parallel or alternate forms reliability, (3) internal consistency, and (4) scorer reliability.

Test-retest reliability is the degree of consistency of scores for the same test given to the same individuals on different occasions. In this case, reliability is assessed with respect to time and the conditions of the test taker and of testing. The higher the test-retest reliability, the less susceptible the scores are to random changes in the conditions of test takers or testing situations.

Alternate-forms reliability is the consistency of scores for the same individuals on different occasions on different but comparable forms of the test. In this case, reliability is being assessed with respect to the specific content of items included in the test in addition to time. The higher alternate-forms reliability is, the less susceptible the scores are to changes in the conditions of testing over time and to peculiarities of the specific test content.

Internal consistency is the degree of consistency of test scores with regard to the content of a single test. The idea behind internal consistency is this: If each test task is measuring the same ability, then a total score based upon many of these tasks will be quite stable and free from random errors. There are a number of ways to estimate the internal consistency of a test. The easiest to understand is split-half reliability. To calculate split-half reliability, the same individuals are tested on one occasion with a single test. A score is calculated for each half of the test for each individual and the consistency of the two halves is compared. You can think of split-half reliability as a special case of alternate-forms reliability in that each half of the test constitutes an alternate form. If a test has high internal reliability or consistency, the items are measuring the same skills and, therefore, they correlate highly with one another.

Scorer reliability is the degree of consistency of scores from different scorers for the same individuals on the same test or from the same scorer for the same individuals on the same test but on different occasions. Scorer reliability is an issue when scores are based on subjective judgments. It indicates the degree of agreement among independent scorers (i.e., interrater reliability) or for the same scorer on different occasions (intrarater reliability).

Different forms of reliability thus pertain to different sources of possible error. For example, test-retest reliability assesses error related to time and the conditions of testing and of the test takers; alternate-forms reliability assesses error related to time and the content of the test; and scorer reliability pertains to error arising from differences in scorers.

Measuring reliability

We have been talking about test reliability as if tests are either reliable or unreliable. In fact, reliability is a quality of tests that varies. Thus, a test can be more or less reliable. There are two commonly reported measures of reliability: (1) the reliability index and (2) the standard error of measurement.

The *reliability index* is a number ranging from .00 to 1.00 that indicates how free from random error a set of scores is. An index of .00 indicates that the scores are nothing but error; they are not really measuring anything at all. An index of 1.00, on the other hand, indicates that measurement is being made without the slightest trace of error. More precisely, the reliability index tells you what proportion of measurement is reliable and, therefore, how much is random error. An index of .80, for example, means that your measurement is 80 percent reliable and 20 percent error.

A reliability index can be calculated for any of the different sources of error mentioned earlier, and the manual may report indexes for retest stability, alternate-forms equivalence, internal consistency, or scorer agreement. For example, an interrater reliability index of .75 for a writing test consisting of a single writing sample tells you that a set of scores from one rater will agree 75 percent with the scores from another rater. An alternate-forms index for this writing test might be .60. That is, if learners took two forms of the test − forms with different writing topics − the scores on the first test would agree only 60 percent with scores on the second. Most standardized test manuals will report reliability indexes for internal consistency. These are estimates of how well a set of scores would agree with a second set if a group of learners were to retake the same test − assuming that there would have been no effects from taking it the first time − no learning, no boredom, no fatigue.

It is very important to recognize what source of error an index refers to. A slight error from one source does not guarantee small errors from other sources. You must always be alert to where error is likely to be a problem for any type of test you are considering. You then want to check the reliability related to that error source.

Standard error of measurement (SEM) is another way of reporting the reliability of a test. Like the reliability index, it is based on the idea that test scores include an error component. It is an estimate, in test score units, of how large the error component is likely to be. Thus, it is particularly useful in the interpretation of test scores.

An example of using the standard error of measurement may make the idea of this index clearer. Suppose that a test manual reports the SEM for some standardized test of second language proficiency as 3.5 points. This tells you that two-thirds of all test scores are within 3.5 points of the test takers' true score (that is, the scores they would have achieved if the test were completely without measurement error). Similarly, random error affects scores more than 7 points (2 SEM) for fewer than 1 percent of all test takers.

If you know the standard error of measurement, you can estimate the likely range within which an individual test taker's true score falls. For example, if the SEM for a test is estimated to be 3 points and the score an individual obtained on the test is 50, then the person's true score adjusted for any possible error effects is likely to fall between 47 and 53. The smaller the SEM for a test, the more reliable the test and, therefore, the more confidence you can have that the scores obtained by individuals on the test are close approximations to scores that would show their true abilities.

There are several important practical consequences of knowing and understanding the SEM. One very important consequence is that no score should be interpreted in an absolute way since there is always the possibility that part of the score is due to measurement error. This might influence the decisions you make using test scores. Take as an example a score of 49 on a test with an SEM of 2 points. Conventionally, teachers in many schools accept a mark of 50 as a passing grade. Taking the error of measurement into account, a student who got a score of 49 might have a true score greater than 49 (as high as 51). On this basis, you might decide to pass the student. However, the true score might actually be lower than 49. In this case, you might decide to fail the student. Whether you decide to pass or fail this student will depend upon the consequences of your decisions to the student and to the educational institution. If a foreign student would be deported because he failed his English screening test, then you might decide to give the student the benefit of the "measurement doubt" by assigning a passing grade. In contrast, if passing this student were to result in some hardship or negative consequence to the student or to the educational institution, then you might decide to fail the student.

Another consequence of knowing the SEM is that you know that differences in students' scores that are smaller than the SEM may not reflect real variations in true ability but rather errors of measurement. Continuing with our example, if student A obtained a score of 65 and student B a score of 67, you would know that this might not be a true difference in ability – rather, it could reflect measurement error. As a result, you would not likely make decisions about these two students that differ significantly, such as giving an award to student B but not to student A.

The question is often asked, How high should reliability be? The easy answer is, The higher the better. Other than that, there is no correct answer, but a few guidelines may be helpful. In all cases, these guidelines refer to estimates of reliability for the students you are concerned with:

1. If the test will be used for making important decisions about individuals that cannot be easily revoked or amended, reliability should be above .90, and preferably .95 or higher. An example is admitting a student to a program of study or to a profession that requires knowledge of a second language.
2. For decisions about individuals that can be rather easily changed or that have minor importance and consequences, reliability should be above .80. An example is placement into one of a number of language course sections according to ability in the language.
3. For decisions that are based upon an average score of a fairly large number of individuals, reliability should be above .60.

Task 5

Identify the kinds of reliability reported for the standardized test selected for Task 4 and assess their adequacy.

---

6. Validity

Validity is the extent to which a test actually measures what it is supposed to measure or is being used to measure. As noted earlier, a test cannot be highly valid if it is unreliable due to measurement error. However, a test can be reliable but not necessarily valid for the purposes it claims. In this case, it might be reliably measuring something other than what it is designed to measure. Validity, like reliability, is a quality of tests that varies from very little to very much. As noted in Chapter 4, there are three general procedures for gathering evidence of validity: (a) content relevance, (b) criterion relatedness, and (c) construct validation; some people also include face validity (that is, the appearance of validity) but face validity alone is insufficient to validate a standardized test.

Sources of invalidity

Sources of invalidity that you should bear in mind when examining standardized tests or how they have been used are related to: (1) test content, (2) test use, (3) test taker behavior, (4) reference group, and (5) criterion selection. We explain each briefly now.

A test that does not include items that are a comprehensive representation of the skill or knowledge being tested lacks content relevance and, therefore, may not measure what it claims to measure. A test that does measure what it is supposed to measure will be invalid if it is used to make decisions other than those for which it was designed. For example, a test of reading achievement in English would not be valid for screening students on the basis of *general* English language achievement. Lack of validity in this case is not a property of the test, but rather of the way it is being used.

The validity of test scores can be lowered if the test is not administered or the test takers do not perform as the test developers intend. For example, if only 50 minutes instead of the specified 60 minutes is given to students to do the test, the validity of the results will be lowered. Or if the students do not cooperate and take the test seriously, then their scores will not be a valid indication of their abilities.

Validity can also be threatened if a test is designed for one type of learner (e.g., adults) but is used with a different kind of learner (e.g., high school students). This is a special case of invalidity due to test use.

Some standardized tests are validated by showing that scores on the test correlate with another measure of some interest; the latter measure is referred to as the criterion. If an incorrect or inappropriate criterion is used, this procedure would fail to establish the validity of the test. For example, a test that is designed to permit the test user to make decisions about who will be a good teaching assistant can be validated by correlating the test scores of a sample of teaching assistants with student ratings of their effectiveness. Such a procedure would not provide a complete picture of the test's validity because students' ratings of their teaching assistants can be influenced by many factors unrelated to their actual effectiveness with the language (e.g., whether they are likeable or assign high grades regardless of how much work the students do).

Assessing and reporting validity

The publisher of a standardized test is responsible for assessing the validity of the test and for reporting this information in the test manual. Other information about validity may be found in journals or research reports. One should never use a standardized test to make important decisions without carefully considering the available information about its validity. If there is no demonstration of validity for the purposes you have in mind, use of the test must be considered experimental.

There are several ways of assessing validity. We have introduced them already: content relevance, criterion relatedness, and construct validation research. In addition, there is the impression or intuitive sense that a test is valid. This latter evidence of validity, frequently called face validity, is very weak and is better considered as evidence of a test's acceptability to the public. The publishers of standardized tests will most often provide information about criterion relatedness. Less often they will report on content relevance and construct validation studies.

CRITERION RELATEDNESS

Criterion relatedness is shown by correlations between test scores and criterion measures. A criterion measure may be another test of the same ability whose validity is already well established. For example, when introducing a new form of an established test, a publisher will want to show how the new version correlates with the older one, the criterion measure. In another instance a new test that is designed with greater efficiency, economy, or administrative ease is correlated with an existing test. For example, a live interview test of speaking ability is difficult to arrange and administer. Trained interviewers may be hard to find and schedule in some places and at some times. A semidirect test, in which test takers respond on audiotape to prerecorded questions, has many practical advantages. Scores on the semidirect test can be correlated with scores on the live interview test, the criterion measure, to show the criterion relatedness of the new test.

The two previous examples have illustrated relatedness to criteria in order to show that the new test measures what it claims to measure. Criterion relatedness can also show how well a test serves in making decisions. In these cases, the criteria are measures of something different from the ability the test claims to measure. For example, a proficiency test of English may be correlated with various measures of ESL students' performance in English-medium courses, such as history. These correlations will indicate how valid the test is for student selection. The standardized test manual should report criterion relatedness of this sort for each use for which the test is recommended.

CONTENT RELEVANCE

Content relevance is the extent to which a test provides an adequate representation (coverage) of the language domain it intends to test. Matching test tasks to instructional objectives and activities when making classroom tests is largely a matter of ensuring content relevance – making sure that your test is an adequate representation of the domain (i.e., course content) it intends to test. Because standardized tests are not designed to measure achievement in particular courses of study, a somewhat different approach must be taken. The ability that the test is designed to measure is first described. Then a panel of experts in that field judges the relevance of the test content to the most current conceptions of that ability. Content relevance is assessed logically. There is no statistical way in which it can be determined.

Standardized tests are not generally useful for measuring achievement in individual courses because, as stated before, their contents are not representative of any one course. They may occasionally be useful, however, precisely because of this unrepresentativeness. One may administer two tests: one a test whose content fairly represents the objectives of a course, the other a standardized test whose content represents expert judgment about the nature of some ability. Comparing results on the two tests can permit inferences about the nature of the course.

CONSTRUCT VALIDATION

Construct validation is achieved through a program of research that defines constructs by showing what tests of different constructs are and are not related to. Judgment is called for in deciding whether the research has been well done and whether the knowledge or language skills that have been investigated have been put into operation appropriately. Some training and skill in research methodology are required to assess construct validation procedures.

Construct validation is especially important when the exact content of the skill being measured by a test cannot be specified, or when it is difficult to specify a single criterion that can be used to validate the test. Let us consider the example of second language aptitude. According to theorists, learners with high levels of second language aptitude are likely to achieve higher levels of second language proficiency than those with low aptitude. Aptitude is thought to be a distinct factor, unrelated to general intelligence, motivation, personality, and so on. A number of tests of second language aptitude have been developed to measure this quality. Second language aptitude is a hypothetical construct in that it is not possible to observe it directly, and there is no single behavior that can be used to prove that it exists.

Nevertheless, if the construct of second language aptitude is valid, it should be possible to find evidence that it has some psychological reality. This can be done by conducting research to show that the construct is related to performance on other tests that it should be related to. For example, second language aptitude should be related to second language achievement, as the theory of aptitude predicts. At the same time, it is important to show that the construct of aptitude is not the same as other constructs. For example, it would be important to show that aptitude is not the same thing as intelligence. If performance on an aptitude test were related to performance on an intelligence test, then aptitude and intelligence might be the same thing. Therefore, the notion of aptitude would be unnecessary; it would be redundant with the notion of intelligence. Since we already have tests of intelligence, we would not need aptitude tests.

The notion of construct validity is acquiring greater significance in language testing as increasingly abstract and complex notions of language proficiency are used. The notion of sociolinguistic competence, for example, requires a process of construct validation since there is no single, or simple, content domain or criterion that can be used to validate it. The same could be said of all language skills, even relatively simple ones, such as vocabulary.

Task 6

What evidence is presented that the standardized test used in Task 5 is valid? Assess the adequacy of the norms presented for this test for your students.

Summary

Using standardized tests effectively calls for an understanding of how they are developed and the qualities of sound standardized tests. To this end, we discussed how standardized tests are developed, and we identified and discussed six criteria to use to assess them: (1) test content and purpose, (2) appropriateness, (3) practicality, (4) user qualities, (5) reliability, and (6) validity (see Table 1 for a checklist for assessing standardized tests). Although reliability and validity are technical in nature in that they require some knowledge of statistics and research methodology, judgment is called for in assessing standardized tests even on these criteria. Standardized tests are useful for certain purposes under certain circumstances, and, if used wisely, they can complement the information provided by classroom-based tests. It is important to understand the limitations as well as the potential benefits of standardized tests if you are to use them to full advantage.

Discussion questions

1. If you are taking a course on second language evaluation, have your instructor administer a standardized language test of English at a relatively advanced level for adults (e.g., the TOEFL) to the students in your group. After taking the test, discuss your experiences with one another.
2. Select two standardized language tests and then use the six criteria discussed in this chapter to critically assess each.
3. Have each student in your group, if you are reading this book as part of a course on second language evaluation, select three standardized language tests and ensure that no one selects the same tests. Then report to the other members of the group the following information about each test: (a) the students it is intended for; (b) the kinds of decisions it is intended for; (c) the types of reliability reported in the technical manual; (d) the types of validity reported; (e) the levels of reliability and validity; and (f) any other noteworthy characteristics of the test.

Table 1.   Checklist for assessing standardized tests

1. *Test content and purpose*

   a. Does the test assess skills described in my objectives? _____
   b. Is the test designed to make the kinds of decisions I want to _____
      make?

2. *Test appropriateness*

   a. Is the test appropriate for the age (and grade) level of my _____
      students?
   b. Is the test appropriate for use with the educational _____
      backgrounds of my students?
   c. Is the general level of proficiency required by the test _____
      suitable for my students?
   d. Is the test acceptable to my students? _____

3. *Practicality*

   a. Is the test affordable? _____
   b. Is there sufficient time to give the test? _____
   c. Is there suitable space for administering the test? _____
   d. Do I have the qualifications required to give the test _____
      properly?
   e. Is specialized scoring required, and is it affordable and _____
      available?
   f. Are all materials and equipment needed to give the test _____
      available?

4. *User qualities*

   a. Is the purpose of the test clear and appropriate? _____
   b. Are test instructions complete, clear, and specific? _____
   c. Is the layout clear? _____
   d. Are test items unbiased and culturally appropriate? _____
   e. Is there a technical manual? _____
   f. Are administrative procedures described clearly and _____
      completely?
   g. Are test instructions provided? _____
   h. Are scoring procedures explained clearly and completely? _____
   i. Are appropriate norms provided? _____
   j. Are procedures for converting raw scores to norms clear? _____
   k. Are instructions provided on how to interpret test scores? _____

5. *Reliability*

   a. What kinds of reliability are reported, and are they _____
      adequate?

6. *Validity*

   a. What kinds of validity are reported, and are they adequate? _____

4. Consult a book (such as Grant Henning's *A Guide to Language Testing*) in which there are explanations of norm-referenced scores. Report to the group on the meanings of two or three types of norm-referenced scores as defined in the book (e.g., stanine, quartile, percentile). Explain how they could be useful for understanding student performance better.
5. What is the significance of the standard error of measurement for interpreting standardized test scores?
6. For what purposes might you use standardized tests to assess your students' language abilities?

Readings

Airasian, P. (1991). Standardized achievement tests. In P. Airasian (Ed.), *Classroom assessment* (pp. 357–408). New York: McGraw-Hill.

Henning, G. (1987). *A guide to language testing.* New York: Newbury House.

Hopkins, C. D., and L. A. Richards. (1990). Published tests. In C. D. Hopkins and L. A. Richards (Eds.), *Classroom measurement and evaluation* (pp. 437–476). Itasca, Ill.: F. E. Peacock.

Paris, S. G., T. A. Lawton, J. C. Turner, and J. L. Roth. (1991). A developmental perspective on standardized achievement testing. *Educational Researcher, 20,* 12–20.

Popham, W. J. (1978). *Criterion-referenced measurement.* Englewood Cliffs, N.J.: Prentice-Hall.

14 *Summary and integration*

- Effective classroom-based evaluation
- Planning evaluation
- Summary

Effective classroom-based evaluation

Evaluation is a purposive activity that includes the collection of relevant information, interpretation of that information, and making decisions about teaching and learning. In the past, discussions about second language evaluation, particularly when testing is involved, have often focused on making decisions about students – their placement, promotion, advancement, and certification. Certainly, these are important reasons for doing second language evaluation, but they are not the only ones. In fact, the majority of decisions teachers make concern instruction – decisions about how and when to teach particular objectives; about the instructional needs of individuals or groups of students; about the appropriateness of instructional objectives and plans; and so on. Even decisions about students often call for choices regarding instruction. For example, decisions to admit particular students to a class or to promote students to the next level affect the composition of the classroom and may alter instruction plans for that class. *Effective classroom-based evaluation thus requires an understanding of the role of evaluation in planning and delivering instruction.*

Much discussion about evaluation has also focused on assessment of student achievement. This makes sense if the primary reason for evaluation is to make choices regarding students. Decisions about instruction, however, require more than data on student achievement. They require information about students' needs, goals, preferences, and attitudes toward school and learning. They often draw on students' previous linguistic experiences, educational history, and cultural background. They utilize information about the coherence of instructional objectives and plans, the feasibility of instructional plans given an instructor's qualifications and the resources available in the classroom or school. They require knowledge of current research and thinking about second language teaching and learning. *Effective second language evaluation in the classroom calls for the collection and interpretation of a wide range of information.*

The range of information needed to make the many decisions that crop up in second language classrooms cannot be obtained from any single assessment procedure. A variety of methods for collecting assessment information are needed. Disillusionment with the shortcomings of tests has led to a great deal of discussion about alternative methods of assessment. It is certainly true that tests alone are not sufficient. This is not to say that they cannot be useful, but rather that additional methods of assessment are also important. In fact, no single method of assessment would be sufficient to provide all the information teachers need to plan effective instruction. Teachers need a repertoire of assessment methods. In the preceding chapters, we saw that some methods of assessment provide many different kinds of information, depending on how they are used, whereas others provide very limited data. Some provide information about student achievement along with learning strategies, but others do not. Some provide information about students' views, attitudes, and motivations, whereas others do not. Some engage students actively in the process of self-assessment and thereby encourage student ownership of and responsibility for evaluation and ultimately learning; others do not. The nature of the information you need will determine the method or combination of methods of assessment you select. *Effective classroom-based evaluation calls for familiarity with a variety of different methods of assessment and for competence in using these methods creatively.*

The chief shortcoming of standardized tests and, indeed, of many classroom tests, is their failure to mesh with instructional objectives, plans, and practices. If tests and other methods of assessment are to be instrumental in improving second language teaching and learning, they must reflect important aspects of teaching and learning in your classroom. As we noted in Chapter 3, classroom-based evaluation is like a feedback loop – assessment activities are motivated and shaped by instructional purposes, plans, and practices in the classroom, and the decisions that arise from the results of these activities, in turn, lead to reshaping of these instructional purposes, plans, and practices (see Figure 1). *Effective evaluation reflects important features of classroom instructional purposes, plans, and practices and leads to improvements in second language teaching and learning.*

There is often no simple or single way to interpret assessment results or to make instructional decisions based on these results. Thus, classroom-based evaluation calls for a great deal of judgment, which can be enhanced if the logic of evaluation is understood. This consists of comparisons between observed or actual states of affairs and desired states of affairs. When there is a mismatch, change is called for that will reduce the mismatch. This is not as complex as it sounds – we do this when we make everyday decisions. The difference between personal and professional decision making is that the latter must be systematic, explicit, and well documented.

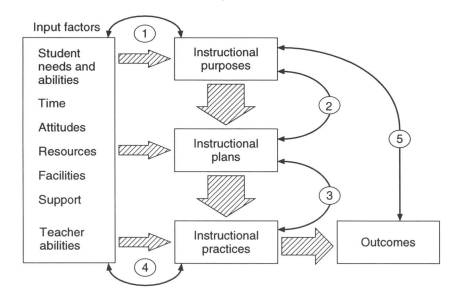

Figure 1   A framework for classroom-based evaluation.

In many cases, teachers need to demonstrate to others – parents, other educators, and students themselves – what information they have collected, how they have collected it, and how they have used this information to make choices. Teachers must also keep records of this process for themselves, so that modifications to instructional purposes, plans, and practices that are indicated by their evaluations are made. Otherwise, important information will be forgotten and needed changes will not be made. *Effective evaluation calls for careful and systematic record keeping and judgment.*

All too often, classroom tests are given, the results reported to students, and instruction proceeds unchanged. In such instances, the results of assessment are not used to improve instruction; rather, they are used only as indicators of student achievement. As a result, student learning becomes disconnected from the learning environment in which it occurs. Effective classroom-based evaluation is part of a process of continuously monitoring and modifying instruction to enhance second language learning. This calls for teachers to take charge of and responsibility for their instructional purposes, plans, and practices. *Effective evaluation calls on teachers to become agents of change in their classrooms – actively using the results of assessment to modify and improve the learning environments they create.*

Planning evaluation

In this section, we discuss planning by synthesizing the material that has been presented since Chapter 3. One approach to developing a plan is to identify the kinds of decisions you need to make or the sorts of questions you seek to answer at different times during the course of instruction. Here it can be useful to organize your plan around decisions to be made (1) before, (2) during, and (3) at the end of instruction. Once this has been done, you can identify the types of information and methods of information collection most suitable for your purposes.

Preliminary to planning for evaluation, it is important to understand the capabilities and uses of alternative methods of assessment, including those we have discussed as well as additional methods that you may be familiar with. Collectively, the methods we have discussed are useful for a variety of purposes:

1. To monitor students' language proficiency in and outside class
2. To understand students' learning styles and strategies
3. To know students' interests and attitudes about learning
4. To know students' background experiences (linguistic, educational, cultural, and medical) that can influence their learning in the classroom
5. To ascertain students' understanding and perceptions of classroom activities
6. Develop students' self-assessment skills
7. Promote student responsibility and ownership of evaluation
8. Involve students in identifying instructional goals and planning instructional activities

Specific methods of assessment that can aid in accomplishing each of these purposes are shown on the next page. We have placed an asterisk next to the methods we think are generally most useful for accomplishing these purposes. These are general opinions; individual readers must decide which method of information collection would be most helpful for their particular purposes.

The mere use of each of these methods will not necessarily achieve these purposes. Special care must be given during the planning and implementation of them to ensure that they serve these purposes effectively. Moreover, these suggestions do not exhaust all possibilities. With creative adaptation, other possibilities are also possible; for example, tests could be included under (6), develop students' self-assessment skills, if teachers were to include students in the construction, scoring, and interpretation of test results.

1	2
Monitor proficiency	*Understand styles and strategies*

Observation*	Conferences*
Objectives-referenced tests*	Portfolios*
Conferences	Observation
Journals	Journals
Portfolios	
Standardized Tests	

3	4
Know student interests and attitudes	*Know students' backgrounds*

Journals*	Questionnaires*
Conferences*	Interviews*
Observation	Conferences
Questionnaires	Journals
Interviews	

5	6
Know students' perception of classroom	*Develop students' self-assessment skills*

Journals*	Portfolios*
Questionnaires*	Conferences*
Observation	Journals
Conferences	Questionnaires

7	8
Encourage student ownership and responsibility	*Encourage student involvement*

Portfolios*	Portfolios*
Conferences	Conferences*
Journals	Journals*

It should now be evident that (1) different methods of collecting information lend themselves to different purposes, (2) assessment activities can do more than monitor student achievement, and (3) by planning evaluation you can take maximum advantage of the variety of purposes that different methods of assessment afford.

Having a repertoire of assessment methods and an understanding of their specific uses, you can now elaborate a plan for evaluation. In what follows, we have identified the kinds of decisions that might be made before, during, and after instruction, and then we have indicated the kinds of information that could assist in making those decisions and the methods of assessment that would be appropriate for collecting this information. We have included information and methods of assessment not discussed in this book. Recall that our earlier discussions excluded methods of collecting information that did not require any special or technical expertise, such as checking school records, examining curriculum documents, and consulting with medical experts and other teachers. We have included these other types and sources of information here in order to be comprehensive in our summary and to illustrate that the material in this book does not rule out other possibilities.

The synopsis that follows is not exhaustive. Individual readers may be able to think of additional sorts of information or methods of data collection for each kind or type of decision. Nor is this synopsis applicable without modifications to any group of learners or classroom setting. It would need to be adapted to be appropriate for particular classroom settings. It serves only to illustrate very generally how to put together much of what we have discussed in the preceding chapters into a plan for evaluation in your classroom. Individual readers need to elaborate their own plan, using this as a guide. Once again, we have identified with asterisks the kinds of information we believe to be generally useful for making each type of decision. We have not done this for methods of information collection since deciding on these depends critically on the classroom context and, therefore, cannot be done without more information. Only individual teachers can make those choices.

Before instruction

1. Decision: whether to modify the instructional objectives and plans based on their coherence

Kinds of information	Methods of information collection
Detailed description of instructional objectives and plans	No special method required: careful review of plans and instructional documents

2. Decision: how to place or screen students for participation at particular levels or in particular courses or programs

Kinds of information	Methods of information collection
Students' SL proficiency*	Proficiency tests Self-assessment by students Prior school records Interviews with previous instructors

Kinds of information (cont.)	Methods of information collection (cont.)
Students' needs*	Questionnaires Interviews Language proficiency tests
Students' educational and SL learning experiences	Questionnaires and interviews Interviews with previous instructors and parents Examine school records
Students' cultural background	Questionnaires and interviews with parents and previous teachers
Students' preferred learning styles	Questionnaires and interviews with students

3. Decision: whether to modify the instructional objectives or plans based on their suitability for incoming students

Kinds of information	Methods of information collection
Same item as 2 above	Same item as 2 above

4. Decision: whether to modify the course of study or curriculum based on its feasibility given the resources available in the classroom and school

Kinds of information	Methods of information collection
Description of instructional objectives and plans*	No special method: logical analysis of instructional documents
Technical and physical resources available in classroom or school*	No special method required
Professional expertise of teachers	Self-assessment by teachers Standardized language proficiency tests for teachers

During instruction

5. Decision: whether to move on to the next unit or lesson of instruction

Kinds of information	Methods of information collection
Student achievement	Objectives-referenced tests Observations of student performance in class Portfolios Conferences

6. Decision: whether and how to modify instructional plans and practices based on your experience with your current students

Kinds of information	*Methods of information collection*
Students' current language proficiencies*	Tests Portfolios Observation
Students' interests and goals	Portfolios Journals Observation
Students' current cultural and social skills and understandings	Observation Conferences Journals

7. Decision: how to modify instructional plans that did not work

Kinds of information	*Methods of information collection*
Current language abilities*	Observation
Students' understanding of and reactions to instructional activities	Conferences Journals
Students' learning strategies	Observation Conferences
Students' interests and likes	Observation Journals Conferences
Students' study habits	Interviews Conferences Journals

8. Decision: how to individualize instruction for students having difficulty

Kinds of information	*Methods of information collection*
Nature of their difficulty, including information about their learning strategies and styles*	Conferences Observations Portfolios Tests
Students' attitudes or feelings about learning and school	Conferences Interviews with parents Journals
Preexisting learning or perceptual disabilities	Examine school records Results from language development specialist

Kinds of information (cont.)	Methods of information collection (cont.)
Prior educational and language experiences	Interviews with parents and teachers School records
First language ability	Interviews with parents Proficiency tests in first language Prior school records

After instruction

Decision making after instruction is finished is different from making decisions before and during instruction because, once instruction is finished, no more information can be collected. Indeed, in principle, all relevant information has been collected. After instruction, decision making is a matter of reviewing all relevant recorded information, interpreting it with respect to each of the decisions to be made, and making decisions. The decisions to be made after instruction is finished are concerned largely with grading students and modifying instructional purposes, plans, and practices for the next group of learners; these include questions such as:

- Do I need to modify my general instructional objectives to be appropriate for the next group of students?
- Do I need to modify my instructional plans to be more effective?
- Do I need to modify the way I taught any of my specific lessons so that they will be more effective next time?
- Do I need to modify my evaluation plans and procedures to be more effective?

Without careful, detailed, and systematic records, decision making after instruction can be difficult, fuzzy, and, worse, arbitrary. Thus, when developing an evaluation plan, it is useful to begin at the end: imagine what kinds of information you would like to have in order to make the instructional decisions you want to make at the end. Then, formulate a plan for collecting and recording that information during the course of instruction. Don't wait until the end to identify what information is needed. In all likelihood, if you wait until the end, you will discover that important pieces or types of information are missing, and it will be too late.

Summary

Effective second language evaluation:

- Is a process that improves decision making in the classroom
- Focuses on improving second language instruction

- Entails the collection of a variety of information
- Calls for understanding of and competence using a variety of assessment methods
- Requires the careful integration of assessment with important and salient aspects of teaching and learning
- Calls on teachers to become agents of change in their classrooms

To be effective, second language evaluation must be planned. An overall evaluation plan is essential in order to:

- Schedule the time needed to engage in necessary assessment activities
- Coordinate evaluation with decision making about instructional planning and delivery
- Organize the classroom to accommodate evaluation
- Take advantage of the multiple purposes afforded by alternative assessment methods
- Ensure that there is open and clear communication among all individuals and groups who are concerned with your students' language learning and, where appropriate, their general education; this includes other teachers and educational professionals, students themselves, and parents

Several themes have recurred throughout this book. We think it may be useful to mention them explicitly here. The first of these we call the "no right way" idea. Teaching and evaluating are very complex enterprises. It is misguided to think that we have discovered the best of all possible ways to undertake those enterprises. Added to that inherent complexity are the facts that (1) courses are designed to accomplish different goals, (2) teachers vary greatly in their individual strengths, personalities, and teaching styles, and (3) learners differ extensively in the skills they are ready to acquire and in the ways that they learn. In short, what might be highly effective for one teacher with one group of learners may be a disaster for another teacher with another group of learners. Professional development includes learning what works best in general for you. Furthermore, even your general approaches to teaching and evaluation must evolve together with changes in curriculum and methods. Finally, these evolving approaches have to be adapted and fine-tuned for each new learner you teach.

The second theme is to compare the actual with the ideal. Evaluation calls for action when an actual state of affairs does not correspond with the state you want. Assessment is guided, therefore, by what you aim for, what you need, or what you expect. These are the ideals of a second language course. Learner needs are ideals to which course objectives should correspond; lesson plans are the ideals that actual lessons should match; learning objectives are idealizations of learner abilities that we hope to see realized. It should be obvious, therefore, that evaluation requires not only means for assessing actual states of affairs, but also a very clear conceptualization of the ideals.

The third theme, related to the first two, is the need to plan evaluation. Without a plan for evaluation, you will find that all too often opportunities have passed you by. Without a plan, important observations may go unrecorded and be forgotten. This can lead to failure to create a better teaching program.

The fourth theme is the need to multiply and vary in your methods of assessment. All assessment procedures give you error together with accurate information. Therefore, you want to multiply your assessments; important decisions should not be made on the basis of first impressions, even when these come from a careful assessment. Furthermore, all of the methods for getting information that you have read about in this book have their own strengths and weaknesses. Sound decisions are much more likely to be made when a variety of assessment methods produce the same set of facts. The different perspectives elicited by different methods combine to provide a truer picture of your teaching and your students' learning.

The final theme is that good intentions aren't enough. While a high degree of success in language teaching probably cannot be attained unless teachers are motivated and well intentioned, these qualities are not by themselves enough. Motivation and intentions must be directed toward the development of the competence of an individual teacher. An important function of evaluation is to guide this development. This is something that teachers can do for themselves. Like successful second language learning, successful teaching is a creative, ongoing process, and classroom-based evaluation is an essential component of this process.

Index